EXPERIENCING LEONARD BERNSTEIN

The Listener's Companion
Gregg Akkerman, Series Editor

Titles in **The Listener's Companion** provide readers with a deeper understanding of key musical genres and the work of major artists and composers. Aimed at nonspecialists, each volume explains in clear and accessible language how to listen to works from particular artists, composers, and genres. Looking at both the context in which the music first appeared and has since been heard, authors explore with readers the environments in which key musical works were written and performed.

EXPERIENCING LEONARD BERNSTEIN

A Listener's Companion

Kenneth LaFave

ROWMAN & LITTLEFIELD
Lanham • Boulder • New York • London

Published by Rowman & Littlefield
A wholly owned subsidiary of The Rowman & Littlefield Publishing Group,
Inc.
4501 Forbes Boulevard, Suite 200, Lanham, Maryland 20706
www.rowman.com

16 Carlisle Street, London W1D 3BT, United Kingdom

British Library Cataloguing in Publication Information Available

Library of Congress Cataloging-in-Publication Data

LaFave, Kenneth.
Experiencing Leonard Bernstein : a listener's companion / Kenneth LaFave.
pages cm. – (The listener's companion)
Includes bibliographical references and index.
ISBN 978-1-4422-3543-4 (cloth : alk. paper) – ISBN 978-1-4422-3544-1 (ebook)
1. Bernstein, Leonard, 1918-1990–Criticism and interpretation. I. Title.
ML410.B566L33 2015
780.92–dc23
2014024675

Printed in the United States of America

To the memory of Robert Kastenbaum,
writer, music lover, collaborator, and dear friend.

"The sweetest flow'rs
The fairest trees
Are grown in solid ground."

CONTENTS

CONTENTS

SERIES EDITOR'S FOREWORD

The goal of the *Listener's Companion* series is to give readers a deeper understanding of pivotal musical genres and the creative work of its iconic practitioners. Contributors meet this objective in a manner that does not require extensive music training or any sort of elitist shoulder-rubbing. Authors of the books in this series are asked to situate readers in the listening environments in which the music under consideration has been or still can be heard. Within these environments, authors examine the historical context in which this music appeared, exploring compositional character and societal elements of the work. By positioning the reader in real or imagined environments of the music's creation, performance, and reception, readers can experience a deeper enjoyment and appreciation of the work. Authors, often drawing on their own expertise as performers and scholars, are like tour guides walking readers through major musical genres and the achievements of artists within those genres, replaying the music for them—if you will—as a lived listening experience.

Can there ever be another total musician like Leonard Bernstein? The door may have closed behind him upon his death in 1990. As a pianist he was skilled enough to present and conduct concertos from the keyboard as was done in Mozart's era. As a conductor he soared to the heights of the craft, leading many of the world's best orchestras. As a composer he left a catalog of lasting and compelling works across multiple genres—again, in the model of history's greatest artists. And, rarely found among more heady artists, as an educator and orator Bernstein communicated the essence of music to a swath of the population less accustomed to being talked to about serious music than being talked at.

In many ways, the world of classical art music had already transitioned into the twenty-first-century paradigms by the end of Bernstein's career. The age of the specialist, which had begun in the 1800s, was firmly embedded by the mid-1900s. Bernstein's contemporaries commonly surrendered ambitions of being composer, performer, conductor, and educator at once. To succeed, one focused on a single area; two, if lucky. To do otherwise was to find yourself quickly overshadowed and overtaken by those who did not waste time casting such wide nets. Thinking broadly became synonymous with lacking focus and falling, ultimately, into obscurity. In the twenty-first century, this view is all but carved in academic stone. From young ages, faculty and teachers guide musicians toward performance or composition or conducting or education, and little is the encouragement offered to meld these increasingly disparate fields. For the young lion or lioness yet to emerge with the multidisciplined potential of Bernstein there is no longer any sort of institutional wherewithal to accommodate such an oddity. Bernstein was himself already a century out of step, and now in the century beyond his life, it would seem he is one of the last of that class referred to as the Renaissance Man.

As a master of both serious art music and popular styles, listeners across the world can still hear Bernstein's music, so his inclusion to the Listener's Companion series hardly needs justification. His works for ballet, choir, chamber groups, piano, orchestra, and theater all place him among world-class composers for his era. But it was Bernstein's ability to create music accessible to popular tastes that ensured his success across different audiences. His contributions to *West Side Story, On the Waterfront*, and *Candide* gave him critical success and forged his reputation as a household name. None of Bernstein's contemporaries can claim such demonstrative accolades across genres.

For such a giant among giants, this Listener's Companion volume is well served by its author Kenneth LaFave, who not only holds a keen interest in all facets of Bernstein's life and work, but actually knew and interacted with the maestro himself. A former publicist for the New York Philharmonic in the late 1980s, LaFave personally knew Leonard Bernstein. Professionally, LaFave is a proven music journalist writing for the *Arizona Republic*, the *Phoenix Gazette*, and the *Kansas City Star*. He is also a teacher and a doctoral student of the prestigious European Graduate School. This combination of skills and personal experience make LaFave ideally suited for writing *Experiencing Bernstein: A Listener's Companion*, offering to all a major contribution to the understanding of the composer's lasting music.

Gregg Akkerman

ACKNOWLEDGMENTS

For their various contributions of encouragement, patience, critical observation, and stores of information, the author would like to thank Gregg Akkerman, Jamie Bernstein, Kristie Byrum, Marie Carter, Bennett Graff, Emmett LaFave, Max LaFave, Janet Oates, Craig Urquhart, and, in her role as proofreader, Susan Simpson.

TIMELINE

1918	August 25, born to Jennie and Samuel Bernstein, Lawrence, Massachusetts.
1928	Begins piano lessons.
1929–1935	Student at Boston Latin School.
1931	Bar Mitzvah, Temple Mishkan Tefila, Boston, Mass.
1935	Graduates Boston Latin, begins undergraduate study at Harvard University.
1935–1939	Earliest compositions, including Piano Trio and incidental music for Aristophanes's *The Birds*.
1937	Meets Aaron Copland and Dimitri Mitropoulos.
1939–1941	Study at Curtis Institute; teachers include Randall Thompson, orchestration, and Fritz Reiner, conducting.
1940	Meets conductor Serge Koussevitzky and begins his lifelong association with the Tanglewood music camp.
1941	First published work: transcription of Copland's *El Salon Mexico*. First professional conducting engagement, leading a single work (Wagner's Prelude to Die Meistersinger) with the Boston Pops Orchestra.
1942	Premiere of Sonata for Clarinet and Piano, first published original work. Composes Symphony No. 1, *Jeremiah*.

1943   Premiere of song cycle *I Hate Music*. Publication of
            first set of *Anniversaries* for piano. Named assistant
            conductor of the New York Philharmonic, Bernstein
            leaps to stardom when he substitutes for an ailing
            Bruno Walter.

1944   Composes ballet *Fancy Free*, and the Broadway musical
            On the Town.

1944–1951   Tours and records as conductor, building an
            international reputation.

1945   Composes *Hashkeveinu*.

1949   Premiere of Symphony No. 2, *Age of Anxiety*.
            Composes *Prelude, Fugue and Riffs*.

1950   Incidental music for Broadway production of *Peter Pan*.

1951–1955   Visiting professor of music, Brandeis University.

1951   Marries actress Felicia Montealegre. Composes one-act
            opera *Trouble in Tahiti*.

1952   Birth of daughter Jamie.

1953   Premiere of Broadway musical *Wonderful Town*.
            Becomes first American to conduct at La Scala Opera
            House, Milan.

1954   Premieres of film *On the Waterfront* and violin
            concerto *Serenade After Plato's Symposium*. First
            television appearance, CBS *Omnibus*.

1955   Birth of son Alexander. Premiere of Symphonic Suite
            from *On the Waterfront*. Incidental music for Lillian
            Hellman's *The Lark*.

1956   Premiere of Broadway musical *Candide*.

1957   Premiere of Broadway musical *West Side Story*.

1958   Begins eleven-year tenure as music director of the New
            York Philharmonic, youngest appointee in the
            orchestra's history, and the first American.

1959   First book published: *The Joy of Music*.

1961	Premiere of Symphonic Dances from *West Side Story*. Film of *West Side Story* released.
1962	Birth of daughter Nina.
1963	Premiere of Symphony No. 3, *Kaddish*.
1965	*Chichester Psalms* composed and premiered.
1966	Book published: *The Infinite Variety of Music*.
1969	Concludes tenure as music director of the New York Philharmonic, is named to the lifelong position of the orchestra's Conductor Laureate.
1970	Fund-raising party for the Black Panthers becomes notorious when Tom Wolfe publishes *Radical Chic*.
1971	*Mass: A Theatre Piece* initiates the John F. Kennedy Center for the Performing Arts, Washington, DC.
1973	Premiere of the reduced, one-act version of *Candide*.
1973–1974	Delivers six lectures at Harvard, titled *The Unanswered Question*.
1974	Composes ballet with Jerome Robbins, *Dybbuk*.
1976	Broadway musical, *1600 Pennsylvania Avenue*. *The Unanswered Question* published as a book.
1977	Premieres of *Songfest*, the overture *Slava!*, and *Three Meditations from "Mass"* for cello and orchestra.
1978	Death of Felicia Montealegre Bernstein.
1980	Premieres of *Divertimento* and *A Musical Toast*.
1981	Premieres of *Halil* for flute and orchestra, and *Touches* for solo piano.
1983	First version of opera, *A Quiet Place*.
1984	Second version of opera, *A Quiet Place*.
1987	Workshop of musical, *The Race to Urga*, not produced.
1988	Premieres of *Missa Brevis, Arias and Barcarolles*, and the Scottish Opera version of *Candide*. International telecast of Bernstein's seventieth birthday celebration.
1989	Premiere of Concerto for Orchestra *Jubilee Games*.

1990   Final concerts. Announcement of retirement from
             conducting October 9, followed by the death of
             Leonard Bernstein on October 14.

INTRODUCTION

I barely knew Leonard Bernstein. We exchanged perhaps 200 words over a period of five years, and most of those regarded professional matters. My connection to him, like that of most Americans, was via his extraordinary *Young People's Concerts* on television, lifelines of musical culture to this Tucson, Arizona, music student. By the 1980s, I had moved to New York, and in 1985, I took a job as publicist for the New York Philharmonic. My job was to write press releases, coordinate photography, and sometimes assist backstage before concerts at Avery Fisher Hall. That is where I saw Leonard Bernstein, the orchestra's Conductor Laureate, in action, and it was through his actions that he truly spoke to me. To echo Bernstein's written notes for his flute concerto, *Halil*, I did not know Leonard Bernstein, but I knew his spirit. Here are some illustrations from those years:

During rehearsals, music was piped in from the stage to my desk on the fourth floor. That way, I knew when there were breaks and could run downstairs to get musicians' sign-offs on publicity photos and releases. One day, a conductor was leading the Philharmonic in Copland's *Fanfare for the Common Man*, in preparation for an upcoming concert celebrating Copland's eighty-fifth birthday. It went along, coherent but unremarkable. Then came a silence, and following that silence came . . . Copland's *Fanfare for the Common Man*! It made me almost jump out of my chair. The same piece was suddenly transformed, re-energized, re-imagined, re . . . everything. Bernstein had taken over the rehearsal. If anyone doubts the difference a conductor makes, tell this story.

One night before a concert of Lenny leading Mahler's Seventh Symphony, we couldn't find him backstage. By "we," I mean the backstage personnel, including Yours Truly, who were responsible for making sure everyone was in place and ready to go at concert time. Lenny wasn't in his dressing room, nor was he in the wings. Panic was about to set in when finally we found him in a stairwell just offstage, talking animatedly about Mahler . . . to the janitor. The janitor was mesmerized—and perhaps a little baffled—as he listened to Lenny exult about music and what it means to be a musician. If anyone doubts that Leonard Bernstein was sincere in his rabbi-like devotion to spreading the gospel of music, tell them this.

Then there was the press luncheon in the lobby of Avery Fisher, an event designed to assuage the passions that had flowed between Lenny and a certain recording label. Bernstein and the label had disagreed about the amount of revenue the label retained, and now the parties had come to an agreement. The public nature of the luncheon was meant to put a good spin on what had been a discordant relationship. Bernstein attended, sitting uncomfortably at a table with the label execs for all of thirty minutes, at which point he rose from his chair and stormed out, yelling for all to hear (the press be damned): "This has nothing to do with the art we serve!" I do think I loved him more at that moment than at any other. If anyone doubts that Leonard Bernstein treated music as a holy endeavor, tell them this.

The publication of Bernstein's letters in 2013 prompted a lot of second thoughts about Leonard Bernstein, and many of these focused on an old question: Was Bernstein authentic? Or some kind of pop culture simulacrum? Robert Gottlieb in the *New York Review of Books* called it "the Lenny problem": "Is he for real? Or is he an act?" Based on everything I saw of Leonard Bernstein, he was for real, and then some. For real, he wanted to make music. For real, he wanted to make people love music. For real, he wanted to change the world. To be sure, he could be arrogant. I witnessed some of that. He also owned a "mean streak," as his biographer Humphrey Burton has documented. Like everybody else, he was human, all too human. But Lenny deeply and without the tiniest hint of insincerity wanted everyone to love music as he did, and so he spared no energy performing music, championing music, and educating people about how music relates to our most fundamental experiences and emotions.

Sometimes, that meant his own music got lost in the shuffle. Leonard Bernstein was a composer. He was not a composer "among other things." He was a composer whose prodigious musical gifts often led him to sacrifice time and energy that might have been spent writing a symphony to writing a script for a Young People's Concert or preparing the score of a world premiere composed by someone else. When one thinks of the concerts Bernstein conducted and the recordings he made of other people's music, not to mention the books he wrote and the time he gave to nurturing the next generation of talent, it is remarkable that he composed as much music as he did. *West Side Story*, *Candide*, and *Mass* are all acknowledged miracles of musical creativity, works unique in their form and impact. Still other Bernstein scores await discovery or re-discovery by performers and critics. This book is intended a guide to understanding them, and to grasping something of Bernstein's life as a composer. It is not a biography, though biographical information is included as it pertains to his compositions.

For nearly twenty years after leaving my job at the New York Philharmonic I worked as a classical music critic, first for the *Kansas City Star*, and later for the *Arizona Republic*. Since 2008, most of my writing has consisted of program notes for such organizations as the Philadelphia Orchestra, Lincoln Center for the Performing Arts, and the Juilliard School. The trick of writing a program note is to tell people about a composition without undue complication, but without misrepresenting it through oversimplification, either. If there were a weeklong festival of the music of Leonard Bernstein, I'd like to think of this book as the program note.

Listeners who are relatively new to classical music sometimes make the mistake of believing they cannot "get" classical music without knowing and being able to recognize tricks-of-the-trade. This misconception arises primarily, I think, from classical music arrogance. Many writings about classical music and some teachers of the genre appropriate a know-it-all attitude that takes great pride in knowing a Neapolitan Sixth chord from a secondary dominant.

To be clear, it is very important to know a Neapolitan Sixth from a secondary dominant and other similar distinctions *if* one is a professional musician. But the lingo of a musician is no more necessary to the enjoyment of music by a typical listener than knowledge of key grips and green screens is necessary to enjoying a movie. If the composer has done his job—and Bernstein always does his—then the listener will *feel* the music in all its mercurial changes or formal stability or rhythmic vivacity. I introduce technical terms only to help explain how the composer has made you feel the way you feel. As a listener, your sole obligation is to open your ears and heart to the beauty and power of the music. As a writer, my job is to guide you in understanding how the composer's life, talent, and craft have shaped the beauty and power you hear.

I

FATHER, SON, AND MUSIC

It's September 26, 1957, and at New York's Winter Garden Theater, the curtain has just rung down on opening night of the most talked-about musical to come to Broadway in years. Intermission left two dead bodies onstage, and now the show has ended with the corpse of the hero carried off to the sorrowful sound of a yearning song called "Somewhere." Audience reaction: perfect silence. For several seconds. And then applause—applause that will not stop. It's a thunderous ovation for the most unexpected musical in the decade and a half since *Oklahoma!* changed the music theater landscape. And it's just the beginning. *West Side Story* will go on to tour, to be revived, to become a major motion picture, and to provide countless professional and community theaters around the globe with a matchless blend of story, song, and dance.

What made *West Side Story* a watershed? The show boasted a strong story line and the most adventurous choreography imaginable. However, it was the songs that colored the piece with unprecedentedly intense hues of joy, excitement, violence, tragedy, and solemn, all-too-human hope. The lyrics were by a young man named Stephen Sondheim. The music was by a young man named Leonard Bernstein.

Leonard Bernstein was, arguably, the most complete musician of the twentieth century. Other musicians have combined the various roles of composer, conductor, pianist, and teacher, but few if any, save Bernstein, have done all of them at the highest levels of professional achievement. As a conductor, Bernstein led the greatest orchestras on the planet, including the New York Philharmonic (the only orchestra for which he ever served as music director), the Boston Symphony Orchestra, the London Symphony Orchestra, the Vienna Philharmonic, and the Israel Philharmonic Orchestra. His interpretations of Beethoven, Mahler, Schumann, Sibelius, Haydn, and the composers of the American school are indispensable, and the dozens of world premieres led by him include works as prestigious as Olivier Messiaen's *Turangali- la-Symphonie* and Charles Ives's Symphony No. 2. As a teacher, he instilled the love of music into hundreds of hopefuls at the Tanglewood Music Center, and left the personal stamp of his mentorship on such conductors as Lorin Maazel, Seiji Ozawa, Michael Tilson Thomas, John Mauceri, and Marin Alsop. But Bernstein's teaching carried far beyond the boundaries of young classical music professionals to embrace the education of millions via more than sixty televised concerts-with-com- mentaries in the 1950s, 1960s, and into the early 1970s. He also transcribed these and other explorations of music into five books that reached countless readers. One of them, *The Unanswered Question*, comprising his lectures at Harvard, attempted nothing less than the presentation of a coherent philosophy of music. If his accomplishments as a pianist did not quite reach the heights he attained as a conductor and teacher, they were nonetheless sufficient to define a major career. Bernstein appeared in concert with major orchestras as soloist in Gersh- win's *Rhapsody in Blue,* and in concertos by Mozart and Ravel. Though he did not play solo recitals, he served as an accompanist to many ranking singers and instrumentalists.

Yet the one criteria by which he considered himself to be above all others was none of these. Leonard Bernstein was first and foremost a composer. And not just the composer of *West Side Story*—a score so popular that it throws most of his other works into shadow—but of three other musicals, a pair of operas, three symphonies, a trio of bal- lets, a film score, and a range of hard-to-define symphonic, vocal, and chamber music compositions that stand among the last scores to have entered the classical repertoire.

This last is an important point, because it puts the music we are about to examine into a real-world, material context. Classical music, which once maintained an open catalogue to which new works regularly were added, is today (2014) a closed book. Up through the middle of the twentieth century, new compositions had a shot at becoming part of a continually growing classical repertoire. Stravinsky's ballets from 1910 to 1913 muscled their way in. In the 1920s and 1930s, numerous works by Ravel, Prokofiev, Gershwin, and others took their places easily. Most symphony orchestras will even acknowledge the 1940s with such scores as Copland's *Appalachian Spring*, Bartok's Concerto for Orchestra, and Shostakovich's Seventh Symphony. After that, things grow pretty thin. Only a handful of pieces composed in the 1950s and 1960s maintain a regular presence on symphony orchestra programs today, including a few late scores by Britten and Shostakovich, and four by Bernstein: Serenade after Plato's Symposium, the overture to *Candide*, Symphonic Dances from *West Side Story*, and Chichester Psalms. One can think of only a few works from the 1970s forward that recur from time to time, among them John Corigliano's *Pied Piper Fantasy*, Philip Glass's Violin Concerto and a pair of overture slot pieces—John Adams's *Short Ride in a Fast Machine* and Arvo Part's *Cantus in Memoriam Benjamin Britten*. The very newest work tends to be premiered and then forgotten. This is not to imply that it is inferior in any way; to the contrary, a great many fine composers now live and write music for symphony orchestra. But new music has become a special event. A premiere is no longer potentially a part *of* the mainstream, it is apart *from* the mainstream, an occasional occurrence for the purpose of fulfilling the obligations of conscientious advocates. Bernstein, then, was among the last classical composers in the old sense, a composer whose work challenged and, if successful, entered, the progress of musical history.

But wait . . . weren't we talking about Broadway musicals? Was Bernstein a Broadway composer, or a classical composer? The answer is yes. The man whose music we are about to hear composed for any format in any genre he chose to write. He tore into the writing of music for the stage or the concert hall or the movies the same way he tore into life—with an all-consuming appetite that would admit no bounds. "Lenny was omni-everything," violinist and Bernstein friend Isaac Stern told me in an interview shortly after Bernstein's death in 1990. He embraced the world, and to a large degree, it embraced him back. No better illustration of the astonishing range of his professional achievement can be cited than the fact that, at almost the same moment *West Side Story* was opening on Broadway, the New York Philharmonic announced that its next music director would be none other than the very same Leonard Bernstein, a thirty-nine-year-old New England–born musician with a penchant for Beethoven, jazz, and chain smoking.

The man who would someday compose *West Side Story* and become the first American to conduct the great symphony orchestras of the world was born Louis Bernstein on August 25, 1918, in Lawrence, Massachusetts. He was the son of Russian Jewish immigrants with no special ties to music or music making. As a little boy, he was called "Leonard" or "Lenny" around the house, as that was the parents' preference over "Louis," a name insisted upon by a grandparent. At sixteen, the boy would legally change Louis to Leonard, but not until after he had been subjected for a decade and a half to an ambiguous nominal identity. It is strangely apt that an artist committed to ambiguity in all things—his career, his art, his sexuality, the very ideas he held about existence—should so begin his life.

A musician's biography (which this is not) usually begins with an explanation of the subject's youthful precociousness: the music in the home, the lessons that started at age five, and so on. Not so with biographies of Leonard Bernstein. They don't start that way because young Louis/Lenny was not raised in a musical family. When, on his own, little Lenny discovered the powerful attraction of music, he had to beg for piano lessons. These finally started at ten, a respectable enough age to begin, though rather late for someone pointed toward a profession in classical music, let alone star status. Consequently, Bernstein's career was enshrouded by the feeling of having to play catch-up. In later life, Bernstein famously uttered the *bon mot*: "To achieve great things, two things are needed: a plan and not quite enough time." Along with persistent ambiguity, it was one of the great themes of his life.

A look at young Lenny's life reveals the strands of a richly woven texture that will become the music of the mature composer. During the week, music around the Bernstein house was popular songs on the radio: the tunes of Irving Berlin, the Gershwins, and Cole Porter. On Saturdays, it was religious music at the Conservative synagogue, the intoning of the cantor and the swelling sound of the choir. When piano lessons started, a third musical stream sprang up in the form of classical masterpieces. Lenny read music easily and grew his skills quickly. He thus went through several early piano teachers before finding the one who was his strongest childhood musical influence, Helen Coates. (Coates later became Bernstein's secretary.) Despite his relatively late start, the child's gifts at the piano might have blossomed into a keyboard career, had he not discovered composing and conducting. While he was still in his teens, Lenny played the piano on a local radio show sponsored by his father, and made his formal professional debut in 1937 at age nineteen, playing Ravel's then-nearly new Piano Concerto in G with the State Symphony of Massachusetts. (He would perform and record that piece throughout the decades to come.) Lenny also exhibited intellectual gifts beyond music. As a student at Boston Latin School, he developed a penchant for literature and languages that served him all his life and influenced the choices he made as a composer, an enthusiasm that deepened during his years as a Harvard University undergraduate (1935–1939). All but a handful of Bernstein's mature compositions involve words, either sung, or present in the background as a "program."

What was the family context for his upbringing? The Bernsteins were well to do, thanks to the thriving hair business established by Lenny's father, Sam, an immigrant from a small town in Ukraine. Sam's company made and sold wigs and hair care items with great success. When he wasn't doing business, Sam was studying the Talmud, the central scholarly work of Rabbinic Judaism. Music was part of his life only as it pertained to worship services at the local Conservative synagogue. (Had Sam Bernstein remained an Orthodox Jew, which he was until coming to the United States, there might well have been no music at all, since Orthodox communities limited and sometimes outright prohibited exposure to any form of secular music.) Lenny's mother, Jennie, had also emigrated from Ukraine, coming to America to marry Sam in a family-forged arrangement. From all accounts, it was not a happy marriage, a fact appropriated later by Bernstein when he wrote the libretto for his one-act opera, *Trouble in Tahiti*. The father in that piece is a cold, removed man who thinks only of business. His name is Sam.

It is necessary to address Bernstein's relationship with his biological father and, by extension, his relationship to father figures and, most especially, to God. Although this book is not a biography, it is hardly possible to write about an artist's work without taking into account that artist's life, and it would be utterly mistaken to examine Bernstein's music and not look hard and long at his relationships, starting with the experience of Sam. "Lenny told me he hated his father" (*American Masters*), Michael Wager, a friend of Bernstein's later in life, has said in a televised interview. That Bernstein expressed such feelings even into his old age says something about their intensity. Yet, as always, ambiguity reigned. Bernstein would dedicate his first symphony to Sam, and dedicate each of his next two symphonies to father figures.

What was the source of this hatred? For one thing, Sam opposed the idea of his eldest son becoming a musician. This opposition was based on the older man's limited understanding of a musician's life and potential, which he had carried with him from the Jewish ghetto in Ukraine. A musician there was a *klezmorim*, a beggar with a clarinet or violin who went from house to house playing for weddings and bar mitzvahs. Even when Sam's vision managed to clear the limit of his upbringing, he was uncomfortable with the idea of his son becoming a musician due to the financial risk involved, and this was not unreasonable. Lenny was no child prodigy and his relatively late start meant extra years of study and, therefore, expense. Besides, Sam had built a lucrative business from the ground up, and he dreamed of handing it over to his eldest son.

Beyond opposing Lenny's musical career (a position on which he waffled; see the reference above to the radio show of Lenny's that Sam sponsored), Sam exhibited a personality his family fond morose. In Humphrey Burton's official biography of Bernstein, Lenny's little sister Shirley says their father was a "manic-depressive" who would sometimes "pace the floor in melancholy" and "act mean" toward their mother. Whatever the origins of Lenny's much talked-about paternal antipathy, one gets the feeling that the son craved something from the father that he never got, and that this something was nothing less than the radiant presence of a final and affirmative truth. "To a child, a father is God," Bernstein later said, in seven revelatory words. If Sam was God, he was a flawed deity indeed, a bitter disappointment, a fraud. He was, to use a phrase the narrator in Bernstein's third and final symphony (the *Kaddish*) will hurl at Jehovah Himself, a "tin god." Faith—the loss of it and the need to get it back—will be the recurrent theme of Bernstein's catalog. Both in works with religious subjects, such as the *Kaddish* symphony and *Mass*, and in seemingly secular scores such as *Age of Anxiety* and even *Candide*, faith or its lack will play a crucial role. It seems almost certain that this concern sprang from young Lenny's disappointment in his own, biological father and, by extension, disappointment in the Father of the universe. Turning away from the failed Father, Bernstein instead placed his love and faith in people.

A single human figure on the side of an Alp "makes the Alp disappear for me," Bernstein once said. People were more than just important to him. In a way, they were everything. He made friends, not easily, but forever, and early on assembled a cast of characters who accompanied him through the drama of his life. These included his sister Shirley, close to him in childhood, close to him in adulthood; Shirley Gabis, his first girlfriend, who would later marry the composer George Perle; Coates, who went from piano teacher to secretary; Sid Ramin, Lenny's first piano student (Bernstein began teaching at age twelve) and an invaluable musical assistant throughout his adult career; Dmitri Mitropoulos, whom Bernstein met in 1937 when the great Greek conductor visited Harvard; mezzo-soprano Jennie Tourel, who championed Bernstein's music; composer-lyricist-activist Marc Blitzstein, whose controversial *The Cradle Will Rock* Bernstein produced at Harvard; and Aaron Copland, one of the greats of modern American composition. (We are not including conductor Serge Koussevitzky, whose role was that of Bernstein's musical father figure, and whom we will meet shortly.)

By his senior year at Boston Latin (1934–1935), when he wrote a paper attacking Freud's case for the "abnormality" of homosexuality, Bernstein had discovered yet another ambiguity in his makeup, one that would inform his life and to some extent his music: bisexuality. In the 1930s, the Kinsey scale of sexuality, which essentially establishes everyone as bisexual to one degree or another, from almost completely heterosexual to almost entirely homosexual, with a lot of shades in between, was still twenty years in the future, and religious tolerance of sexual variety was unheard of. Lenny had been brought up in a conservative religious household, so one can only imagine the angst that must have plagued the high school senior as he courageously wrote: "Why should beautiful relationships like these be smutted with talk of abnormality?" Yet, for four decades to come, Bernstein would maintain his characteristic ambiguity about intimacy, dating both sexes (his own surreptitiously), and then marrying and establishing a family, only to see this accommodation tragically explode in the 1970s.

After graduating Boston Latin, Bernstein did undergraduate work at Harvard University. While studying harmony, counterpoint, and orchestration, he also composed his first pieces, a string of chamber music scores largely derivative of the major composers of the recent past. Scriabin seemed to have been a favorite. His breakout piece was incidental music for a Harvard production of Aristophanes's *The Birds* that drew positive remarks from professors and friends alike. Bernstein also made his conducting debut leading the music in the pit, and this brought accolades as well. From the start, then, conducting and composing vied for attention, as ever they would.

It's significant that Bernstein attended a major university as an undergrad, rather than a conservatory. This fit perfectly his intellectual hunger to know and understand as much as possible. Among the humanities professors at Harvard, one stood out: David Prall, whose course on aesthetics struck Bernstein with great force. The larger aspects of music—its potential to express things otherwise inexpressible, its social and political significance—took on vast importance for the budding composer. The majority of Bernstein's pieces will not be content to exhibit species counterpoint or advanced harmonic techniques: they will look hard at the human condition, explore the follies of history, advocate for peace, address God.

Lenny's education continued with graduate studies at the Curtis Institute in Philadelphia where he studied conducting with Fritz Reiner and orchestration with Randall Thompson. He later claimed that he never studied composition per se, and that advice from his friend and older colleague, Aaron Copland, was as close as it got. In a television documentary from the 1980s about teachers, Bernstein related how he worked with Copland:

"The closest I came to [having a composition teacher] was with Aaron Copland, whom I met by accident on his birthday in November, 1937, on one of my rare trips to New York [from Harvard]. . . . Everything I wrote from then on, every bar I ever wrote [for many years], I would bring to Aaron. He would say, 'This is rewarmed Scriabin or second-hand something. Throw it away. But these two bars are fresh. They are you. Work on those, develop those.' That sort of criticism. I revere and worship Aaron Copland for what he taught me about what not to write, what to throw away" (*Teachers and Teaching: An Autobiographical Essay by Leonard Bernstein*). Bernstein also got his first work as a published composer—or least, arranger—through Copland. The elder composer had been to Mexico and brought back with him a bunch of folksongs that he turned into an orchestral piece called *El Salon Mexico*. Simply because he liked the work, or perhaps to impress his friend and mentor, Bernstein arranged it for solo piano and played the result for Copland, who in turn suggested that Bernstein take the arrangement to his publisher, Boosey & Hawkes. To Bernstein's surprise,

Boosey & Hawkes not only bought the arrangement for a whopping $25, they commissioned him to write a two-piano version for $50. "I was the richest guy in the world," Bernstein later recalled. More important than the money was that the *El Salon Mexico* arrangements were his entrée to Boosey & Hawkes, later to become his major publisher.

The budding composing career progressed side by side with a blossoming conducting career. In 1940, a summer music institute was established at Tanglewood in the Berkshires, in Bernstein's home state of Massachusetts. Lenny studied there with conductor Serge Koussevitzky, who exercised a deep influence on Bernstein throughout his life, beginning a legendary, lifelong association with the institute, first as student, then as teacher. Bernstein's final appearance as a conductor would be with the student orchestra at Tanglewood.

Bernstein's early scores are a search for self, for a voice. In a way, the Bernstein oeuvre itself will continue this search, turning the quest for a voice into the voice itself. Here is Bernstein's so-called eclecticism, a word thrown at him by critics throughout his career, culminating in the insipid attacks made upon the composer's *Mass* in 1971. This so-called eclecticism only means that, once he got past emulating Scriabin and company, the young composer turned naturally to the music of his time and his life: to Gershwin and Copland, to jazz, to the variety of folk music sources made available by the new technology of sound recording, and last, but far from least, to the music of Hebrew worship. These disparate influences did not remain distinct, but blended into an emergent style. If the influences sometimes "stick out," it's because the ambition of the composer is to embrace them all ("Lenny was omni-everything"), and somehow make them work inside his own musical impulse, even when they don't. Eclectic? Yes. But the flip side of eclectic is universal, and the very fact that the Bernstein fabric contains so many threads makes it a garment to be worn by all. "Who Am I?" is the name of a song Bernstein will later write (both music and lyric) for a production of *Peter Pan*. In it, Bernstein has the character of Wendy wonder aloud if her life was something "planned in advance," or if she had been born "by chance." In addition to being a childlike admission of the songwriter's quest for a personal self, it's an example of how Bernstein's musical language could make a home in any number of houses. Born on Broadway, it has been featured in classical recitals, and was later given a highly personalized and embroidered cover by avant-garde jazz singer-

pianist Nina Simone. Similarly, Barbra Streisand expanded one of the
songs from Bernstein's first "classical" song cycle, *I Hate Music*, into the
title number of her celebrated TV special and album, *My Name Is
Barbra*. For that matter, the list of Bernstein's most-performed symphonic works is topped, not by one of his symphonies, but by the Symphonic Dances from *West Side Story*.

Bernstein's earliest mature compositions were: a sonata for clarinet
and piano; a set of brief piano pieces called "Anniversaries"; a "kid's"
song cycle for voice and piano; and a symphony for orchestra with solo
voice. Most of the music Bernstein composed as a student had consisted of chamber scores (a violin sonata, a piano trio, etc.—works for
small ensembles). When, at Tanglewood, Lenny befriended the brilliant young clarinetist David Oppenheim, it seemed natural for him to
write a work the two of them could play. As it happened, another
clarinetist—and another David as well, this one David Glazer—played
the world premiere of Bernstein's Clarinet Sonata in Boston in 1942,
though Oppenheim gave the New York premiere the following year.
Bernstein was the pianist both times. The work now seems slim, its
eleven minutes not particularly redolent of Bernstein's personality. But
compared to the student works, it was a major step forward into the
realm of an individual style. Here's an overview.

The first movement of Bernstein's initial opus is marked *Grazioso*.
The use of an Italian tempo designation is one of very few things about
it not redolent of the music of Paul Hindemith, who would've used his
native German instead. This is Bernstein's announcement to the world
of his intent to be a composer. Yet here he is, so clearly emulating the
neoclassical formalism of Hindemith that almost every review of the
piece spotted it. Nor does the brief *Andantino* that follows make any
better case for Bernstein's individual voice. It is clearly a tribute to
American composer Aaron Copland, a close friend and mentor. But
then, after little more than a minute, the *Andantino* is tossed aside and
out of the blue comes a new movement-within-a-movement, marked
Vivace. This is where the piece has wanted to be all along. We have
traversed the homage to Hindemith, we have acknowledged the presence of Copland, and now we are skating rapidly over an unfamiliar
terrain that is half jazz-gesture and half playful abandon. The time
signature changes from 5/8 to 3/8 to 7/8 and back again, a free employment of metrical morphing that would become a Lenny trademark.

Bernstein's Opus One, as it were (though he did not use opus numbers), is a journey of self-discovery. Its uniqueness lies precisely in its struggle to assert the composer's musical selfhood. If it is impatient to get there, that too is part of the piece's charm. As Bernstein grew into musical maturity, he borrowed less, and did more to develop a distinctly personal style. But inherent in this style was a search for musical identity, and this, in turn, owed to the music he experienced in childhood.

Though the Clarinet Sonata is today an accepted part of that instrument's repertoire, it has had its critics, and indeed the overall feeling of the piece is rather tentative. It is slightly rushed and the borrowings are obvious. But it dances. It announces itself as one thing, does a sonic striptease in the brief slow section, and re-emerges in the *Vivace* reborn. Remarkably, though instrumental chamber music was the dominant genre of Bernstein's work between 1935 and 1942, he all but abandoned it thereafter. Some little brass pieces from 1959 and the curious Variations on an Octatonic Scale from the last year of his life are the only chamber scores Bernstein wrote after the Clarinet Sonata.

What would become Bernstein's Symphony No. 1, *Jeremiah*, began as a "Hebrew song" for soprano and piano that Bernstein wrote in 1939 based on excerpts from the Old Testament Book of Lamentations. It is significant that this first of many times he set Hebrew to music, Bernstein chose a tragic passage about the fall of Jerusalem; significant, because the fall of Jerusalem is emblematic of the loss of faith, a theme that will persist throughout the composer's life. The song sat in a drawer until 1942, when the New England Conservatory announced a contest for a new symphony. Bernstein leapt at the opportunity to use the contest as an excuse to write his first, large-scale orchestral work. The idea occurred to orchestrate the song as the last movement of a three-movement symphony, the first two movements of which would be purely instrumental evocations of prophet Jeremiah's dire warning, and the "profanation" or sacrilegious acts of the Hebrew people. Whether because he found out about the contest late, or because his many obligations led to procrastination, Bernstein found himself in a panic to make the deadline of December 31, 1942. He even got friends and family to help him copy the parts. In the end, he had to deliver the piece personally to the conservatory, with just two hours to spare. The symphony lost the contest. A verbal outline of the *Jeremiah* Symphony follows:

I. PROPHECY

Jeremiah begins in anguish, with a protest and a cry. The protest is heard quietly at the start, in eighth-note dissonances in the strings and timpani. In three iterations, the eighth notes go from *piano* to *forte* and then, at their last sounding, the first horn enters in the wailing expression of a cry like a human voice making grim pronouncement. The woodwinds take this up in shrill high register, and our brief introduction is over. The strings, in dramatic unison, utter a subject distinguished by steep intervals of the fourth and fifth. This will play out over the next several measures in richly harmonized elaborations from the strings and woodwinds, while the brass and timpani punctuate it from time to time with the two-note protest motive.

A solo flute softly takes up the horn's initial subject over an even softer snare drum roll, leading to a gathering of clarinets and bassoons in thick conversation. A plangent little English horn solo of declamatory nature is followed by a cadence into E minor, the key center of the movement. The twin eighth notes of protest now become a gentle accompaniment, upon which the flutes build a long-lined melody that emphasizes the fall of a step or half step, followed by a deeper fall of a fifth or fourth. This gesture will be echoed in the last movement, but flipped, when the central orchestral melody, first in the flutes and then the violins, falls a sixth and then a step. The entire orchestra takes up the development of the central ideas and harmonic tension grows and intensifies until it is released in what certainly must be the musical equivalent of the prophet's words of doom: a *fortississimo* blast of the earlier stepwise statement by the English horn. The orchestration thins and harmonic entanglements fall away until we are left with a bare E minor triad in the lower strings.

II. PROFANATION

In clock time, the second movement is not quite as long as the first movement and a great deal shorter than the concluding, sung movement. Yet it occupies 314 of the symphony's 529 measures, and each of those measures is busier than the last. Here is Bernstein's first musical statement as himself, fully and truly. The final movement of the Clarinet Sonata says mildly the name "Bernstein," and the first movement of the present work announces his intention to be a symphonist of real mettle. But this masterful scherzo has depth of feeling, originality of means, and sheer brilliance in the orchestration. While still very young, Bernstein learned a great deal about orchestration, perhaps from score study or maybe from that subject's teacher at Harvard or both. He knew how to color a string line by doubling a wind instrument, how to exploit the various characters of instruments in their different ranges, how to use the range of non-pitched percussion instruments to fullest effect. As his conducting career took off and he experienced firsthand the capabilities of the modern symphony orchestra, this aspect of his composing art only deepened.

The title of this movement and its role in the score's dramatic scheme may indicate the portrayal of a people in rebellion against their God, but buoyancy and irresistible rhythmic abandon make it an entirely genial musical companion. Again, we encounter the ambiguity of values in the Bernstein cosmos: the profanation may be sacrilege, but it is also ecstatic. Bernstein is now completely free of metric constraints, of the accepted measures of four or three or two beats, one after the next. Nor are we talking of simply creating rhythmic grooves of repeated bars in odd counts like seven or five (though Bernstein will do this). No, the rhythms of *Profanation* shift as they will, creating patterns that elude any effort to identify a regular beat. Seven shifts to five, then to four, then to six and to seven again, and on and on. The rhythms that evolve over this metric flux are, to use a word that will attach itself to the composer again and again, *mercurial*.

When Bernstein composed *Jeremiah*, modern composers had already enjoyed "freedom from the barline" for nearly three decades. Many pages of Stravinsky's *Le Sacre du Printemps* (1913) exhibit exactly this kind of constant meter-shifting; ditto the first movement of Bartok's *Music for Strings, Percussion and Celesta* (1936); and there are many other examples. So what is significant about Bernstein's use of this device? Because in his case, it flows from the additive, non-metrical rhythms of Hebrew. Meter is not an aspect of Hebrew poetry, as has been pointed out by scholar Donald Broadrubb. The alternation of syllables in Hebrew does not naturally shape itself to regular beats. In Hebrew, Broadrubb writes, "The line between prose and poetry is often more indistinct than we might like" (93). He cites a passage in the book of Jeremiah, the very source of Bernstein's inspiration, that appears first as poetry and then, without the change of a syllable, as prose. When poetry does appear in Hebrew, it fits no metered scheme: "There is no known poem in biblical Hebrew which fits any metrical theory completely" (Broadrubb 93). In other words, accents in Hebrew—poetry as well as prose—follow the same irregular patterns as the constant time signature shifts in *Profanation*.

But there is an even more intimate connection between *Profanation* and traditional Hebrew: the melody is "derived, note for note" from the melody assigned to a tune Bernstein had sung at his bar mitzvah. In a video interview with Humphrey Burton, Bernstein explains how he sped up and "rhythmicized" the tune that makes up the central idea of this movement.

III. *LAMENTATION*

The "Hebrew song" that began it all has been changed from a soprano solo to a mezzo-soprano solo. The melody bends downward, ever downward in its melodic contours. Jerusalem lost is a people lost. The emotional range, however, is not limited to guilt-ridden grieving. By turns, the music evokes loss, outrage, compassion, remorse, and even, in the cradling melody that emerges, between verses of the song, in woodwinds and strings, some shard of hope. Defiance hangs at the edge of sorrow's expression, as is nearly always the case when Bernstein approaches God/father. The symphony ends with the three-note motive of the "hope" melody softly repeated. In a last, quiet melodic gesture, the downward turn of the motive is quietly reversed.

Bernstein dedicated the *Jeremiah* Symphony to his father, yet another instance of the emotional ambiguities surrounding his and Sam Bernstein's relationship. The dedication and the ultimate success of the work resulted in what the composer later called "a great reconciliation" with his father. Though it did not win the contest, Bernstein's *Jeremiah* Symphony entered the repertoire and is today performed, while the contest winner has been long forgotten. Two conductors vied for the right of their orchestras to premiere the symphony, and both were the composer's teachers: Fritz Reiner in Pittsburgh, and Serge Koussevitzky in Boston. Reiner won, arranging for Bernstein to lead his Pittsburgh musicians in the world premiere on January 28, 1944. The Boston premiere was scheduled for the following month, the composer once again conducting.

When these performances were planned, Bernstein was a total unknown. A certain event in the fall of 1943 changed all that and catapulted the young musician to fame, in turn throwing a spotlight on the premieres that otherwise would not have been shown. We'll encounter that event in the next chapter.

Meanwhile, Bernstein composed and composed and occasionally earned a performance or got a score published. The *Seven Anniversaries*, short piano sketches dedicated to various friends, relatives, and colleagues, came out in print in 1943, the same year he wrote, published, and premiered his first song cycle, *I Hate Music*. *Seven Anniversaries* initiated a lifelong series of pieces so named; sets of *Four Anniversaries* and *Five Anniversaries* and *Thirteen Anniversaries* would follow. We'll take a look at all twenty-nine of these miniatures in a section following this chapter.

The curiously named *I Hate Music* (the title comes from a phrase thrown at Bernstein by a roommate when he played the piano too late at night) was a set of five "kid's songs" to the composer's own lyrics. The words are baby-simple but also full of wonderment at the world around and within, as befits their purported speaker/singer, a ten-year-old girl. The five are "My Name is Barbara," the song that was later changed by Streisand into "My Name Is Barbra," "Jupiter Has Seven Moons," "I Hate Music!," "A Big Indian and a Little Indian (Riddle Song)," and "I'm a Person Too." The five trace a little journey of self-discovery. It's not the last time Bernstein will write kid's songs. In his final song cycle, *Arias and Barcarolles*, he will set a silly poem by his mother called "Little Smary," and in the songs for a 1950 production of *Peter Pan*, he will have the character of Wendy explore her burgeoning selfhood in songs that include the aforementioned "Who Am I?" Bernstein's kidsong style is a different strand from his Hebrew-influenced or jazz-influenced music. Deliberately a little on the side of being "sing-songish," the melodies stick to familiar turns of direction for the most part, but then suddenly go sideways with rhythmic surprises or shifts of range. It is yet another stylistic arrow in the Bernstein quiver so frequently described as "eclectic."

Bernstein had by this time befriended a mezzo-soprano named Jennie Tourel. Her dark, smoky sound would inform not only "I Hate Music" but, the following year, the last movement of *Jeremiah* and, much later, the original version of Symphony No. 3, *Kaddish*. With the composer at the piano, Tourel premiered the cycle on August 24, 1943, the eve of Lenny's twenty-fifth birthday, at the Public Library in Lenox, Massachusetts, his old stomping grounds. World premieres anywhere are important, but New York premieres trump them, so when Tourel announced that she would include "I Hate Music" in her New York recital of November 13, 1943, it was a major coup for the young composer. One imagines Lenny looking forward to November 13 the way one might to a special holiday or feast. As it turned out, that day would be his last on earth as an unknown musician. Celebrity was about to come crashing down on Leonard Bernstein.

THE *ANNIVERSARIES* FOR PIANO

In 1943, Bernstein wrote the first of four sets of *Anniversaries* for solo piano. These are snippets of expression, sketches of ideas that the composer would sometimes pick up and expand in other, larger works. Reflecting the importance he placed on the people in his life, each *Anniversary* is dedicated to a friend, relative, or colleague, either on the occasion of a birthday or some other happy event, or in memoriam. Bernstein continued to write *Anniversaries* throughout his early years, stopped writing them during the busy middle decades of his career, and returned to them late in life, composing a total of twenty-nine in all. We will jump the timeline here and present tiny individual descriptions of these brief but engaging pieces, several of which will later become parts of larger compositions.

SEVEN ANNIVERSARIES (1943)

I. For Aaron Copland (November 14, 1900)

The first anniversary is a fleet, light piece that announces a three-note motive in clear A major, then toys with the idea as it slides into other tonal spaces (but not too far) before coming to rest via a few "wrong" notes.

II. For My Sister, Shirley (October 3, 1923)

An angular, yet lyrical melody in octaves fills the right hand, while the left comments in descending eighth notes shaped in quartal harmony—chords made of fourths rather than the usual thirds. One feels the steeliness beneath the grace.

III. In Memoriam: Alfred Eisner (January 4, 1941)

Alfred Eisner was a brilliant fellow student and close friend at Harvard who died young of cancer. Bernstein remembers him in a piece that first grieves in a quiet little gesture that starts, stops, and starts again. This brief statement is followed by a quiet, stabbing little quotation of the *dies irae*, the chant for the dead. The motive of interruption repeats, flowing into a short, plaintive, upward-reaching melody based on the opening gesture. The motive of interruption returns again, this time stepping on itself in an attempt to grow out of its confined space—to proceed and to grow, uninterrupted. This increases until at last it breaks, and then . . . the *dies irae* again, this time in strident triumph. The piece concludes with the plaintive melody and a final allusion to the *dies irae*. This is one of the most touching and fully realized of all the anniversaries.

IV. For Paul Bowles (December 31, 1910)

Bowles, a composer and author (he would write *The Sheltering Sky*), is honored with a perpetual-motion sort of piece that finds the left hand in a motoring mode and the right soaring up into the stratosphere and staying there.

V. In Memoriam: Nathalie Koussevitzky (January 15, 1942)

Serge Koussevitzky's second wife, daughter of a wealthy tea merchant, was his right arm for decades. She is remembered here in a slow-tempo piece alternatively sweetly singing and sepulchral. This music will reappear in different garb in Bernstein's Symphony No. 2, *Age of Anxiety*.

VI. For Sergei Koussevitzky (July 26, 1874)

Bernstein's conducting mentor/musical father is commemorated with a rather austere, note-against-note piece that references, perhaps, Koussevitzky's lifelong dedication to new music. There is no definite feeling of key until the very last chord, which, when it finally arrives, comes as a shock. (Koussevitzky's first name is here spelled in the fashion of transliterated Russian; it is more frequently spelled in the French form, without the "i.")

VII. For William Schuman (August 4, 1910)

Bernstein's tribute to his colleague and fellow composer William Schuman is a brief burst of energy in triplets, mostly monodic (one note at a time, no harmonies), suggestive of a busy and original imagination.

FOUR ANNIVERSARIES (1948)

I. For Felicia Montealegre (February 6, 1922)

Chilean-born New York actress Felicia Montealegre accepted Bernstein's proposal of marriage in late 1946, but the couple called it off at the end of 1947. Four years later, they would reunite and marry. It is clear from this portrait of charm and spirited strength that in 1948 Bernstein still found in Felicia much to admire, despite the dashed wedding plans. A serenely beautiful theme in 3/8 time but with perfectly "misplaced" accents pronounces a kind of solemn joyfulness. The more animated middle section doesn't take us far away, and the return to the lyric "A" section, which occurs beneath the continuing—and even intensifying—flood of sixteenth notes, is inevitable and right. The indication "dolce"—"sweet"—appears three times in the piece's forty-seven measures. This is one of the more substantial of the twenty-nine *Anniversaries*.

II. For Johnny Mehegan (June 6, 1920)

The dedicatee was a Tanglewood pianist with whom Bernstein often played four-hand piano jazz. A picture of jazz-flavored whimsy, this is one of the shorter anniversaries. It zips past, mostly at *piano* or an even softer dynamic, all jagged rhythms and blue-note harmonies.

III. For David Diamond (July 6, 1915)

A reflective piece written for his friend and fellow composer, David Diamond, who was once a next door neighbor and piano/four-hands partner. A simple four-note motive is announced, mulled over, developed along lines both rational and mildly adventurous. The ascending perfect fifth of the opening melody becomes a brief but majestic harmonic statement near the end.

IV. For Helen Coates (July 19, 1899)

This is the first of two *Anniversaries* written for the woman who was first Bernstein's beloved piano teacher, then his lifelong secretary. The second, in the final set of thirteen, will be dedicated in memoriam. This *Allegro giocoso* boasts octaves and scales and runs, just as you might expect in a piece dedicated to a piano teacher. An overall feel of driven-but-loving, no-nonsense purposefulness comes across.

FIVE ANNIVERSARIES (1949–1951)

I. For Elizabeth Rudolf (b. January 23, 1894)

Elizabeth Rudolf was the mother of a Tanglewood friend from Wyoming. One imagines her a sprightly woman, as she inspired this slick little Allegretto that slips from C major to C-sharp major and back again. The piece will show up as the "A " section theme of the second movement to the composer's soon-to-come *Serenade After Plato's Symposium*.

II. For Lukas Foss (b. August 15, 1922)

Piquant and pointed, in alternating measures of four and three, this fleet portrait of another of Bernstein's fellow composers roams the keyboard freely with only the gesture of a strong pick-up note to unify. This one, too, will show up as a part of the *Serenade*'s second movement, its "B" section to be precise. (Such self-borrowings are not unusual among composers. Handel recycled portions of Messiah through a series of organ concertos; Beethoven's ballet *The Creatures of Prometheus*, became the last movement of his Eroica Symphony, etc.)

III. For Elizabeth B. Ehrman (b. January 22, 1883)

Our second Elizabeth was the mother of Ken Ehrman, a Harvard friend who remained in touch with Bernstein throughout the years. She must have had a lively personality to have inspired this rollicking Allegro, which will later reappear in the party scene in *Serenade*'s last movement.

IV. For Sandy Gellhorn (b. April 23, 1951)

The final pieces in this set were composed for the children of two of Bernstein's closest female friends. Author Martha Gellhorn was Ernest Hemingway's third wife, and when she met Bernstein in Israel in 1948 they hit it off. The pair lived together for a time in Mexico, but it's unclear whether they were lovers. Sandy was Gellhorn's son, and this graceful piece has the feeling of a cradle song in which a disconsolate child is slowly assured of safety and comfort, and coaxed to sleep.

V. For Susanna Kyle (b. July 24, 1949)

Susanna was the first-born daughter of Bernstein's friend and collaborator Betty Comden. Quiet and meditative, this *Anniversary* relies for its sweetness on a simple gesture that is reset in different implied keys throughout.

THIRTEEN ANNIVERSARIES

These were published in 1988, but composed between 1964 and 1988.

I. For Shirley Gabis Rhoads Perle (b. April 7, 1924)

A girlfriend in the early 1940s and a lifelong friend afterward, Shirley Gabis Rhoads Perle is here given the most nostalgic of *Anniversaries*, a piece built on a simple dotted-rhythm motive that insists, throughout brief attempts to be changed, on staying the same.

II. In Memoriam: William Kapell (September 20, 1922–October 29, 1953)

William Kapell was the great hope of American pianism when he died in a tragic plane crash while on tour. The burst of energy that is this tiniest of pieces does something to suggest the steeliness and command of his playing.

III. For Stephen Sondheim (b. March 22, 1930)

Bernstein's salute to his *West Side Story* lyricist is a gentle blues that meanders to and fro, changing its direction but never losing its essentially wistful character. He will also use the piece in his 1983 opera, *A Quiet Place*.

IV. For Craig Urquhart (b. September 3, 1953)

Pianist-composer Urquhart headed the Bernstein Office for a number of years. This crisp *Allegretto*, a mock-waltz, is one of the happiest of all the *Anniversaries*. Bernstein lets accents fall where they may, and the result is a dizzying dance. Mostly in cut time, one hand will occasionally carve out a three-beat phrase against the two-beat of the other.

V. For Leo Smit (b. January 12, 1921)

For this pianist-friend, Bernstein had provided a tiny, rapid-fire two-part invention that begs to go on, but stops anyway. The motive is a twelve-tone row that Bernstein manipulates to come out tonally.

VI. For My Daughter, Nina (b. February 28, 1962)

Played at the indicated metronome, this is the longest of all the *Anniversaries*, and is certainly one of the more enigmatic, as well as one of the most fully developed. The tempo indication is "Slow and a bit melancholy," not the sort of thing you might expect from a piece dedicated to his youngest child. But the feeling is more bittersweet than melancholy, and there is a sense of wanting to hold on to something that time makes slip away. Intensely chromatic (but not twelve-tone), it ends the most ambiguous chord in the harmonic catalogue, a minor triad with a major seventh on top.

VII. In Memoriam: Helen Coates (July 19, 1899–February 27, 1989)

Dated "17 July 1970," this is the "Meditation No. 1" from *Mass* (1971), arranged for piano solo. When Coates, his piano teacher and longtime personal secretary, died shortly before the publication of the *Thirteen Anniversaries*, Bernstein inscribed it to her memory. Here is one of Bernstein's most pungent expressions of despair, only marginally offset by loving beauty. At a painfully slow *Largo*, an aching melody tries to hold on to its highest note, but falls inexorably, underpinned by severe intervals of the seventh. A brief middle section marked "Tranquillo" offers comfort, but the despair returns, and even a coda of the comfort music does not dispel its effect.

VIII. In Memoriam: Goddard Lieberson (April 5, 1911–May 29, 1977)

The written date (1964) precedes the death of the "in memoriam" dedicatee, so Bernstein must have written the piece while Lieberson, a record producer and friend, was still alive, publishing it only after his death. It's a jolly, optimistic little dance in crystal clear F major, no clouds in sight.

IX. For Jessica Fleischmann (b. September 19, 1965)

The dedicatee, daughter of London Symphony Orchestra administrative head Ernest Fleischmann, was not yet twelve at the time Bernstein wrote this fey, sweet-yet-probing piece in June of 1977. The pianist is at times instructed to make "a sound like 'tsk' or a light tap or snap." Was Jessica a frustrated piano student who made little "tsk" sounds when she played a wrong note?

X. In Memoriam: Constance Hope (December 23, 1904–June 13, 1977)

Hope was an artists' representative and the wife of Bernstein's optometrist. Spare and honest in its mourning, the piece broods over a handful of notes, then suddenly all falls away and we hear a twelve-tone row, over which are written corresponding words from Edgar Allen Poe. The experience repeats, with changes, and the second time we hear the row the words from Poe are: "No more shall bloom the thunder-blasted tree. No more."

XI. For Felicia, On Our 28th Birthday (& Her 52nd)

Bernstein met his future wife on her birthday in the year 1946, thus the dedication of this 1974 piece. Short, by turns sweet and a little feisty, a pall hangs over it when one realizes that the trauma of Bernstein leaving her for a male lover was shortly to come.

XII. For Aaron Stern (b. November 3, 1949)

With Bernstein's help, young Stern, an educator who befriended Bernstein late in life, later established the Academy for the Love of Learning, an alternative teaching institution in Santa Fe, New Mexico. This straightforward piece, patient in its clear unfolding, seems the perfect piece for a teacher.

XIII. In Memoriam: Ellen Goetz (June 16, 1930–January 27, 1986)

The final *Anniversary* of this set and the last of the twenty-nine is a plaintive-but-pretty waltz, Chopinesque in the simple chromatic working-out of its harmonies. The dedicatee was a fan who became a friend.

2

CELEBRITY

Bernstein's composing career took a small but significant step forward that Saturday night in New York. Tourel's American debut was greeted by critics as a major event, and *I Hate Music* was called by Virgil Thomson of the *New York Herald Tribune* "witty, alive and adroitly fashioned" (qtd. in Burton 114), generous words from a normally waspish critic. For the first time in the composer's young life, a score by Bernstein—albeit only a whimsical, seven-minute song cycle—had been performed by a major artist in an important venue. If not for the life-shaking event of the very next day, the date of November 13, 1943, surely would have gone down in the Bernstein saga as the most important of the decade. But November 14, 1943, would eclipse everything that had happened before, and cast both light and shadow over everything that was to come. It essentially decided Bernstein's musical fate. That was the day he became a conducting celebrity, the day he was made both freeman and slave. To echo Schopenhauer, November 14, 1943, was the day Bernstein was made free to do whatever he wanted—but not free to want what he wanted.

Throughout his life, Bernstein proclaimed composing to be his real and ultimate goal. Not merely to compose music, but "to be a composer" was his desired aim. In a 1963 speech honoring French composer Edgard Varese, Bernstein wrote words that would later be prominently quoted in a PBS special about him. They echo the Gospel according to John: "In the beginning was the note. And the note was with god. And whosoever could reach for the note—reach high and bring it back to us on earth—to our earthly ears, he is a composer" (Bernstein, *Findings* 210). Bernstein believed his life would be spent reaching for that note. To be sure, the intervening discovery of conducting had led him down a twin path, and yet, as of the fall of 1943, both paths were roughly parallel. The one—conducting—could have been abandoned, or at least marginalized, had the other narrow trail suddenly opened up into an avenue. This, however, was not to be. As it turned out, it was the conducting path that would open wide, and in spectacular fashion.

In the summer of 1943, Bernstein had accepted a position as assistant conductor of the New York Philharmonic. It was a singularly inglorious job. For $125 a week (a small, but not unreasonable salary at the time) he studied the scores for every concert and sat in on rehearsals. Should music director Artur Rodzinksi or a guest conductor fall ill at the last minute, the assistant conductor would step in, so Bernstein needed to know every note. Without an illness or other unanticipated absence, however, the assistant conductor's preparations might never come to fruition. Bernstein was an understudy, and understudies rarely take the limelight.

But fate trumps all statistics. The conductor scheduled for a concert the afternoon of Sunday, November 14, 1943, was the great Bruno Walter. Walter was to lead a program comprising Schumann's *Manfred* Overture; the Theme, Variations and Finale of modern Hungarian composer Miklos Rozsa, known today primarily for his film scores; Richard Strauss's *Don Quixote*, and Wagner's *Meistersinger* Prelude. The challenging program demanded a conductor with a knack for navigating tricky rhythms (in the Rozsa), the ability to coordinate diverse forces (the Strauss included extensive dialogue between solo cello and orchestra), and a feel for grand Romantic gesture (the Schumann and the Wagner). So it's understandable that, when informed Sunday morning that Walter had come down with the flu, Philharmonic manager Bruno Zirato called Rodzinksi to see if he could take the helm instead.

Rodzinski was at his country home in Stockbridge, Connecticut, and though it wasn't yet Thanksgiving, Stockbridge, normally a four-hour drive from New York, was already snowed-in, making a return trip arduous and that much longer. Rodzinski's answer to Zirato: "Get Bernstein. That's what he's for" (Burton 114). Bernstein was asleep in his Carnegie Hall apartment when he got the call at 9 a.m. By that time, there was no opportunity to arrange a last-minute rehearsal. Bernstein simply went over the scores at Walter's bedside and showed up in the hall, ready as he ever would be. This was no ordinary concert, but one in a series of programs to be broadcast over national radio. Bernstein would be conducting, not only for a couple thousand people in Carnegie Hall, but for an audience of millions, nationwide.

It can be difficult to understand the place of classical music in America more than seventy years ago, given our view from a culture that relegates it to a place of marginal status, looking at it as an acquired taste with seemingly little relevance to popular culture. But in the first half of the twentieth century, the middle class grew up taking piano lessons and going to symphony concerts. The demand for classical music was great enough that the National Broadcasting Company even formed an orchestra of its own—the NBC Symphony—and hired the great conductor Arturo Toscanini to conduct it. American radio audiences listened to Toscanini broadcasts with almost religious fervor, making them one of NBC Radio's most popular items, and creating competition from other orchestras, including the New York Philharmonic broadcasts, which aired over CBS Radio. A twenty-five-year-old, last-minute substitute conductor leading such a broadcast was therefore a very big deal, and not least for the reason that here was an American-born and educated musician doing a job usually reserved for older Europeans such as Toscanini and Walter. World War II was raging, and the idea that a young American might lead a concert of such venerated music had a distinctly patriotic aspect. The event also boasted the two necessary ingredients of Bernsteinian greatness: there was a plan, and not quite enough time. He didn't even own the proper formal wear for the event, and without time to purchase same, had to make do with a gray business suit.

Was he nervous? Bernstein later recalled: "Out I strode, in my funny double-breasted suit, and—polite smattering of applause—went wildly into the crazy three opening chords of *Manfred*, and it was like a great electric shock. From then on, I was just sailing. I don't know what happened, but those three chords I will never forget. *Dum dum DUM!*—pause. And in that pause I knew that everything was going to be all right" (*Newsday* interview, 1967).

Thus began the Bernstein mode of becoming lost in the music. Throughout his conducting life, the act of leading an orchestra seemed to confound Bernstein's left brain to the point that only his right brain functioned, albeit at the highest level. Here's an example from later in Bernstein's career: This writer once accompanied Bernstein to the Juilliard School, where several students worked at preparing an orchestra in the intricacies of Mahler's Symphony No. 7, a score Bernstein was to conduct that very week. The orchestra and student conductors were on that day preparing the second of the two *Nachtmusik* sections (*Andante amoroso*), orchestral nocturnes that offset what Bernstein termed the "parodistic" mood of the Seventh's other movements. The maestro said a few words about Mahler and the Seventh and how difficult a symphonic nut it was to crack, then he picked up his baton and began. Several minutes passed, the music ended, and Bernstein looked out at the orchestra and at the students, as if coming out of a swoon. With utter sincerity he asked, "Tell me, what did I do?"

On that Sunday afternoon in the fall of 1943, twenty-five-year-old Leonard Bernstein got lost in the music in the actual or virtual presence of millions of listeners. He had awakened that morning the writer of a short, well-received song cycle, a nascent composing talent with a somewhat promising future and some nice words from America's most important music critic. He would awake the next day a superstar, an overnight sensation with an all-but guaranteed future on the podiums of major orchestras worldwide. The *New York Times* of Monday, November 15, featured coverage of the concert, not in the arts and entertainment section, but on the front page. Reviews in all the press were glowing, citing the conductor's attractive combination of vigorous youth and mature self-confidence. Leonard Bernstein was on the way to becoming a household name.

The rest of Bernstein's professional life would consist of tug-o'-war between the fame and fortune of conducting and the inner compulsion to "reach for the note." It might have been easier had he looked upon conducting as merely a way to make money while supporting his first love, composition. But in truth, Bernstein aspired to conduct every bit as much as he wanted to compose. The urge to lead musicians in performance came from a different place than the urge to compose, and the two activities spoke to contrasting personal elements in the man. Conducting must have appealed to Bernstein's love of people, crowds, and excitement. Composing on the other hand was a lonely task. Creating a piece of music meant patient solitude, and the ability to "go inside."

This extrovert/introvert dichotomy was not absolute, of course. One drifted into the other. On the podium, with a hundred musicians before him and two thousand listeners behind him, Bernstein of necessity withdrew into that secret, inner sanctum where his ego evaporated and only the music existed, the place he went when he conducted Mahler for the Juilliard students. Living the music inside of himself, Bernstein-the-conductor "became" the composers of the scores he led. Bernstein often said that as he conducted an orchestra he felt he was Beethoven or Shostakovich or Elgar creating the music inside his own body, as it were. This close identification with composers' creative processes charged Bernstein-led performances with high energy and spontaneity.

On the flip side, did Bernstein borrow from his public persona to feed the inner workings of Bernstein-the-composer? Certainly the composers he championed on the podium were often the composers who influenced his own style. Among these were three who shared a Jewish heritage: Mahler, Copland, and Gershwin. The influence of Gershwin shows in the incorporation of jazz influences in such works as *Fancy Free*, the early musicals, the Masque section of *Age of Anxiety*, and *Prelude, Fugue and Riffs*. From Copland, whose mentorship guided him from very early on, Bernstein inherited a love for folk song of all ethnicities, as demonstrated in the *Danzon* from *Fancy Free*; the faux-tango in *Candide*; the plaintive, and the folkish line of *Somewhere* in *West Side Story*. From Copland also came the spare voicing of chords, the "prairie sound" so closely identified with the elder composer. Bernstein was aware of this indebtedness. He is reported to have said to Copland at the conclusion of the premiere of *Mass*, apropos its closing chorale, "That's you, baby."

Mahler's influence was both formal and personal. As Mahler's symphonies stretched the idea of what a symphony can be, so (more modestly) would Bernstein's three essays in that form challenge the traditional notion of what a symphony is. Bernstein championed Mahler's symphonies, recording all of them twice, and introducing them to audiences from New York to Vienna. He felt a strong connection to the earlier composer for a variety of very good reasons. Like Bernstein, Mahler was a professional conductor whose primary passion was composing, but whose career limited him to composing between conducting engagements. The similarity intensified when Bernstein was named music director of the New York Philharmonic, the very position Mahler held from 1909 until his death two years later. Both men were Jewish, though Bernstein's Judaism was more spiritual than that of the cynically secular Mahler, who never got a bar mitzvah and who converted to Catholicism in midlife in order to qualify for a professional position. (He never took first communion, either.)

As they had for Mahler, conducting and composing would vie for attention throughout Bernstein's life. But at this moment of total triumph on the podium that Sunday afternoon, the two disciplines must have seemed in perfect balance. Conducting, the far more lucrative enterprise of the pair, suddenly had the potential of financially buttressing the composing. Bernstein must have felt a sort of vindication, a green light telling him to go ahead. A project was already underway, and he now turned to it with unleashed youthful energy. That project was the ballet, *Fancy Free*.

The genesis of *Fancy Free* was as fateful as that attending Bernstein's legendary New York Philharmonic debut. One day in the fall of 1943—it's unclear whether before or after the great date of November 14—Bernstein sat in the Russian Tea Room nursing an earworm. A jazzy, impudent little tune had thrust itself into his head and wouldn't go away. Surrendering to its insistent charm, he wrote it down on a napkin and took it home to ponder. That night, a knock came at the door of his Carnegie Hall apartment. It was a young choreographer with Ballet Theatre (later "American Ballet Theatre") who had heard about Bernstein through a series of mutual connections. He had an idea for a ballet in which three sailors on twenty-four-hour leave do the town. Would Bernstein have any interest in writing a jazzy score for such a ballet? "Funny you should ask," Bernstein is purported to have said, and he played the tune from that day. "That's it!" yelled the choreographer, whose name was Jerome Robbins. Thus was born one of the most important collaborations in twentieth-century performing arts. The team of Bernstein and Robbins would cocreate three ballets and three musicals, including one of the most indispensable works ever made for the American stage.

In various press stories through the years, Bernstein described his composing method as lying on the floor or a couch in a darkened room and staring straight up until ideas came to him. A famous Bernstein family story has his wife, Felicia, opening the door to the study to find him in the middle of this practice. "Oh," she says, "I thought you were working." His retort: "I am!" That may have been the method for composing his symphonies and other concert works, but it was not the mode of writing *Fancy Free*. As they began work on the project, Robbins was on tour with Ballet Theatre. So Bernstein had to mail tape recordings of piano four-hands reductions to him wherever he was dancing in order for Robbins to use the music could in turn round up dancers after a performance and create the choreography to the music on the recording. (Bernstein's second pianist for the recordings was no less than Aaron Copland.) When Robbins returned, the collaboration continued as Bernstein sat at a piano in the studio, improvising and composing on the spot, as Robbins set the steps. This kind of composing "live and in person" doubtlessly appealed to the extrovert in Bernstein, the people-loving, party-going artist.

Fancy Free premiered April 18, 1944, and was a smash hit. A "hit ballet" may seem improbable today. But in 1944, it was a marketable entertainment commodity, and the spunky dance ode to the healthy impulses of American Naval personnel enjoyed over a hundred performances in New York, followed by a national tour. It remains today in the repertoire of many ballet companies worldwide. It was no isolated event, but the first of many Bernstein scores used for dance works. Some of these were composed directly for ballets, while others were lifted from their homes on the concert stage. We sometimes divide composers into "singing" composers and "dancing" composers. For example, Verdi was a singer, and Stravinsky was a dancer. Bernstein's combination of vivacious rhythms and poignant melodies made him both. That's part of what makes *West Side Story*, a show that depends heavily for its expressive power on both dance and the singing voice, such a success.

We'll now outline the thirty minutes of music and the choreographic action in *Fancy Free*. While it's possible to hear the score as "just music," there is value in understanding what's supposed to be happening as the music plays. No matter the quality of a ballet score, the accompanying story (if there is one) clings to it like dye to fabric. Even Stravinsky's venerated *Rite of Spring* goes "beyond the music itself" to evoke the primitive, ritual sacrifice of the work's title. This issue of music's meaning—of whether notes can have reference to anything outside themselves—will become a recurrent theme in Bernstein's life.

Fancy Free opens with a lonely bartender in a Manhattan bar. On the jukebox we hear "Big Stuff," a blues ballad written by Bernstein to his own lyric. For the original production, the singer for the recorded song was the composer's sister, Shirley. Bernstein had wanted to hire Billie Holiday, but her price proved too high. A year later, Holiday recorded the song, and it is she that is heard on the first commercial recording of the work. The song is interrupted (too soon, some would say, as the piece has charm) by four rapid-fire rim-shots on the snare drum. Our three sailors make their entrance doing literal cartwheels. To the tune Bernstein penned that day on a Russian Tea Room napkin, they throw themselves headlong into the bar. They dance out their expectations for the coming twenty-four hours of leave. The lusty theme bounces back and forth between full orchestra and solo piano, as Robbins's choreography swings between classical steps and broad mime. One sailor outlines the curvaceous body of a woman, another tries a tap dance routine, and so on. The feeling is of physicality unleashed after weeks of discipline.

This opening trio comes to an end as we hear a more plangent, almost wistful, theme start up in the woodwinds. This alternates with a fast, two-note syncopated motive from the piano: a sonic picture of desire mixed with longing, or even a certain sadness. They have a drink. They chew gum. They stand and wait—but not for long. A new, low-down jazz theme announces the entrance of the first woman. She struts her stuff and the sailors put the moves on, becoming obnoxious in their aggression. In a brilliant choreographic strike, Robbins has the woman "dance" them back and away from her. The flirtation then morphs into a game, as one sailor grabs the woman's purse, slings it over his shoulder, and parades in mimicry of her. At length, she retrieves her purse, knocking down the sailor who took it, and exits, pursued by the two sailors still standing. The remaining sailor is not alone for long. The second girl enters and he regales her (in mime) with stories of his exploits. They dance to a languorous orchestral take on "Big Stuff," the jukebox song. The ensuing duet is a study in seduction that veers off into a more orchestral/classical passage before returning to the song in a bold way. Robbins's choreography includes such flashes of virtuosity as the woman's "fish dive" into the sailor's arms.

The duet ends with a gentle kiss. The other two sailors re-enter with the first woman. The woman has more or less attached herself to one of the sailors, creating the untenable situation of three sailors and two women. Suddenly, the women recognize each other and bond, leaving the sailors perplexed. The five of them retire to a table, and the sailors take turns dancing with the women to the jaunty opening theme. One of the sailors dances an *allegrissimo* solo, a *Galop* showing his prowess in best sailor style, replete with jumps and turns and occasional stops at the bar for drinks. The next sailor dances a more lyrical variation, a *Waltz* over sensuous strings that segues into a jazz dance section, with isolations of knees and hips, and popular dance allusions. It remains for the last sailor to perform the *Danzon* variation, choreographically a canny blend of bravura and sultriness, musically one of Bernstein's sweetest takes on Latin-American style. (When *Fancy Free* is heard in the concert hall, it is in the form of these last three dances as excerpts, only.)

Of course, this has all been for the benefit of the ladies, who must now decide upon which two of the three sailors to bestow their favors. As the women confer on their choices, the sailors grow impatient and at last throw themselves behind the bar and into a fistfight. As the men fight, the women slip out of the bar and into the night. The sailors are left with only their wounded dignity and glasses of whisky. The sad theme from near the start returns, as the men make up and become friends again—albeit lonely ones. Then, the third woman enters. To a spiky little piano solo, she dances for the men's attention. They try not to notice her—they don't want a repeat of what has just happened—but of course, they fail. She floats out of the bar, and they follow in hot pursuit to the sound of a repeated trumpet note that seems to call them into action.

Fancy Free was such a hit that Robbins and Bernstein decided to expand the idea into a full-blown musical. Things fell into place naturally, as they seemed to do so with regularity in Bernstein's young days. Bernstein's friends Betty Comden and Adolph Green came on board to write the book and lyrics. Veteran producer George Abbott took up the project and scheduled it for production by the end of the year. And so, Leonard Bernstein's first musical followed quickly on the heels of his first ballet, the first symphony, and his wildly successful conducting debut. That musical was a brash, bold, youthful show that announced not one, but four fresh musical talents to Broadway: Comden, Green, Robbins, and, of course, Bernstein. Though its premise was identical to

that of *Fancy Free*, the length was quadrupled, all of the music was
new, the story was greatly expanded, and the range of feeling was greater. As with all ballets, the "plot" of *Fancy Free* was mostly an excuse for
dancing, and the music existed primarily to support the dancing. But in
a musical, the songs—both music and lyrics—are the heart of the matter, and expression is limited only by the aims and abilities of the songwriters.

In the songs for *On the Town*, which opened December 28, 1944,
Bernstein let loose a torrent of imagination and talent. The bolting,
masculine rhythms of the show's opener, "New York, New York" (not to
be confused with the 1975 song of the same name, written for Liza
Minnelli by John Kander and Fred Ebb) burst open the doors of popular song with an angular melody that charged up and down and up again
to end at its highest, most exuberant point on the words "New York,
New York—it's a helluva town." The familiar bass-line pattern of boogie
-woogie got pushed to new harmonic and rhythmic levels in the comic
"I Can Cook, Too." The haunting "Some Other Time" turned a diving
octave into a sigh of regret. This is the craft of writing melodies: a
songwriter who knows how to reflect words' emotions in music will
show great care in how the words "fall" on the music. It is no mistake or
random choice that Bernstein chose angular intervals for most of the
songs in a show about youthful adventure and vibrant sexuality.

When we say that a melody is "angular," or that it contains harmonic
surprises, or that a certain melodic gesture (such as a downward moving
octave) expresses this or that emotion, what do we mean? How does the
composer turn the material of music—scales and rhythms and harmonies and such—into the experience of music? And how, specifically,
does Bernstein accomplish this in *On the Town*? Let's take one song,
the mid-tempo love ballad, "Lucky to Be Me," and see what Bernstein
did to make this alchemical conversion of matter to spirit—of chords
and beats and notes to expression of feeling.

Early in the show, Gabey, the wide-eyed romantic one of the three
sailors on shore leave, sings about the "Lonely Town" that New York is,
"when you pass through / And there is no one waiting there for you."
But then he sees a poster on a subway station wall. It's a picture of
"Miss Turnstiles," and for him it's love at first sight. Suddenly, he is on a
mission to find the real Miss Turnstiles. With the finale of Act One fast
approaching, he at last tracks her down and meets her in person. She's

Ivy Smith, an ordinary and, in fact, rather wistful girl who falls in love back at him. This prompts Gabey to shout about what a lucky bum he is. And that's our song.

"Lucky to Be Me" uses a melody Bernstein had originally set to his own, quite different lyric the year previous, but had never used or published. In the context of the new Comden-Green lyric, it's a simple statement of Gabey's ecstatic happiness in finding Ivy. It's a "stand-and-sing" song in which nothing happens to advance the plot or character. Rather, it's a moment in which we bathe in the emotion of one of the show's characters, like Curly singing the beauty of the countryside in "Oh, What a Beautiful Morning," or, for that matter, most of the protestations of love in both opera and musicals. In a stand-and-sing, action stops and goes inside the character. If the song's successful, we go there with it.

Gabey's love song is cast as a perfect A-A-B-A ballad, with an opening verse. The verse is there to introduce the song, to make transition from dialogue to music. The core of the song is A-A-B-A, which is just a way of saying that there is a musical idea (A), followed by the repeat of that idea (A again), followed by a contrasting idea (B), and a final return to the opening "A" once more. There sometimes follows an extension, in which the composer pulls at the A idea like taffy until it stretches into a coda, or endpiece. Richard Rodgers was a master of the extension. If you have time, listen, for example, to "It Might as Well Be Spring." The wistful singer of this lovesick song sings "A," then sings "A" again, and goes on to "B" ("I keep wishing I were somewhere else") and returns to "A" ("I'm as busy as a spider spinning daydreams"), but where the tune has gone before, it does not go again. Instead, on Hammerstein's words "I haven't seen a crocus or a rosebud," it shoots off (just like one of those rosebuds—Rodgers was a canny tone painter) in a new direction, leading to the song's final sentiments and a satisfying end to the song. "Lucky to Be Me" will not have a coda, but it will exhibit one other formal tendency of the typical Broadway song: at the end will come a key change, lifting the singer to an even higher level of punchdrunk Eros.

Why is all this important? Because the songs for Broadway musicals sound the way they do for reasons like these. Popular music in the early to mid-twentieth century (which was interchangeable with the kind of music written for the theater in that era) depends for its effect on form, such as the A-A-B-A form mentioned above, and the flirtatious play of tonal harmonies. In well-crafted songs from those days, the chord structure will frequently "flirt with" other keys, or even slip into them, as in the closing key change of "Lucky to Be Me." Contrast this with the celebrated three-chord song typical of early rock 'n' roll, given in musical shorthand as "I-IV-V," meaning the first, fourth, and fifth chords of any given key. For example, in E major, a typical guitar key, the I, IV, and V chords would be the E, A, and B major chords, respectively. But every one of those chords is potentially a *different* numbered chord in another key. In other words, the E chord is an I in E, but a V in the key of A and a IV in the key of B. The A chord is IV in E, but I in its own key of A, and so on. In other words, chords have no homes except the ones composers choose to give them. Songwriters in the classic era of American popular song liked to move those homes around quite a bit within a song.

Back to "Lucky to Be Me": Gabey starts the verse of the song by remembering that he used to like to "wake up as a couple of other guys." But with the discovery of Ivy has come two things: the feeling of being blessed, and the chorus (the main part of the song). "What a day" sits on the song's first notes like a happy shout. The melody plunges down, but in amazement, not despair, and in the very next measure it races back up to a note higher than the song's beginning. This is what might be called the Bernstein rollercoaster: a melody that constantly pushed to go higher and higher, while sometimes falling first in order to get there. We hear all three primary chords (I, IV, and V) within the first two measures, creating a sense of hurried excitement. The rate of harmonic change has a technical name: "harmonic rhythm." It means simply that the feeling of a piece of music is affected by how quickly the chords change. If Bernstein had written a song that kept the I chord for two measures or more, it would not have had the same effect. In another *On the Town* song, "Lonely Town," the I chord does sit in place for the first two measures, which helps shape a feeling of stasis and abandonment. Harmonic rhythm as an expressive device is largely lost in current (ca. 2014) popular music. The chord changes in most popular songs today are almost universally very slow; the songs rely for expression on other elements, such as vocal inflection and production.

In the first eight measures, "Lucky to Be Me" races up and down and up again in a melodic contour that virtually defines good feeling.

The harmonies shift ever so slightly toward a different, related key, and then scoot back again. The A section repeats, and the B section (called the "bridge" or "release") contrasts about as sharply as you'd want. Instead of big jumps between notes, the melody now slithers chromatically up, up, ever up, coming to rest at just the right place to make the return of the A section seem natural. The B section is repeated, and then, when A returns, it bolts up into a key a minor third higher. This is a stunning change, one that goes way beyond the generic, stereotypical key change of going up a half-step—the minimum possible. The ecstasy felt by Gabey becomes our ecstasy as he sings his final proclamations of love at the high end of his range.

So goes the score of *On the Town*, song after song. In the course of the story, each of our three sailors finds a girl and each, inevitably, must say goodbye to her as he returns to his ship and who-knows-what fate. The goodbye song, the glowingly sad "Some Other Time" is, along with "Lucky to Be Me" and "New York, New York," a favorite of cabaret singers. The 1949 film version starring Frank Sinatra and Gene Kelly is, unfortunately, Hollywood butchery. Only two Bernstein-Comden-Green songs, "New York, New York" and "I Can Cook, Too," made it into the movie. Other songs were replaced by blander numbers, penned by a Hollywood hack. But the show has been frequently revived, and part of its fresh and mercurial breeze of a score has found its way into the concert hall by way of the *Three Dance Episodes from On the Town*. (As of summer 2014, a new Broadway revival of *On the Town* was in the planning stages for an opening in the fall of that year.)

It's not going too far to say that 1944 was the keystone year for Leonard Bernstein as composer. His sudden celebrity as a conductor made possible the highly successful premiere of his Symphony No. 1, *Jeremiah*, in January, followed immediately by hugely popular debuts both as a ballet and musical comedy composer. The commercial successes of *Fancy Free* and *On the Town* must have triggered in Bernstein some need to balance these secular works with something spiritual, something to say, "I am not all nightclubs and sailors." The result was his setting of the Hebrew evening prayer, "Hashkiveinu," for cantor (tenor), SATB chorus, and keyboard (usually organ in performance). Unlike *Jeremiah* or Bernstein's later works in Hebrew such as *Chichester Psalms*, "Hashkiveinu" was intended for service rather than concert. Here there is no doubt, no drama, only worship and belief. Written as it was in 1945, as news of the horror of the Holocaust was at last being made known, this exhortation to God to "spread a shelter of peace over us" must have had especially tragic significance. After the composer's death, Bernstein's longtime assistant Jack Gottlieb found notes in which Bernstein had contemplated a full-length cantata for the synagogue to express the "Jewish roots I long for." It never happened.

The collaboration with Robbins next found expression in a work now virtually forgotten, the ballet *Facsimile*. Based on their understanding of human psychological frailty, as explored through years of psychoanalysis undergone by both men, *Facsimile* was the reverse of *Fancy Free*. No healthy, fun-loving sailors and girls in this piece, but rather three people—two men and one woman—in the act of what we might now call "looking for love in all the wrong places." Robbins's choreography consisted, according to reviews of the October 1946 premiere by Ballet Theatre, of a great deal of "rolling around on the floor" and "indiscriminate kissing." Bernstein's score begins with the most obvious of all his homages à la Copland, "prairie sound" in the woodwinds, answered by low, mournful strings.

A little lost flute solo ensues that introduces us to the woman, a similarly lost soul in search of . . . something. Bursts of rhythm from the trumpets announce the first man, and at length a *pas de deux* begins that is at once playful and cautious. The opening theme becomes at first a lumbering, off-beat waltz and then a real waltz, but for the briefest of moments. The action and the music reach a real Hollywood climax, and then—a smattering of seemingly random notes on the piano, and quiet afterthoughts from the strings. A solo violin elaborates in a passage that is half real, half sentimental. But then, that is the idea behind the piece, as given in its title: that what accept fakes in our life, substitutes for the real thing—whatever that is. The second man enters and the *pas de trois*, the longest section of the piece, follows. The music is now bright and faux-cheerful, in an almost *Til Eulenspiegel* way. One suspects the tempo has changed, not so much to portray the vacuous energies of the trio, but to provide Robbins the opportunity to set some real allegro steps on his dancers. In dance, the composer's ultimate responsibility is to the choreographer's vision.

The piano cascades, the flute returns in chirping happiness, and the strings, accented by rolling timpani and crash of cymbals, seem to provoke a genuine ecstasy. But an explosive chord right out of *Appalachian*

Spring (which premiered in 1944, the same year as *Fancy Free*) strips the veneer from the folderol and reveals our trio to be fakes after all. The piano admits his error, the strings remind us of the sorrow underlying everything, and *Facsimile* comes to a close. The ballet was quite the downer after *Fancy Free* and the reviews were not positive. Unlike the earlier Bernstein ballet score, this one provided no excerptable tunes (the *Danzon* from *Fancy Free* is often done as a pops piece), nor did it stand alone as a concert suite. Furthermore, and more pertinently, it prompted chastisement from Koussevitzky, who had already lectured Bernstein on "wasting his time" on things such as *On the Town*. A serious conductor, Koussevitzky intoned, devoted his life to mastering the repertoire, not to a "side activity" like composing.

First, Bernstein's biological father had tried to keep him from the profession of music. Now, his musical father upbraided him for choosing to compose when he should be conducting. Bernstein had answered his biological father by composing a symphony in his honor. Clearly, the answer was to do the same for Koussevitzky.

3

AGE OF ANXIETY

Bernstein's relationship with Koussevitzky mirrored the troubled relationship he had with his own father, and in many ways the senior conductor held a position of command over the younger one as a paternal figure. In the mid-to-late 1940s, under Koussevitzky's guidance, Bernstein learned and conducted the great classics as music director of a part-time orchestra, the New York City Symphony; as music adviser to the new Israel Philharmonic; and as an in-demand guest conductor around the world. For Koussevitzky, this was his protégé's career, and no other. Not only did Koussevitzky chastise Bernstein for the "frivolous" *On the Town*, he turned a furrowed brow to any composition projects whatsoever. Bernstein's biological father had denigrated the profession of musician, and now his musical father denigrated his ambitions to "reach for the note" and bring it back to earth from God. Conducting, the great Russian maestro proclaimed, demanded one's full energies.

On the one hand, Koussevitzky's insistence that Bernstein focus solely on a conducting career flies in the face of music history. The list of great composer-conductors includes Mendelssohn, Berlioz, Schumann, Wagner, and Mahler. Why shouldn't Bernstein aspire to add his name to that august list? On the other hand, Koussevitzky was in hindsight prescient, at least to a degree, for times were changing. In the nineteenth century, little star status was afforded conductors. Soloists—virtuoso pianists and violinists—were the superstars, while conductors simply supplied accompaniment. The demands of celebrity did not settle on them, sucking their energy and time, and therefore musicians like Mendelssohn and Schumann could conduct when they wished, with plenty of time leftover for composing. The flamboyant Hector Berlioz (1803–1869) may be said to have changed that, and by the time of Gustav Mahler (1860–1911), conducting had taken on the dimension of a "career" in the modern sense. The demand for Mahler's baton made him into a "summer composer," someone who wrote music only in the off-season. By the 1940s, the commodification of music had made it even harder to make a serious conducting career without a 100 percent commitment to it.

Bernstein insisted to Koussevitzky, as he insisted to everyone throughout his life, that he was a composer first and a conductor second. Furthermore, he had a plan to make Koussevitzky see the light of his error. Bernstein needed to show that he could compose substantial music while maintaining a demanding conducting schedule. So, without canceling a single conducting engagement, he would compose a "serious symphony" for his beloved mentor and dedicate it to him. The idea for his Symphony No. 2 came once again from a literary source, this time a contemporary English-language poem.

The Age of Anxiety is a book-length poem by W. H. Auden, one of the twentieth century's greatest poets, an Englishman by birth, and, from 1939 on, an American by choice. Auden subtitled his poem "a baroque eclogue," an ironic designation in one respect, given that "eclogue" refers specifically to an ode to rural or pastoral life, while *Age of Anxiety* addresses solely urban concerns: the setting is Manhattan, first in a bar, and later in an apartment, near the end of World War II. But "eclogue" also indicates that the characters in the poem will be represented by language far beyond their natural or realistic capacities. In other words, in an eclogue, the sentiments of ordinary people are translated into words of sophistication they would not use in "reality." In Auden's eclogue, the characters number four: a woman named Rosetta, who is a buyer for a department store, and three men with highly unlikely names: Malin, a Canadian airman; Quant, a store clerk; and Emble, a naval recruit. This quartet will analyze their lives and proclaim the age they live in to be one of emptiness and worry. They will grapple with the march of history and the meaning of life, and they will do so, not in their own voices, but uniformly in that of the poet.

Published in 1947, *The Age of Anxiety* won the Pulitzer Prize. In spite of this, the poem was controversial from the start and was dismissed by many critics, including one, writing anonymously for London's *Times Literary Supplement*, who called it Auden's single failure in a lifetime of successes. Bernstein adored it, calling the work "fascinating and hair-raising." He found in Auden's examination of contemporary culture and the vacuous existence it cultivated the perfect symbol of "our difficult and problematic search for faith." (This theme of faith lost and the restless desire to regain it will recur in Bernstein's oeuvre, most notably in Symphony No. 3, "Kaddish"; in *Mass*; and in some sense in everything he wrote.) How did the poem become the basis of Bernstein's next symphonic score? Twenty years after Bernstein's death, letters to him from an anonymous friend were found that could provide a clue. In one letter, the friend had scribbled in the margins this suggestion: "Why don't you try a tone poem of 'Anxiety'?" In another letter, the same friend wrote:

> What do you think of the "Anxiety" idea? There is so much musical-subtlety in it, and those various metres brought about by the different roads the couples take and their differing means of transportation, to say nothing of the moods, and the separateness that becomes Oneness under alcohol and/or libidinal urges. You mentioned it being good ballet material, yes, but I think, first, it should be composed as music by itself and therefore protect it from being too obvious program music, and then if some clever choreographer can put the musical composition to work, with what added quality good music may give to the themes and material, well and good. I would rather have "it" in the concert hall, where it can be less "handled" than in the ballet school where many different talents brush it up. It's too good a thing for many hands. (www.leonardbernstein.com)

It's strange to think that Bernstein initially thought of *Anxiety* as a ballet, given he had just addressed the very theme of Auden's poem—the fakeness of contemporary existence—in another ballet, his most recent work, *Facsimile*. Although the score would at length be used as the basis for a ballet by Jerome Robbins, *Anxiety* began life as the symphonic tone poem suggested by Bernstein's anonymous friend, and it is in that form that it is best known today. In fact, the symphony is now more widely regarded than either the poem or the ballet. After six-plus decades, the poem has faded from favor, the ballet is rarely done, but the symphony has been given a new burst of life by conductor-champions such as Bernstein protégé Marin Alsop. Increasingly, Bernstein's symphony is considered the strongest work of the three named *The Age of Anxiety*. In an article for *The Guardian* April 9, 2012, commentator Glyn Maxwell offered an explanation as to why the symphony bests the poem: "Throughout the piece instruments explode into life, peter out suddenly or are drowned out by others, yet the same fragile theme struggles on. This gives the symphony the concision and cohesion wanting in the poem. It is short (for a symphony) and electrifying. Its voices hear each other."

The interpretation of written words via instrumental music has severe limits. Except for the division into six distinct sections, little of the structure of Auden's poem found its way into that of Bernstein's symphony. It would simply have been impossible. For instance, Auden used an early English structural device called alliterative verse, in which alliteration substitutes for rhyme as a cohering element. The beat is largely tetrameter, four to a line, which sets up the expectation of rhyme, but this is deliberately frustrated, as the poem never rhymes. Instead, each line draws attention to initial consonants through alliteration. Consider these examples: "Our bodies bound to these bar-room lights"; "Dull through the darkness, indifferent tongues"; and "The rents are rising in the river basins." There is simply no musical parallel for this device, no way Bernstein could have translated it into music. Instead of form, then, it is content—emotional and thematic content—that Bernstein is out to capture. This is well within in the tradition of the symphonic tone poem.

A tone poem is the evocation, in musical form, of some extra-musical event or literary source. Beethoven's Symphony No. 6, the *Pastoral*, is a tone poem in which Beethoven "describes" a peasant festival interrupted by a storm and the serenity that follows the storm's end. Berlioz's *Symphonie Fantastique* "tells the story" of a young man who takes drugs after being disappointed in love. The words "describes" and "tells the story" are in quotes here because, of course, music can neither describe something nor relate a story. This was a point Bernstein made over and over again in lectures and in Young People's Concerts and in books: music, by itself, without the aid of words or pictures, cannot convey anything outside itself. One might associate images or stories with a particular tune or a certain rhythm, but that is due to the imagination of the listener, not the music itself. Music, strictly speaking, is a self-contained entity. This was the modernist view of music, and Bernstein adhered to it loudly in many commentaries. When it came to composing, however, he ignored it completely. Only a handful of Bernstein instrumental compositions lack an accompanying story of some kind, and many of those are juvenile works.

Bernstein's sole nod to the form of Auden's poem is also the most controversial element of the symphony: the use of solo piano as the "voices" of the four characters. You might think, "Why not four different instruments to represent the four characters in the poem?" But remember what an eclogue is: a poem in which the ordinary language of the characters is replaced by the more sophisticated cadence and tone of the poet. All four characters in *The Age of Anxiety* speak with the same voice—Auden's. The choice of piano as a stand-in for the characters is therefore the perfect one: a piano "speaks" with a single sound, and yet, the ability of the pianist to produce many tones at the same time also suggests several voices subsumed in one. In Auden's poem, the four characters who meet in a bar struggle against the war environment, the cynicism of their time, the weight of history, and their own, innately flawed humanity. In Bernstein's symphony, the piano and the orchestra are similarly, though far from precisely, related.

Some commentators aver that the employment of solo piano perforce makes *Age of Anxiety* a concerto. That's incorrect for two reasons. Number one, a work is whatever its composer says it is. This is important not only because of the relationship of an artist to his/her created work, but because form evolves, and the most important element of that evolution is the innovations an artist brings to it. Two: there is precedent for solo instruments in a symphony, most famously the use of solo viola in Berlioz's *Harold in Italy*.

Bernstein's Second Symphony divides into two parts and six sections (three in the first part, three in the second), named after the six subtitled parts of Auden's poem. Part I of the symphony contains *The Prologue*, *The Seven Ages*, and *The Seven Stages*; while Part II comprises *The Dirge*, *The Masque*, and *The Epilogue*. What follows is a description of the symphony, section by section. Each description is followed by a brief reference to the corresponding part of Auden's poem.

THE PROLOGUE

It begins with a "triple p" dynamic marking (*ppp*), a quietness further emphasized by the indication "echo tone," for two clarinets in haunting dialogue. Tempo is "Lento moderato" with a metronome of sixty, or one beat per second, a pulse Bernstein would elsewhere note was roughly that of a beating human heart. Listeners who know the twentieth-century piano concerto repertoire might find the opening akin to that of Prokofiev's Third Piano Concerto, which also opens with a two-clarinet dialogue. But the mood of the Bernstein is much lonelier and its working-out much longer. Humphrey Burton has identified the origin of the dialogue as a violin-cello duet Bernstein penned for a Harvard production of Aristophanes's *The Birds*, transcribed for clarinets. Whatever their origin, these eighteen measures create the frame for the symphony, and their feeling of empty longing will color the entire first half.

The first clarinet's initial utterance is a motive that will reoccur throughout the symphony in many guises; we'll call it the central motive of the piece. It holds a single tone, embroiders it a bit, then tries to climb higher, only to drift down again. The dialogue concludes with the quiet entrance of a handful of other instruments. Principal flute invokes a long, slow, downward scale that Bernstein said "acts as a bridge into the realm of the unconscious, where most of the poem takes place." Its importance throughout the symphony requires us to name it the supporting motive. These two motives—the central motive of a plaintive melody that moves obsessively around one note, climbs and falls, and the supporting motive of a steady, descending scale that cannot immediately be identified as major, minor or anything else recognizable—will be subjected to variations throughout the remainder of Part I.

Though relatively brief, the *Prologue* aptly conjures the mood of sadness among the four strangers who meet in a 52nd Street bar, their emptiness and their fear.

THE SEVEN AGES

Variation I. The piano's entrance on a single note signals the beginning of the four characters' discussion of life and its potential meaning, or lack thereof. Bernstein's score asks the pianist for a "pure and singing" tone. The central motive wanders almost aimlessly about the piano in this variation without orchestra, which continues the pensive tempo of the *Prologue*. The sense is of a plangent longing without any defined aim. The variation ends with a harp entrance that reprises the descending flute scale (supporting motive) of the *Prologue*.

The first words of the First Age section of Auden's poem are Malin's: "Behold the infant, helpless in cradle." It goes on to describe the continued helplessness of youth, which youth masks through compromise with the grown-up world.

Variation II. The piano, whose plaintive harmonies have until now conjured the clarinet dialogue, picks up on the descending scale motive, turning it into a torrent of notes. Marked with the indication "romantically," the piano part makes a sudden shift from the "pure and singing" sound of Var. I to this more effusive declamation. This is the first of Bernstein's depictions of the characters' self-indulgence, one of their many modes of forgetting the emptiness of their existence. We hear for the first time most of the instruments of the orchestra playing together: woodwinds, horns, and timpani, punctuated by strings and harp. For one short, astonishing moment, the scale motive achieves an instant transformation of mood. This happens when the orchestra, sweetened by the bright colors of glockenspiel (orchestral keyboard bells) and celesta, plays the scale as straight or "diatonic." That's the equivalent of an all-white note scale of the piano, and it contrasts with the "chromatic" nature (white and black notes together) of the scale motive. The effect on the listener is a feeling that, suddenly, shape and identity have emerged, where before there had been only a fog of confusion. The moment goes by swiftly, however, and at variation's end, the downward-plunging scale returns to its state of indefinable chromaticism, signifying the angst underlying the characters' attempts at wholeness.

In the Auden poem, Rosetta remembers being sixteen and dreaming of the beautiful house she would one day own by the sea. "Smiling and singing I sailed till dawn." This memory of optimistic innocence parallels the diatonic-scale moment in the symphony.

Variation III. Presaging the dirge of Part II, this variation is played by the orchestra without piano, over the incessant, funereal, two-beat pulse of low harp and cellos-with-double-basses, pizzicato. It is warm music—almost overwhelmingly so—with bowed strings in their low registers dominant. Near the end, a solo violin intones a melody that presents an especially melancholy take on the central motive.

In Auden's poem, Rosetta puts a nickel in the jukebox and sings "a sad little tune" with the first line, "Deep in my dark the dream shines."

Variation IV. Marked *piu mosso* ("a little faster"), this movement exhibits Bernstein's love of odd-beat meters, in this case 5/8. The inherently off-balance feeling of a five- or seven-count time signature allows for greater rhythmic expression, as a bar of five, for example, can be accented 3+2, 2+3, or even 2+2+1. This variation uses 3+2, a kind of happily lopsided dance that starts off innocently and grows increasingly frantic as the initial piano and pizzicato strings are joined by more and more instruments until the dance breaks down in a tumble.

The variation illustrates what one character in Auden's poem calls "the clown cosmos."

Variation V. It's hard not to hear the influence of Shostakovich in this wildest, loudest, most insistent variation that finds the full orchestra and piano hitting sixteenth notes hard against a cloddish 2/8 meter. As if to offset the rhythmic invention of the Fourth Variation's failed clown dance, this movement nails the meter to the wall and makes you watch it.

The variation reflects the characters' admission of the weary world's triumph in all matters material. As Quant observes, there is nothing but "a continuous Now / As the clock turns."

Variation VI. The piano, suddenly alone, clears the space with a spare, cadenza-like solo that embroiders the scale motive with little thirty-second-note ornaments, displacing the notes in different octaves along the way.

The corresponding part of Auden's poem is very long compared to the few measures of Bernstein's variation. One line from Emble, however, summarizes the feeling of the piano solo: "I've lost the key to / the garden gate."

Variation VII. Oboe and English horn dialogue in a passage that could be the opening clarinet dialogue in a distorted mirror. At length, the two clarinets enter, as if to remind oboe and English horn of the original dialogue they have transmogrified. Piano enters with the descending scale motive, which combines perfectly, if briefly, with the central motive. *The Seven Ages* ends with the scale taking us deep into the piano's bass register while a halo of flutes and clarinets intones a simple, cleansing, C major triad.

This section of the poem ends with the four characters "occupied with memories of a distant or recent, a real or imaginary past."

THE SEVEN STAGES

The next set of seven variations will fly by much faster than the first seven. We have now reached a point of imagined frenzy in the story of our four characters and their random evening together. In Auden's poem, the four have drunk themselves into a stupor. They dream, separately and yet somehow together, dreams rife with images of various forms of transport—horses, trains, planes, a bicycle, a trolley, and a canoe—that take them into landscapes suggestive of human history, from early hill-dwellers to mediaeval monks to bourgeois families living in homes with "Frock-coated father framed on the wall"—one of the lines that Bernstein cited in his enthusiasm for the poem.

Variation VIII. From the concluding C major of *The Seven Ages*, we are lifted into D-flat major at the start of *The Seven Stages*. This is accomplished through a two-measure ostinato (repeated figure) in the bass instruments. Viola and English horn fight this at first, insisting on the C major of their "distant or recent . . . real or imaginary past." It is largely absorbed in the new key of D-flat, but not altogether erased. The piano makes a "quietly singing" entrance in little pairs of baby-step eighth notes, as the struggle for a single key center continues, and continues to end in a draw. Twice, the composer uses Italian words for "melancholic" to indicate the mood of the piece. The first is "malinconico" (for the flutes) and the second "melancolico" (for the piano). Whether Bernstein intended different connotations for these synonyms is unclear. A composer's Italian is a very personal thing, and depends on the level of his/her education in languages. Bernstein spoke fluent Italian, as well as German, French, Yiddish, and Hebrew, and was very exact in his use of language in conversation, so it's likely that he indeed intended the two words to mean slightly different things. But it would take a reincarnated Bernstein to describe this to his musicians—and to us. Meanwhile, a massive crescendo ends this variation and leads us to the next.

The bitonality of the variation—C major fighting against D-flat major—conveys aptly the "groping through fog" of the characters in their drunkenness.

Variation IX. A mad, rushing waltz, the melody a distended version of the central motive and the accompaniment a rough inversion of the supporting motive (the scale rises instead of falling), this variation takes us into the heart of recent history, with its Romanticism and its revolutions.

Rosetta here dreams of "ex-monarchs" who remember "wars and waltzes as they wait for death."

Variation X. Screaming octaves at a feverish tempo in an off-balance meter (a measure of cut time followed by a measure of three-four time) spell "lost and scared." The notes are roughly those of the scale motive, but now they are no longer a scale. Dispersed to this octave or that, they begin to resemble a twelve-tone row—a set of all dozen chromatic pitches arranged deliberately so as not to imply connection with each other. And sure enough, when the original statement of the descending scale is reexamined, it turns out that this innocent little motive contains all twelve tones, and while their order doesn't fully comply with the rules of twelve-tone writing (in which one pitch may not reappear until all others have been sounded), the effect is similar.

(Bernstein's relationship to twelve-tone music, or dodecaphony, is crucial to his compositions and to his vision of music. It will be discussed in chapter 9.)

"Our train is traversing at top speed," Quant says, matching the frenzy of Bernstein's top-speed music. The railroad passes images desolate and lonely, but the speed of the train and the rain outside keep them from being clearly seen.

Variation XI. At the end of the previous variation, a brittle, angular gesture has grown out of the scale motive's displaced notes, and, in one of the clearest examples of the composer's belief that a variation should grab hold of some aspect of the previous variation, the piano now declaims it with renewed force and vigor. The whole orchestra takes this up, with xylophone underlining the variation's edginess.

"The scene has all the signs of a facetious culture," says Quant, observing the commuting workers, slums, and suburbs.

Variation XII. Solo piano continues the idea of the previous variation with a magically reharmonized, transparent mini-scherzo, played in very high register and *pianissimo*.

Rosetta relates the dalliance of two middle-class, middle-aged people in a bush.

Variation XIII. Variation XII is over in a flash, and XIII begins with the entrance of low brass. The eighth-note insistence of the last two variations continues and intensifies. A chorale-like gesture evolves from this in the brass, as this penultimate variation plunges directly ahead into the final one.

Malin hankers after Emble, and Emble after Rosetta. Malin speaks of the ego: "The aim of its eros is to create a soul."

Variation XIV. The energetic push that began with Variation X now reaches a climax. The piano zooms ahead in fiery octaves. The brass has transformed one part of the fractured scale motive into an eight-note subject that sounds a great deal like, but is not yet quite, the "Dies Irae," or Catholic chant for the dead. And at last, piano and orchestra smash headlong into a group of defining, concluding chords, *fortissimo*.

They wake from their collective dream to find the bartender closing down the bar. Rosetta asks everyone back to her place for a nightcap, hoping only Emble will accept. But suddenly they are all out in the noise and tussle of the street, and Emble hails a cab.

Now let's take a look at Part II.

THE DIRGE

Now the supporting motive, that quietly descending chromatic scale, reveals itself at last for what it has always been—a twelve-tone row. But instead of descending quietly, the motive, in its newly unmasked state, rises fiercely to engulf the listener in bitter emotions and fearful weariness. This is the great despair: nothing connects. A twelve-tone row or series constitutes the deliberate undermining of necessary connection between pitches; such was the intent of dodecaphony's founder, Arnold Schoenberg, though his desire was to make a new kind of music from this disconnect. Even as Bernstein was composing his second symphony, the musical world was coming under the spell of Schoenberg's idea: that the music of future belonged to compositions that turned away from major and minor and triads and melody, and toward the objective manipulation of the twelve individual tones. The idea would grow considerably in sheer chicness before phasing out.

Bernstein never wrote twelve-tone music. Instead, it might be said that in limited circumstances he composed a kind of anti-twelve tone. That is, he employed the idea of twelve-tone music, which was sometimes called "atonal," in the context of tonal music—the music of major, minor, etc. Of course, there could be only one place for the deployment of a twelve-tone row in tonal music, and that was precisely the use to which was putting it here. The row that rises in the opening measures of the dirge blankets the real world with its unreal disconnections. It signals hopelessness. All meaning is lost. The orchestra responds to the piano's declamation of the twelve tones with a funeral march in a woeful Largo. The entire movement is mostly a working out of the piano's tone row and the orchestra's death tread.

In the Auden poem, the characters mourn, "Our lost dad / Our colossal father." God is dead, or at least in hiding.

THE MASQUE

Until now, the piano part has fulfilled its formal role of substituting for the voices of Auden's four characters. Its cries have been their cries, and the world has responded to it/them as the sound of the orchestra. There has not, however, been a great deal of virtuosity. A difficult passage here or there, especially in the faster variations, but nothing to qualify as concerto-level bravura playing. *The Masque*, however, will more than make up for that lack.

The piano part for *The Masque* is somewhere between fiendishly and insanely difficult. The jagged rhythms, the Herculean leaps, and the steely control required for machine-gun passagework are outdone only by the atomic precision necessary to coordinate all this with the orchestra, which for this movement consists only of percussion instruments and the contrabass. What we have here is the pinnacle of Bernstein's use of jazz language to create a sense of frantic dislocation fringed with fun. The movement begins with a quiet beat in the snare and bass drums, picking up on the fading sound of the dirge. From there on, for several minutes, it's a party, one surely more intense and physical than the sandwiches-and-drinks of Auden's poem, and in fact in this movement and the final one Bernstein will move away from his literary model and into territory he creates in response to the poem's themes and situations. Glyn Maxwell, in the *Guardian* article cited above, believes that Bernstein's conception of the party "does magnificently what the poem can't do—spins the characters out beyond reason in their desire to blot out the dismal world." Conductor Marin Alsop has noted that the fundamental material Bernstein uses in *The Masque* is the same row he used in the dirge: "He takes that twelve-tone row and transforms it into a hip, grooving, bebop jazz that is not to be believed."

A note about Bernstein's orchestration: it is both canny and bold. As a hands-on orchestral musician, he knew how to make everything he wrote *sound*—not an easy thing when you are writing complex music. Stuff can get lost, or it can stick out. Not every great composer is a great orchestrator. Beethoven was quite an ordinary one, and at times even less than that. Bernstein's canniness means that he will, for example, sometimes double the violins in their middle register with English horn, knowing that the woodwind instrument will add color and weight to the strings. At several points in this work, he uses the viola—belittled cousin of the violin and the brunt of too many jokes—for the dark lyricism it examples, provided you don't use the bottom string too much. This is Bernstein's practical craft. But he is also bold in sometimes choosing unusual combinations of instruments or in eliminating some instruments altogether, if the sound he wants necessitates it. The choice to use percussion and contrabass only in *The Masque* perfectly suits the mood and the genre-specificity he is after. Later, he will make a similar decision not to use woodwinds in *Chichester Psalms*.

The Masque, in 2/4, is marked "extremely fast," though the metronome marking is merely the quarter note equals 120—about the tempo of a standard march. But the beat is multiple, meaning that for winds and percussion, the meter is actually 4/8. For them, it's the eighth note that gets the pulse, a rate double that of the quarter note; winds and percussion are actually zipping along at a beat equaling 240 counts to the minute! The piano has a parenthetical time signature of 12/16, indicating the sixteenth-note triplets that will dominate its part. This means, in essence, that the piano is also moving to a pulse like that of winds and percussion. Only the strings hold on to the steady, relatively moderate pulse of 120. All this is simply the framework for a dazzling display of rhythmic invention and coordination. Auden's masque is a polite aggregation of strangers in tentative connection, but Bernstein's is a wild party to a beat that can never quite settle on a common count, racing ahead restlessly like a death wish fueled by alcohol and sexual desire.

The movement makes brief reference to a song Bernstein composed for *On the Town*, but which was cut from the show. "Ain't Got No Tears Left" was written as a bluesy torch song. In *The Masque*, it shows up as the first part of a secondary subject that answers the twelve-tone bebop. (It is stylistically apt, too, since the tune contains ten of the twelve tones and the first seven notes do not repeat a pitch.) In the poem, the four revelers listen to a number of popular songs on the radio. Bernstein simply inserted one of his own.

In the poem, Emble and Rosetta kiss, while the unlucky Malin *"builds an altar of sandwiches" in dejection. Emble asks a higher power to "Guard our togetherness from ghostly ills."*

THE EPILOGUE

Here is where Bernstein veers most decidedly away from the poem-model. In the poem, Rosetta walks Malin and Quant to the street to help them get a cab, and returns to her apartment in hopes of continuing her tryst with Emble. Alas, her young recruit has fallen asleep. The evening has ended in the frustration of fulfillment for all. In a final statement, Malin invokes Christ (without naming him) in an attempt, perhaps, to make some sense of the senseless: *"His Truth makes our theories historical sins."*

This is not the first explicitly religious reference in the poem. At the conclusion of *The Masque*, Rosetta, who is Jewish, invokes the great prayer: *Shema' Yisra'el: 'adonai 'elohenu, 'adonai 'echad* (Hear O Israel, the Lord our God, the Lord is One). Grabbing hold of these two expressions of faith from out of the failed evening of attempted distraction, Bernstein shapes a musical paean to faith, a hymn that sails out of the symphony like a rescuing ship in a sea storm. It does not accurately convey the much more ambiguous ending of the Auden, but moves into new territory. It makes the core statement of the piece wholly Bernstein's, not a mere palimpsest of Auden. To quote Maxwell again from his essay in *The Guardian*: "[I]f the grand closing chords seem more resolved than anything at the end of the poem . . . perhaps, at that point where genius in language and music meet, only the latter can seem to mend what's broken."

The Epilogue actually begins with a reference to the immediately preceding *The Masque*. With the party energy of the *Masque* exhausted, the solo piano stops playing, and yet, a pianola—a second piano, within the orchestra—continues to play, as if the frantic intensity of our four characters has left behind a phantom of their desperate energy. Over this fading party music comes a trumpet announcing a new motive in falling fourths, a musical interval that will shortly form the melody of our hymn of faith. This is a *theatricalism*, or device that uses formal elements of the work's presentation to make a point. While there is nothing of particular musical interest in the continuation of the pianist's music by a second pianist, it serves to illustrate the programmatic theme of pathetic diversion. As Bernstein frequently admitted, he was essentially a theater composer—even in the concert hall.

The original form of the symphony called for the pianist to sit out *The Epilogue* until grabbing hold of a chord at the very end. As a literal take on the poem, the lack of the piano at the end could be viewed as the objectivity of faith that replaces the experiences of the subjects. But musically it didn't work at all; it made no sense for a solo instrument that had been wholly engaged with the orchestra from the start suddenly to disappear. In 1965, Bernstein revised the score, bringing the piano back in for one final burst of questioning before the moving hymn dispels any doubt whatsoever.

Some commentators have gone out of their way to distance the symphony from the Auden model. Official Bernstein biographer Humphrey Burton avers that the connection of the music to the poem is "overstated," citing various sketches made by the composer that preceded the publication of the poem, such as the *Birds* dialogue and "Ain't Got No Tears Left." Yet, if the symphony has so little to do with the poem, why did Bernstein bother to name the piece after the poem, and to follow Auden's structure and subtitling so closely? If the symphony was meant to be no more than a generic response to Auden, why bother to shape the symphony in six sections, naming each one after the parts of the poem? Why bother to construct exactly seven variations that correspond to the *Seven Ages*, and another set to match the *Seven*

Stages? On a more local level, why would the word "waltz" in the Auden poem prompt the only waltz variation in the Bernstein symphony, if the composer had not deliberately intended a connection?

Burton's objection depends for its urgency on the idea, mentioned above, that a symphonic composition without sung or spoken words can have "no meaning except itself"—that a piece of wordless music can evince meaning only in the strictly abstract relationship between its notes. Therefore, goes the modernist reasoning, a work that depends on a program is by definition inferior to one that tells no story, describes no events. The latter remains within the bounds of what the medium can do, while the former violates the bounds of the medium. One is tempted to say this is tantamount to claiming that an English translation of a work in another language is "inferior" to one original in English; after all, English has meaning only in and of itself; it does not "refer" to another language; all translation is, as the saying goes, paraphrase. But a programmatic musical work is no mere translation or paraphrase. It's a parallel creation. It lays bare the connection between different modes of human experience.

What we might ordinarily call a single experience—sitting in a bar and meeting a stranger, for example—is multidimensional. Physically, we feel the coldness of the glass in our hand, catch a glimpse of the stranger's eye and hear a song on the jukebox. Emotionally, we are gripped by excitement and a little fear at the back, while intellectually we might be recalling previous experiences with strangers and judging the advisability of proceeding with this one. All this and more happens at once. Why, then, should a work of art that describes this experience in its medium not be described as well in another medium? Each will convey some aspect of the experience without exhausting all the possibilities, for every human experience runs far too deep to be fully described by one poem, or one painting, or one musical composition. As for music's inability to have meaning outside itself, this handily ignores the powerful emotional force of music. Words are best for the physical descriptions of the cold glass and the jukebox music, as well as the mental reflections on the situation. But music plunges deeply into the unconscious to bring out associations that go way beyond the physical and the intellectual.

In *The Age of Anxiety*, and again (as we will see in chapter 5) in the *Serenade After Plato's Symposium*, Bernstein did two things at once.

He shaped pieces that drew on the content of their literary sources, and at the same time created works that can stand on their own, without any necessary literary reference. Just as each individual line of a poem is both an integral unit and a part of some bigger whole, so *Anxiety* and *Serenade* are sonic simulacra of their literary models; also, utterly independent symphonic scores. That said, both pieces are richer for the listener's comprehension of their verbal inspirations. It is possible to listen to *The Age of Anxiety* simply in the mode of its subtitle, Symphony No. 2, without referencing the poem, thus to experience a robustly orchestrated, formally satisfying, and melodically stimulating composition. None of that is lost, and much is gained, when the full title is restored and the listener is made aware of the Auden poem. The awareness not only adds the evocation of a certain time and place in history, it makes explicit the very theme—the extra-musical theme—that its composer explicitly said informed the work. In comments prior to a BBC telecast of the London Symphony Orchestra's performance of *The Age of Anxiety* with pianist Krystian Zimerman, Bernstein conducting, the composer noted:

> They become very close, these four characters, and when the bar closes, they are invited by the girl to come up to her apartment for a nightcap. . . . It's all fake of course, fake hilarity (which comes) not to grief, but to nobility. They pass out, and somewhere in the aftermath of this false hilarity . . . at least one of the characters does find the core of faith, which is what one is after, and *what I am after in, I guess, every work I ever write.* (emphasis added)

As this search for "the core of faith" shows up in some scores more than others, it is fascinating to hear Bernstein generalize so about his output. How can faith be at the center of a work like *Candide*, in which the whole point is that reason, and not faith that ours is "the best of all possible worlds," is the only thing that can save us? Where does faith figure in the *Serenade*, with its amorous interchanges and concluding party mood? Or in the homage to the war dead that is *Halil* or the criticism of middle-class lifestyle called *Trouble in Tahiti*? These works lie ahead of us, and as they unfold, we may see (or not) the underlying theme of faith that Bernstein speaks of.

Symphony No. 2, *The Age of Anxiety*, is Bernstein's masterpiece, in the original sense of the word. In the medieval era of workers' guilds, an apprentice to a given craft would at some point create a work that embodied everything he had learned: this was the craftsman's master-piece, or graduation work. It signaled independence and the ability to move forward. Until the creation of a masterpiece, an apprentice needed a master; after it, he was his own master. *Age of Anxiety* is the culmination of everything Bernstein knew about composition up to that moment, and it is also the seed of much that would come. The varia-tions point to the later orchestral scores, such as the Concerto for Or-chestra; *The Masque* portends the work that would immediately follow, *Prelude, Fugue and Riffs* (the latter even quotes the former); the *Epi-logue*'s sorrowful opening and the hymn of faith that evolves from it will be mirrored in the final movement of *Chichester Psalms*.

That hymn of faith was the first of many to conclude a Bernstein score. We could call this manner of ending the "Bernstein hymn," a trademark of sorts. It forms a kind of benediction at the conclusion of a struggle. We will hear Bernstein hymns again at the end of *On the Waterfront*, the finale of *Candide*, the conclusion of *Chichester Psalms*, and, most famously, in the repeat of "Somewhere" in the final moments of *West Side Story*. The exhortative flute trio near the end of Diverti-mento threatens to become one, before the piece returns to the wildly parodistic tone of its other movements.

At age thirty, Bernstein was now both famous and accomplished. In his Second Symphony, he had shown the mastery of a full-fledged com-poser. He had reached for the note and grabbed it. In *The Age of Anxiety* Bernstein created a voice that was wholly his own, clearing a wide and well-lighted path to future compositions. Or so it seemed.

4

TROUBLE IN TAHITI AND WONDERFUL TOWN

The final irony of Bernstein's second symphony is that the work was not only dedicated to Koussevitzky, it was commissioned by him through his foundation. Once again, we have ambiguity of relation to a father figure. Just as Sam had pushed Lenny away from music, but also taken him to concerts and paid the advertising for his radio show, so "Kousse," as his closest students called him, both complained that composition was a distraction from conducting, and encouraged it by granting him a commission.

The years 1949 to 1954 were transitional for Bernstein as composer. The success of *The Age of Anxiety*, and the blessing given it by Koussevitzky, freed him to compose more, but he did not turn exclusively to composition. Conducting made money where composition did not, and Bernstein in 1949 was contemplating starting a family. After all, that's what one did if one was a respectable man of thirty. A young Chilean actress he'd dated for a time in the mid-1940s came back into his life at exactly the right moment, and in 1951, Bernstein married Felicia Montealegre. They would have three children together: daughters Jamie and Nina, and son Alexander.

Letters from that time show a Bernstein biting his nails over bank accounts and bills, so it is not surprising that conducting occupied him more than composing. Compositionally, those years were a ramping up to the four back-to-back masterpieces of 1954–1957: the *Serenade After Plato's Symposium*, Symphonic Suite from *On the Waterfront*, *Can-*

dide, and *West Side Story*. Still, four notable works came out of the ramping up: *Prelude, Fugue and Riffs* (1949); incidental music for *Peter Pan* (1950); the one-act opera, *Trouble in Tahiti*, premiered in 1952 at Brandeis University, where he was professor of music from 1951 to 1955; and the Broadway musical, *Wonderful Town*.

It might also be said that, even as a conductor, Bernstein was a composer. Acute critics of Bernstein's conducting style found him so entangled with the scores he led that the ontology of writing/performing became confused. A review quoted in Humphrey Burton's biography, though from a later date, encapsulates this phenomenon. London critic David Cairns wrote in 1959: "There is a shrewd truth in the American wisecrack, 'Unfortunately the composer was unable to carry out Bernstein's intentions'" (qtd. in Burton 311). Yet it was precisely this personal identification with the composer that lent Bernstein's performances the exciting feeling of being created on the spot.

Toward the end of this period Bernstein discovered his place in front of the camera. In 1954, he went on the CBS-TV show *Omnibus* with a visually enhanced analysis of Beethoven's Symphony No. 5, and was hugely successful in engaging the American mind in, of all things, classical music. This started a series of presentations exploring everything from "What Is Modern Music?" to "What Makes Opera Grand?" During his years with the New York Philharmonic (1958–1969), these would become the famous televised Young People's Concerts. In more than fifty Young People's Concerts, Bernstein made classical music a part of American life. Subjects did not take the cheap way out: sonata form, the nature of melody, jazz in the concert hall, orchestration, acoustics, and an array of composers including Stravinsky, Shostakovich, Sibelius, Hindemith, Ives, Mahler, Berlioz, Liszt, and—twice—Aaron Copland.

Leonard Bernstein's relationship to jazz was one of great affection and, perhaps, a little envy. Jazz musicians were improvisers, and therefore composers by definition. They do not have to choose between performance and creating new music; those enterprises for a jazz musician are one and the same. The kind of jazz that fed the composer's own imagination, that influenced his compositions, was basically big band jazz of the 1930s and 1940s. As jazz grew away from that idiom and into more progressive realms, it held less interest for Bernstein, or at least for Bernstein the composer. Bernstein the music-lover was always out to hear something new, even if didn't feel inclined to steal it. A story tells of Bernstein in the late 1950s, now the distinguished young music director of the New York Philharmonic, visiting a jazz club after hours to hear Thelonious Monk, and throwing himself against the back of Monk's upright piano to feel the vibrations. Nothing like Monk ever found its way into a Bernstein score, however.

Other jazz influences did. *Fancy Free* is "jazzy," and the rhythmic keyboard skating of the scherzo to *Age of Anxiety* owes to jazz gestures. Both pieces anticipate *Prelude, Fugue and Riffs*, the piece Bernstein was to compose in the wake of his success with *Age of Anxiety*. In the 1940s, jazz clarinetist and bandleader Woody Herman had experimented with commissioning classical composers to write scores for his ensemble, a typical big band of five saxophones, five trumpets, four trombones, and a rhythm section of piano-drums-bass, plus Herman's clarinet as soloist. The most famous result of this was Stravinsky's *Ebony Concerto*. In early 1949, Herman commissioned Bernstein to write such a piece, a score that would combine jazz flavors with classical forms. ("Third Stream" music, which would arrive a few years later courtesy of Gunther Schuller, was slightly different, in that it involved improvisation. The scores for Herman were all written out.)

Bernstein must have taken on the commission with great enthusiasm, for he finished it in November of the same year, a quick turnaround for him. Unfortunately, Herman's band broke up shortly afterward and the piece was shelved. (Bernstein never received the promised check.) It wasn't until Bernstein began his television career that it resurfaced. In a 1955 CBS-TV broadcast, Benny Goodman premiered *Prelude, Fugue and Riffs*, with a studio band conducted by the composer as part of Bernstein's presentation, "What Is Jazz?"

The score starts with a blast from the brass. Bernstein always wrote well for brass instruments, especially the trumpet. The prelude is given entirely to trumpets and trombones, plus drums and bass, an aggressive, four-beat fanfare of sorts that couldn't possibly be mistaken for jazz. The presence of middle-period Stravinsky seems to hang over it. Then comes a sudden shift into a broader swing rhythm and a big-band theme worthy of Duke Ellington. Back to the Stravinsky-like theme we go for some semiserious classical "development" and then, like stopping on the proverbial dime, we're into the fugue, which is given entirely to the saxophones. More reflective in subject matter, the fugue is less a fully developed fugue than a "fugato" passage, in which a subject is tossed around from instrument to instrument, leading to a lyrical episode, which is then in turn treated imitatively and blended with the first subject. The prelude lasts less than two minutes and the fugue is even shorter. With the startling entrance of the piano we come finally to the meat of the score, the "riffs," or short, repeated phrases. In actual jazz, improvisation would occur over the riffs, but since this is written-out music, the composer has given us simulated improvisation. This has always been the challenge of writing jazz-like music: how to make it seem spontaneous, how to give the impression of impromptu musical thoughts.

The central idea of the four-minutes-plus riffs section is a tiny, scurrying figure that climbs a scale in sixteenth-notes and ends with a syncopated flourish on top. This is announced by the solo clarinet in tandem with the piano, who adds a stride bass line. The drum set enters and we hear xylophone, and then vibes add their thoughts to the framework of the repeated riff, followed by woodwinds, brass, and a solo from the drums. There is an unexpected return of the Duke Ellington-ish slow-swing theme from the prelude, this time for the entire band, and then the riff comes back to the clarinet and from here on it's a race to the finish, an increasingly complex fabric of instrumental interaction. We hear the clarinet impose the second fugal subject over the continuing harmonic progression. Then things press on with even more intensity, hitting the central idea again and again until the band finally stops, the solo clarinet holds a high written G for a considerable amount of time, and then, in two staccato notes, it's over.

One reason Bernstein's scores are performed less than they might is that it's hard to know where to "put" them. *Prelude, Fugues and Riffs* is a prime instance of that conundrum. At nine minutes long, for big band, it doesn't natural fit the bill for a symphony concert, though symphony orchestras have gone to the trouble of hiring saxophones (not normally a part of the symphony orchestra make-up) and performed it, incongruously, in formal attire. Nor are there many big bands around anymore to play it.

The songs for *Peter Pan*, for which Bernstein supplied both music and lyrics, are likewise "lost" pieces that have no particular home. For the 1950 production of J. M. Barrie's play, featuring Boris Karloff as Captain Hook, the producer wanted a few songs for the Wendy and

Captain Hook characters, nothing like the full score of a musical. A full-length musical would come just four years later, with music by Jule Styne and Moose Charlap, and lyrics by Carolyn Leigh and Bernstein's old friends Betty Comden and Adolph Green. This would only further obscure Bernstein's already obscure contributions to the history of the play. A complete recording of Bernstein's *Peter Pan* music was not made until 2004, when pianist-conductor Alexander Frey researched Bernstein's archived materials and found more than just the Wendy songs that by that time were the stuff of college voice recitals. Among his discoveries were two major songs, a bravura set piece for Captain Hook and an unabashedly romantic song for Wendy called "Dream with Me." The first had been written for Karloff but was not used. The second, written in 1944 and perhaps intended for *On the Town*, was something Bernstein must have tried to shoehorn into the *Peter Pan* score, because the style of it is out of sync with the childlike songs he wrote expressly for Wendy. "Dream with Me" went undiscovered and unperformed until Frey's discovery of it, and has since become a favorite with classical singers who do crossover. It is an early example of Bernstein's tendency to push a lyrical melody higher, falling back but then returning ever higher, an expressive tool that leads to the emotional experience of "opening up."

"Dream with Me" didn't make the 1950 production, but a number of songs for Wendy did: "My House" is a charmer made of wide intervals and comforting diatonic chords; "Peter, Peter" conveys a tentative flirt with the title character, but one completely innocent; and there is the whimsical "Who Am I?" previously mentioned in connection with its cover by Nina Simone. The 1950 production featured these Bernstein songs and a couple others for Hook, but commissioned incidental music from a completely different composer. Frey found the instrumental music Bernstein intended for the production and included it in his recording. A lot of it is recycled from other pieces. For instance, one cue is identical with the *Anniversary* piano piece Bernstein wrote for Betty Comden's baby.

The *Peter Pan* songs are perfect instances of the composer's love for simple and endearing melodies suggestive of unstained childhood. The most important work from this period, however, satirizes all that is supposedly "innocent" in the American dream: the white picket fence, the happy family, the mother in her comfy home and the father—oh, the father—at his job. *Trouble in Tahiti* is Bernstein's only one-act opera, a piece later (1984) subsumed into his full length opera, *A Quiet Place*, but a stand-alone as well. It is impossible not to notice that he wrote it exactly at the moment he gave his personal life over to social expectations, that is, marriage.

To the composer's own libretto, *Trouble in Tahiti* tells the story of Sam and Dinah, a young couple ensconced in a picket fence quest for respectability, and thrall to the notion that their life together must be the only way to live—could one even imagine another? It opens with a trio singing of the joys of suburbia. It's a popular-style little ditty, a jumpy "shuffle" that extols the virtues of complacency ca. 1950. The excellent 2001 BBC film of the opera accompanies the opening trio with stock footage of the era: women demonstrating kitchen appliances, children gamboling on perfectly manicured lawns, advertisements for packaged foods. After the pleasantness of the opener, we meet Dinah and Sam as they bicker in perfect harmony. They bicker over money. They bicker over "the kid," a son named Junior. They bicker over Sam's secretary at his job. And then Sam does what all good husbands do when faced with such challenges: he goes to work.

At the office, which could sell widgets for all we know, Sam does something ill defined, and he must do it very well. After selling a client on the phone, our trio (which now portrays Sam's coworkers) sings in admiration: "When it comes to the dollar / No one touches marvelous Sam." The scene changes to Dinah, prone on her psychiatrist's couch, relating her most recent dream. She was in a garden, choked with weeds and trees "black against the sky," when her father's voice called out to leave. But she couldn't find a path out until she heard another, different voice sing, "There is a garden . . . a shining garden." This is the ideal father calling, or perhaps the ideal Father in what Dinah calls "a quiet place." These words will later become the title of the full-length opera. (In a side scene, we hear Sam ask his secretary to forget a certain incident.) In the dream, Dinah goes to touch the hand of this man whose face she cannot make out, but who must be "so handsome." She and the man run toward each other . . . and then she wakes up. "I was standing in a garden" is a fully developed opera aria, not a popular song expanded into an aria.

Sam and Dinah run into each other on the street, and each lies to the other just to avoid contact. This becomes a brief but effective duet that conveys the fear they both feel in the face of their estrangement. In an interlude, the trio reminds us that this is not the official version of Sam's and Dinah's life together. The official version is that they are a "happy couple with a sweet little son." Sam then sings an especially ugly (ugly in sentiment, not music) paean to winning at any cost. "There are men," he sings, who follow the rules and get by, and then there are the ones who know how to bend and break them. These are the winners. This is Sam. "There's a law" is another true opera aria, a character number that requires controlled classical vocal technique to pull off. *Trouble in Tahiti* is a "number" opera, made of arias and ensembles linked together with accompanied recitative. It is by turns sarcastic, lyric, brutal, and pathetic. The text hovers on the edge of cliché, but the whole things works because of Bernstein's ability to shape a song or aria (which differs from a song only in relative length and the technique required) that projects character.

Dinah then sings the showstopper, if operas can be said have showstoppers. She has sneaked off to see a movie called *Trouble in Tahiti*, and it was dreadful. "What a Movie! ('Island Magic')" is her summation of the movie's ridiculous plot about south seas natives and the "good old U.S. Navy." The trio joins her in making fun of the movie's theme song, "Island Magic." The movie's title is, of course, code for "trouble in paradise." And indeed, Dinah and Sam have a lot of trouble in their supposed paradise of suburbia. Sam returns home, admitting in song that coming home is "the price" he pays for his success. He doesn't want to face the arguments he knows he will break out, so he suggests they go see the new movie that's just opened, called *Trouble in Tahiti*— the very movie Dinah sneaked off to see that afternoon. Dinah says yes. Better the ridiculous unreality of the movies than the horrible reality of their non-marriage. The couple sings a duet of rather grim hope that someday they might touch another again. As they leave for the movie, the trio sings softly, "Island magic!"

Trouble in Tahiti is sui generis. Nothing else like it exists in the Bernstein catalogue, nor indeed in the opera repertoire. When done alone, as opposed to being subsumed into *A Quiet Place*, it is usually done as the second half of a double bill of English-language one-acts. Samuel Barber's *A Hand of Bridge* and Gian-Carlo Menotti's *The Telephone* are typical of the first halves in such circumstances.

A professor at Brandeis, a conductor with a busy touring schedule, an emerging television personality, and a composer of vocal and instrumental music, Bernstien also wrote thoughtful articles for publications like the *New York Times* and *Downbeat* on the musical subjects that enthralled him—and that was a long, long list. Bernstein used to say he was "overcommitted on all fronts." It was hard for him to say no to a worthy musical project or event.

In September 1952, the Bernsteins welcomed their first child, a daughter named Jamie. Now the bills were bound to mount, and the need for money certain to increase. The composer must have thought it was divine intervention when, just two months later, his old friend George Abbott, who had produced *On the Town*, asked him if he'd liked to reunite with Comden and Green on a project that had a script, a star, investors—everything but songs. *My Sister Eileen* was a famous book of 1930s New York memoirs by Ruth McKenney that was turned into a hit play by playwrights Joseph Fields and Jerome Chorodov in 1940. In 1942 it hit the silver screen with Rosalind Russell in the lead. Now Fields and Chodorov had adapted their script as a musical, with set-ups for songs, but the composer-lyricist team hired to fill in the blanks turned in an unsatisfactory score. Abbott had snagged Russell to star in the musical version of the film she'd starred in ten years previous, but if a score wasn't ready soon, she would be released from her contract. So Abbott asked the impossible: Could Bernstein, Comden, and Green come up with a new set of songs for the show in . . . five weeks? One of our themes makes a triumphant return: here was a plan, and not quite enough time.

The trio of friends closeted themselves up in a hotel room and blocked the windows so they couldn't tell day from night. For the next five weeks, they immersed themselves in the story of a bright woman journalist who comes to New York with her pretty younger sister, Eileen, and learns things about the world, men, and herself. (But not very serious things. *My Sister Eileen* and the musical that came from it are light entertainment in the best sense.) The rehearsal process and try-outs added another ten weeks to Bernstein's commitment. Childhood friend and first piano student Sid Ramin, now a professional musician himself, was brought on board to do the orchestrations.

(A note about orchestrations for theater scores: Bernstein orchestrated his own concert pieces, but found it necessary, because of the scope of theater pieces and the frequent last-minute changes made in the theater, to share orchestration duties for his shows with others. This was customary on Broadway. Over the years, Bernstein's most prominent co-orchestrators for his Broadway shows and for *Mass* would include Ramin, Irving Kostal, Hershy Kay, and Jonathan Tunick. But this should not be taken as some kind of artistic abdication on Bernstein's part. As Kay has observed, Bernstein kept a close eye on the orchestrations, approving and/or correcting them for final use.)

The result of the Bernstein-Comden-Green reunion was an unblemished hit musical comedy called *Wonderful Town*. When the show opened in February of 1953 it garnered rave reviews from every one of the eight New York newspapers then in print. It won Bernstein a Tony Award for best music, ran for 500 performances, and made everyone a lot of money. Artistically, *Wonderful Town* is the least interesting of Bernstein's four major musicals. It is more standard issue than the startlingly youthful *On the Town*, it lacks the musical sophistication of *Candide*, and it doesn't swim anywhere near the depths of *West Side Story*. But its songs never fail to engage the ear, the tunes and words blend effortlessly, and they exude a breezy kind of uncloying positivity about life, love, and living in Manhattan. They also travel well down the decades: *Wonderful Town* was given a successful Broadway revival in 2003, starring Donna Murphy.

The story takes place in the 1930s, but the producers at first told the songwriters it should be updated to the 1950s for greater audience appeal. On hearing this, Bernstein rushed to the piano and began playing 1930s big band music. The time of the show remained the 1930s. Many of Bernstein's songs are largely pastiche; that is, songs deliberately couched in a certain idiom. There's a conga number, titled, logically enough, "Conga!" (if you don't feel like dancing to this driving take on the Latin-beat line dance, check your pulse); a nostalgic country-ish song ("Ohio"); a pseudo-Irish song ("My Darlin' Eileen"); and one flat-out homage to the popular music of the era, "Swing." The love songs are pure Broadway Lenny. "A Little Bit in Love" is a breezy embrace of the early stages of infatuation. "A Quiet Girl" approaches hymn status in its idealization of someone who cannot exist. "It's Love" bursts with the character's realization that he really is in the fabled state of being in love. It's a Bernstein rollercoaster that takes advantage of its form to make the climb to the top especially dramatic.

Earlier, we looked at how Bernstein filled the popular song form of A-A-B-A (refrain, refrain, bridge or "release," refrain) in "Lucky to Be Me." In "It's Love," he uses the shape of another form to make his ascent. A-B-A-C is the second most common form of classic popular song. The singer sings something, and then answers it one way. She sings it again, and this time answers it differently, bringing it to a new, final place. A famous example is Henry Mancini's and Johnny Mercer's "Moon River." The singer sings "Moon River, wider than a mile / I'm crossing you in style / Someday." Then she sings an answer that ends with "I'm going your way." Then the tune starts up again with the words, "Two drifters." This time, when that initial phrase ends, it's answered (starting with "We're after . . .") by a melodic line that takes it to a fresh harmonic place and concludes the song. "It's Love" starts with an upward reaching interval of the fifth, like a trumpet announcing the truth, which is repeated twice on the words "It's love" ("A"). It then proceeds along its way to a second phrase ("B") that levels out our singer's enthusiasm. The first phrase ("A") repeats and when the answering phrase ("C") comes back, it pushes skyward like the character's sudden and irrepressible joy.

Wonderful Town is the last time Bernstein will relax and have fun in the theater. *Fancy Free* and *On the Town* were exuberantly youthful odes to being exuberantly youthful. This unclouded charmer of a show follows suit. But after that, Bernstein seemed intent on making bigger and bigger statements. His score for the ballet *Facsimile* began the trend in 1946, and his last ballet, *Dybbuk* (1974), would be uncompromisingly dark. His works for the lyric stage made steady progress in the same direction. *Candide* may sound like confetti and baubles, but not always, and even its brightest moments are there to make a point. *West Side Story* of course, is not largely a lot of laughs, and by the time we get to *Mass* (1971), Bernstein is writing, in huge letters: "Listen to this, it's important." Like many people who achieve a certain stature and are allowed peeks behind the curtain, Bernstein in later life became convinced that the power structure in place in the world needed to be challenged, and that it could be challenged through art. The idea was there from the start, as when he staged Marc Blitzstein's controversial *The Cradle Will Rock*. The two men became friends, united by their belief that a corrupt capitalism required their attention as artists. Collaboration, however, was infrequent, and usually involved Bernstein, who was more famous, championing the work of his older colleague. In 1954, Bernstein would conduct the premiere of Blitzstein's translation of *Threepenny Opera*, composer Kurt Weill's setting of Marxist playwright Bertolt Brecht's anti-property, anti-capitalist tale of a criminal hero.

Bernstein's last attempt at a stage work also had a Brechtian connection. In 1968, he reunited with *West Side Story* lyricist Stephen Sondheim, *West Side Story* choreographer Jerome Robbins, and young playwright John Guare with the intention of musicalizing Bertolt Brecht's *The Exception and the Rule*. This short, one-act piece, among Brecht's so-called teaching plays, told the story of a rich merchant and his servant who leave for the desert in search of oil. At length, the merchant finds himself stranded, and only his servant has the knowledge and the compassion to save them. The action was meant by Brecht as a lecture on class differences and the superiority of socialist politics. Bernstien, Sondheim, and Guare dubbed their adaptation of the play with the spoonerism of a title, *A Pray by Blecht*.

The show was abandoned when Robbins left to pursue another project. But in 1987, Robbins secured the use of Lincoln Center's Mitzi Newhouse Theatre, then dark, to workshop the piece, now renamed *The Race to Urga*, for three weeks. John Guare came back on board to rewrite the book, Josh Mostel was hired to play the merchant, and the Bernstein-Sondheim songs were tried out in various forms and order, sometimes altered in key or tempo on a daily basis by music director Michael Barrett or by Robbins himself, who was musically adept. (This writer was a pit musician for the *Urga* workshop and witnessed the mercurial changes wrought by Robbins and company.)

After three weeks, the workshop was performed for an invited audience. The audience laughed at the jokes, applauded the songs, and spoke excitedly of the show's prospects after the performance. New York's Broadway community was already ablaze about *Urga*. After all, here were three-quarters of the team that had given us *West Side Story*: Bernstein, Sondheim, and Robbins. The show going forward depended on the composer saying yes to Robbins's stated desire that *The Race to Urga* at last be birthed. The cast and creative team eagerly awaited Bernstein's answer, but when it came, it was a flat "no."

As the bad news filtered down among those involved, rumors of the reasons for his decision were varied. The reason that rang true to those who knew Bernstein was that the show did not have the potential to reach and change the hearts of those in power. There are two ways to look at this. One, it signifies that, at this late stage of Bernstein's life, the composer felt that his music, to have meaning, needed to work major changes in the fabric of society. Failing that, it was useless. *The Race to Urga* may have held the promise of an entertaining evening with a dollop of social consciousness on top, but that was not enough. Two, it suggests that Bernstein's faith in the ability of his music to touch and inspire had waned. Even given the world-shaking ambition of inspiring the collapse of capitalism, it is conceivable that *Urga* could at least have tilted things in that direction. After all, *West Side Story* had contributed mightily to the American consciousness of race relations and cultural differences, and a big part of that effect had been the power of Bernstein's music. *Urga* was a different sort of score, more piquant than dramatic, more vaudeville than opera. Yet the effects of music on the soul, as everyone from Plato to Santayana have proclaimed, are deeper than those of words or pictures, and the possibility of *Urga* creating at least a ripple of social discontent was real. Unfortunately, its composer wanted a tsunami, or nothing.

By 1953, Bernstein had mastered his own compositional voice and was at the peak of his abilities. *Wonderful Town* gave him secure financial footing to strike out in the direction of composing without worrying about being able to support his growing family. The next few years would be a whirlwind of creativity.

5

ON THE WATERFRONT AND SERENADE
AFTER PLATO'S SYMPOSIUM

Bernstein was now at the peak of his composing output. In the wake of *Age of Anxiety*, which can be seen as a breakthrough piece, he had composed a jazz essay, a one-act opera, incidental music for a Broadway play, and a new hit musical. Between 1953 and 1957 he would work on four major pieces nearly simultaneously: *Serenade after Plato's Symposium*, the score for the film *On the Waterfront*, and two major contributions to the lyric stage, *Candide* and *West Side Story*. Not for another three decades would the composer enjoy this level of productivity.

On the Waterfront (1954) was controversial primarily because its director, Elia Kazan, had cooperated with the communist witch hunt waged by Senator Joseph McCarthy. Kazan never lived down his testimony, and even as late as 1999, when he was given an honorary lifetime Oscar, many members of the Academy of Motion Picture Arts and Sciences protested the award. Bernstein's involvement in the project seems an odd choice, given his leftist politics. Not only had the film's director named names before a vicious tribunal, but Budd Schulberg's script portrayed corrupt union practices, something that could easily play into right-wing efforts to discredit unions.

The truth is that the politics of the early to mid-1950s were much more complicated than we can possibly ascertain from a sixty-year distance. Threats were real. Power, under the rubric of "anti-communism," was rampant. Compromises often had to be made just to stay out of prison or even to stay alive. The suicide scene in *The Front*, a 1976 movie about the McCarthy era, is a realistic depiction of the devastation wrought by the investigations. Unlike Kazan, and unlike his friend and colleague Jerome Robbins, Bernstein was not subpoenaed, meaning that he did not have to face the horrible choice of testifying or suffering the consequences. Even without a subpoena against him, Bernstein was stripped of his passport for having consorted with leftists and leftist organizations. To get it back, he was forced to go through the ritual of publicly renouncing communism and to pay a lawyer $3,500, an enormous sum in 1953. Bernstein's involvement in *On the Waterfront*, or for that matter his continued association with Robbins (shortly to result in the composer's most famous score), seems therefore just the continuation of business under new management, as it were. The political-cultural climate had changed, and everybody did whatever they had to do in order to breathe the new atmosphere and stay alive.

More challenging than the politics of Bernstein's choice for this, his first and only incidental score to a movie, was his approach to composing for film. The principle underlying film music (other than film musicals) is that it should be heard but not listened to. A more radical way to say it is that film music should not even be heard, but merely sensed or felt: it should limn a scene emotionally, without making its presence obvious. Think of a scene in the *Return of the Jedi* (1983), when Luke and Leia are talking in the forest. You may recall what they discussed—something about being brother and sister—or even the sound of the actors' voices. But if you try to recall the music, chances are that—unless you are a musician with a special interest in movie music—all you will recall is a certain feeling, a sense of warmth and fulfillment, as if some inevitable and beautiful truth has been revealed. And that is exactly why John Williams is an extraordinary film composer: he knows how to write music that literally underscores the action and, what's more, supports the emotions of the characters. Of course, epic movies like the Star Wars series lend themselves to big openings with grandiose musical themes and finales that call for memorable tunes, so Williams also had plenty of musical capital to haul away from the screen and turn into concert suites. More complex films don't afford this opportunity. The scores best regarded by film music buffs often disappear completely into the movie, so perfectly anonymous yet wholly apt are they to the film's visual and verbal content. Jerry Goldsmith's music for *China-town*, written under pressure in a very short time, is often held up as a prime example of the film composer's art. Try to think of it, and it evaporates. Remove it, however, and you lose a large portion of the film's sense of foreboding, imminent tragedy, and fate.

Exceptions to this rule of musical anonymity are scenes in which there is no dialogue, and the music is the only sound (other than effects) to be heard. The most famous example is the shower scene in *Psycho*, in which the slashes of the knife are accompanied by slashing string instruments in deadly dissonance. Composer Bernard Herrmann managed both to "hit" the cue—meaning match the physical action with a musical event—but also, in the desperately high screech of the strings, to depict musically the horror of the attack. Other such music-only moments run a gamut of emotional states, from T. E. Lawrence scanning the Arabian landscape to the accompaniment of Maurice Jarre's lonely melody in *Lawrence of Arabia*, to Burt Bacharach's anachronistic, yet perfectly apt, pop music backdrop for the hard-riding title characters of *Butch Cassidy and the Sundance Kid*.

Apart from a brief opening scene of workers gathering on the docks, and another, more poignant scene toward the end, *On the Waterfront* afforded Bernstein no such luxurious opportunities. Instead, he created them, sometimes by superimposing his music over the scene rather than under it. That's not to say the music is in any way "bad." To the contrary, Bernstein's score captures with an almost savage intensity the main elements of the story: the brutal life of a working man on the docks; the sinister presence of deadly power; and the transformational potential of love. Yet it sometimes moves the musical statements of these things to the foreground of the movie, which is exactly what a film score should never do. Bernstein even wrung his hands over the genre's priorities in a fantasy dialogue that takes place in "Upper Dubbing, California." Published in Bernstein's first book, *The Joy of Music*, the dialogue finds the composer wearily acquiescing to the fact that film is not a musical form, per se, but nonetheless lodging the complaint that one of his score's best moments had been usurped by "one of Marlon Brando's grunts."

We will first look at the film itself, commenting of each of Bernstein's cues. Then we will consider the orchestral work he arranged from the score, Suite from *On the Waterfront*. If the former is idiomatically strained, the latter is a powerful symphonic composition deserving of much wider exposure.

Even as the familiar Columbia Pictures logo of lady-with-the-torch hits the black-and-white screen, a forlorn, unaccompanied horn announces a theme. Taking a shape typical of early Bernstein melodies, the theme pushes upward, falls and climbs again, falls and climbs yet again, this time higher, and as it climbs, it slips from minor into major by the most unlikely of means: a blue note. A blue note is an altered pitch, a flattened note where a flattened note is unexpected. It comes from the blues, the African-American form that derives its distinct sound from such flattened pitches. Blue notes don't replace their non-flattened or natural counterparts; they exist side by side with them, creating an ambiguity of expression. Bernstein will exploit this ambiguity as a device to convey the subtle emotions of the characters in the film.

Bernstein's twenty-four-note theme takes less than thirty seconds to play, and in that half-minute, it establishes the emotional premise of striving impeded by exterior obstacles. As the main title credits continue to roll, the theme repeats in woodwinds, with muted brass in close imitation. The first scene lights up the screen, and we are thrown into the world of life on the docks. Men of obvious power, men in suits with expensive overcoats, walk past the ships to their cars, and one of them slaps Marlon Brando's character on the shoulder and says, "You take it from here, slugger." Brando, dressed in flannels and clearly not one of them, walks away, and the setting shifts to the streets of Manhattan.

The action seems almost banal, yet Bernstein's music—a muscled knot of percussion overlaid by incisive, two-note jabs from an alto saxophone—overflows with drama. We'll call the quick, two-note jabbing idea the "stabbing motive." It will expand to a three-note version and beyond, but it is always as jagged as a boxer's punch, as now it expands into something abrasive and aggressive, like a dark fanfare. We are about to conclude that the music is overkill, that Bernstein has flooded the screen with music that portends tragedy when all that's happening is a friendly slap on the shoulder and a walk along the shore, when we see Brando call up to someone on the top floor of a tenement, "Joey! Joey Doyle!" Something more is up. At length, the terrible truth is revealed: Brando's character, named Terry Malloy, has been sent by the men in suits to lure Joey to the roof of his building. Terry tells Joey he's found one of Joey's birds, one of the pigeons he keeps in coops on the roof. Terry sends the bird to the roof, Joey follows, and shortly Joey is a bloody pulp in the street, thrown from the roof by thugs waiting there for him. Terry has been party to the killing of a man, though he had not understood, when he agreed to follow instructions from the suits, that murder was the aim. Now the dark music, which ends as Joey hits the pavement, makes a kind of horrible sense in retrospect.

Joey had been planning to talk to "the crime commission." His round trip to the roof was insurance that the people he was about to rat out would not be ratted. Who are those people? Union bosses. Indistinguishable from Mafiosi, the union bosses run the action at the docks, hiring only those workers who agree to take loans from them at usurious rates, and skimming money off the top of workers' wages. One of the bosses is Charley Malloy (Rod Steiger), Terry's brother, second in power only to Johnny Friendly (Lee J. Cobb). In Johnny Friendly's bar, Johnny and Charley try to cheer up Terry, who is feeling awful about Joey. We learn that Terry is a former boxer, who once had a shot at a title. Johnny gives Terry $50 and tells him, "Go get a load on" (i.e., get drunk). Instead, Terry goes back to Joey's building, and to the rooftop where Joey kept his pigeons.

In one of Bernstein's most sensitive cues, a quiet harp sets the scene and low-pitched flute and strings flutter like the pigeons. Terry sits, dejected, next to Joey's coop. An oboe sounds a simple, plaintive, four-note motive borrowed from the "stabbing" notes of the sax in the opening cue, which extends into a melancholy statement. Terry talks with a neighborhood kid about the pigeons, but his feelings are in the oboe cue.

It's Monday morning and laborers throng the docks looking for a day's work. The union rep stands before them, handing out chits to the men he chooses. Work is scarce; most of the hopefuls will be declined. Terry's is the first name called, and after a few more men are selected, some laborers start to surreptitiously hand dollar bills to the union rep as bribes. The laborers begin to clamor and push the union rep, who throws the remaining chits into the air. Union bosses look on and laugh as the men fight for a chance to earn a few bucks. Bernstein's cue is a fortissimo chunk of jagged, rhythmic writing accented by a chime. The chime is a perfect touch, revealing the pathetic nature of what, on the surface, is merely a mad scramble.

Into the mob, someone makes an unlikely entrance: It's Joey Doyle's sister, Edie (Eva Marie Saint). She's come down to the docks with

Father Barry (Karl Malden), her parish priest, to ask questions about the death of her brother, and to be there with her father, who insists on trying to work that day. ("How else will I pay for the funeral?" he asks.) As Edie grabs for a chit for her father, Terry playfully takes one just out of her grasp and then flirts with her, even inviting a slap that makes him smile. A fellow worker says to him, "Hey, don't you know who that is? That's Joey Doyle's sister?" At this moment, the music should suddenly stop, or at least go instantly quiet. But Bernstein punctuates things with a strident, three-note motive from the brass—a cinematic error, to be sure. Those three notes will later become the first notes of a love theme for Terry and Edie, but here they are woefully misplaced.

Father Barry and Edie decide to hold a meeting in the basement of the church to discuss what's happened. Of course, the mob/union leaders get hold of the info and send Terry to the meeting as a plant. Only about a dozen laborers show up for the meeting, including Terry, who sits in the back. Father Barry puts it blankly to the group: "Who killed Joey Doyle?" Nobody answers. One worker says the rule is "stay D and D." "D and D?" "Deaf and dumb." No matter how bad things get, the worker says, "You don't rat." "Ratting to them is truth to you," Father Barry says. "Don't you see that?" They don't. Defeated, Father Barry cedes that the meeting is over, but before a prayer can be offered, a rock crashes through one of the basement windows. The jagged, angry music of the previous cue starts up again, as we see thugs outside the church. To the incessant slicing sound of the violins in rapid unison, the thugs beat the workers from the meeting as they exit. Terry knows a back way out to avoid the beatings, so he grabs Edie and off they go.

In a nearby park, Edie and Terry talk. They are about to part ways when Edie says she remembers Terry from school. That she'd remembered him the moment she saw him. This sparks one of Bernstein's loveliest melodies, the love theme. It reaches far—up an octave—and then, but not as far. Another reach up, to a blue note this time, and down once more. And then, unexpectedly, it soars still higher, and in the harmonies beneath, a chord that was minor becomes major. If this sounds familiar, that's because it's very similar to the shape of the main title theme, described above. Similar—yet substantially different. The love theme is more open, more expansive, more embracing than the main theme. Something of the tight little struggle of the opening subject has been released, and the once-imprisoned passion is readying to fly. The conversation stops before it can take off.

The melody gets a second chance in the next scene. Edie wanders to the rooftop and finds Terry and the neighborhood kid there, looking after the pigeons. "You got a second?" Terry asks, and the love theme starts up in the strings. This time, the ending latches on to a certain gesture and suddenly the melody is being repeated . . . a perfect fifth higher. This built-in transposition, or change of key, is a brilliant musical stroke, and it lifts an already beautifully inspiring melody into a place of uncanny spirituality. After another iteration, it once again repeats, yet another perfect fifth higher. (It would be like starting a song in G major, then, at the end, slipping into D major, and then into A major, etc.) The message to the listener whose ears are open is clear: this could go on forever, growing and changing and yet always being the same melody. It's a perfect musical picture of the devotion Edie and Terry allude to when they talk about pigeons mating for life. In an opera, this could be an extraordinarily effective, even stunning, duet. Alas, it's a movie and the whole thing doesn't work.

It doesn't work because the music doesn't match the dialogue. "You like beer?" Terry asks. "I don't know," Edie says. "You ever have a glass of beer?" Terry asks. "No," Edie answers. Yes, there is talk of pigeons and how they mate for life and the subtext of mutual interest is clear. But the music is a full-out panorama, not of a subtle little hint at intimacy through aviary biology, but of Devotion Itself, of LOVE in all capital letters. If the characters were saying to each other, "I'll love you until I die, I pledge my everything to you," then the music would be apt. But they are talking of beer and pigeons and hinting at a relationship, and the layered, complex, and ultimately distracting music is just wrong.

Edie says yes to a glass of beer, and the music climaxes as Terry releases a pigeon. Terry tells his life story. Dad was "bumped off—never mind how," and they stuck him and Charley in a "dump called a children's home." Terry says things like "Do to the other guy before he does to you" and Edie calls this attitude "living like an animal." The talk turns to Joey's murder and Edie says, "Help me if you can, for God's sake." The love theme starts up again, blunted somewhat and more subtle, in bassoon and strings. This time, it's right. It's a short cue, but the moment when Edie touches Terry's cheek and Brando registers something between shame and ecstatic release, the music does its job.

Edie tries to escape the back room of the saloon where she and Terry are drinking, but she runs into a drunken wedding party and turns back. Terry finds her and gets her to dance to the wedding party's music—"a pretty tune," Edie calls it. It's the love theme played as a dance tune on muted trumpet, without the interlocking transpositions. A thug shows up to tell Terry to go see the boss, and within moments, members of the crime commission deliver Terry a subpoena. Edie wakes up to Terry's probable involvement in her brother's death and leaves, to the accompaniment of the "stabbing" theme re-done as a dance tune for jazz band.

Johnny Friendly and Charley Malloy confront Terry and tell him to stop seeing Edie. It seems that a certain Dugan, who was at the church meeting, has sung like the proverbial canary and testified to the crime commission. The next day, Dugan is in the hold of a ship, unloading Irish whisky—his dream come true, he says—when the mob thugs arrange for an accident. Dugan is crushed to death by falling cases of whisky. Father Barry makes an impassioned speech over Dugan's body and dares the other men to come forward with the truth about the graft and corruption of their mob-run union. At the conclusion, somber strings intone a sort of requiem over the scene. The next scene is that night, and Edie has come to the roof looking for Terry. She wants to give Joey's jacket to him, but it's clear she's come for much more than that. The love theme is heard the way it probably should have been heard the first time—played unaccompanied, by a single flute. It moves to the strings just in time for Terry and Edie's first kiss. The exact moment of the kiss is underlined by a sudden, dramatic shift in the harmony.

The kiss and the cue fade out and we fade in on the church the next morning. Terry and Father Barry take a walk and Terry tells Father Barry about luring Joey to the roof. Father Barry tells Terry to confess this to Edie, which he does, but it goes badly and she runs away. The entire sequence of Terry and Edie is shot right at the waterfront, and as Terry tries to explain to Edie that he didn't know Joey was going to be murdered, a tugboat lets its steam whistle sound and all Edie can hear is it and some vague words of excuse coming from Terry. To the sound of the stabbing motive, Edie runs away. In one of his best cues, Bernstein allows the motive to continue into the next scene, and then soften. It's a transition from the intensity of Terry's confession to the rooftop, where Glover from the crime commission (played by Leif Erickson) has come to confront Terry one more time. Terry reveals that, in a big boxing match at Madison Square Garden a few years before, he'd taken a dive so that his brother, Charley (as well as, presumably, Johnny Friendly), would win a bet they'd placed on the other guy.

Johnny Friendly confronts Charley on Terry's scheduled upcoming testimony. "Will he be D and D ['deaf and dumb'] or a pigeon?" Friendly asks. "I wish I knew," Charley answers. Friendly tells Charley to take his brother out for a little talk and if he doesn't see the light to "give him the Jerry G." We don't know what the "Jerry G" is, but it doesn't sound good, and Charley says, "I can't do that." The scene ends ambiguously and Charley leaves to a cue of sinister-sounding, pyramiding brass. That night, Charley and Terry have their famous conversation in a cab. Terry tells Charley he doesn't know what he's going to do about the subpoena, and Charley pulls a gun on him and tells him to take a cushy boss' job on the docks and keep his mouth shut.

This leads to a conversation about Terry's boxing career. Gently, lovingly, Terry expresses to Charley the enormous hurt and disappointment he felt when he had to throw the big fight at the Garden to another boxer just so Charley could win a bet. It was a "one-way ticket to Palookaville," Terry says. "You was my brother, Charley, you shoulda watched out for me a little." Brass introduces a three-note variation on the stabbing motive which moves easily into a hauntingly tragic theme in the strings. "I coulda had class, I coulda been a contender," Terry says, in the most famous quote from the film and, arguably, all of Brando's career. Bernstein's sorrowful music is effective, though perhaps just a little too interesting in and of itself. In a sense, Bernstein's music is "too good" for the film, at least in spots. Anything less than the stellar performance given by Brando in this scene (aided by the extraordinary Rod Steiger) would have been brought down by Bernstein's too-interesting cue. Back to the story: Charley can't do what he knows he'd better do, given his brother's ambivalence. Charley gives Terry the revolver ("You're gonna need it," he says) and drops him off on a side street, then tells the cabbie to take him to the Garden. But the cabbie has been paid off and drives Charley to Johnny Friendly's. Charley's doom is sealed.

Then comes the most awkward cue of them all. Bernstein reintroduces the rushing strings and punctuating brass that accompanied the end of the church meeting scene. This works fine at first, but it continues into the next scene, when Terry goes to Edie's apartment and demands she open the door. We then hear the love theme in angry dress, counterpointed by percussion, first in the strings and then repeated in the trumpets. Terry forces his way in and Edie shouts at him to leave. In an act that today would be considered sexual harassment, Terry forces Edie into a kiss, saying, "Edie, you love me." The music now shifts to the stabbing motive, which attempts in sound to equal the edgy passion of Brando's visual ardor, but which comes off instead as overly operatic. In fact, by this time, we are beginning to get the idea that Bernstein has conceived of the love scenes in the film as a kind of unsung opera. In opera, a scene of angry lovers, torn apart by circumstance but still passionately, almost violently in love, would be wrapped in precisely this kind of music. In a film, however, this sort of writing goes way overboard. Mercifully, the music stops with the kiss.

After the score's most strained moment comes the finest few minutes in Bernstein's one-movie career as a composer of background music for film. Terry is called out of the apartment by voices who say his brother wants to talk to him. He leaves, to Edie's protests, and a muted trumpet sounds the stabbing motive, taken up in turn by the strings. It intensifies as Edie leaves to take chase and builds still further as a truck tries to run over Terry and Edie in an alleyway. Terry thrusts his hand through the glass panel of a locked door, opens it, and throws Edie and himself to safety behind it, just as the truck catches up to them. As he does, the truck's headlights fall on the horrifying sight of Charley hanging from a meat hook in the alley. Bernstein's music climaxes in an emotional release that leads directly into the deep, sorrowful string music from Terry and Charley's conversation in the cab. We hear now that the sorrow music is intimately related to the stabbing motive, linking the harsh life on the docks to the tragedy of Terry and Charley's hurtful relationship. As Terry wraps his arms gently around his brother to take him down from his death perch, the sorrow music reaches a height of unspeakable grief. It is a perfectly realized coordination of screen action and dramatic music. And here, Bernstein's music actually covers up for the script's most ridiculous line when Terry says, "They got Charley." "*They got Charley*"? What Terry says is not what Terry feels. What he feels is in the music.

Terry testifies and goes to Friendly's bar with the revolver looking for revenge, but Father Barry confronts and stops him. The sorrow music laden with heavier chords accompanies Terry staring at a picture of Johnny Friendly and it builds until Terry throws the revolver at the picture. Terry testifies, but his testimony comes at a price. His former friends won't talk to him. In a scene embroidered with string music that's a softer, sweeter take on the sorrow theme, Terry and Edie talk. Terry goes to the rooftop. The neighborhood kid on the rooftop has killed all the pigeons and when he sees Terry, he hurls one in Terry's direction, yelling, "A pigeon for a pigeon." Edie has followed him. She says she wants to go west and find a farm. "A farm?" Terry answers in disbelief. He leaves for the docks. "I'm just gonna go down there," he says, "and get my rights." The music, continuing, has now changed into the main title theme, played softly in winds and brass, and it takes us back to the docks.

The union boss says, "Everybody works today" and proceeds to call out the name of every man there, except Terry. The French horn calls out the notes of the opening. Terry walks down to the dockside office occupied by Friendly and the rest of the mob, and yells for Friendly to come out. He does, and their confrontation is understandably heated. "You ratted on us!" Friendly screams. "Maybe from where you're standing but I'm standing over here now. I was ratting on myself all those years and didn't even know it," Terry retorts. Friendly goads Terry into a fight and of course as soon as Terry gets the upper hand, the other mobsters gang up on him and beat him to a bloody pulp. The music of the first dock scene, the bursts of brass and percussion, backdrops the beating.

Edie and Father Barry show up, too late to do anything but minister to Terry. A ship's owner starts to scream for workers, but when Friendly orders the men to work, they refuse, saying, "If Terry works, we work." Tussling with one of the workers, Friendly falls into the water and the men laugh uproariously. To Father Barry's urging, Terry gets up and walks to the ship's hold and into work, his painful walk supported by a transformed main theme. That theme is now triumphant, a "Bernstein hymn," like the one at the end of *Age of Anxiety*. When Terry enters the hold, the men at last go to work, to the frantic screaming of Johnny Friendly and the climactic sounds of the main theme, briefly and magically intertwined with the love theme.

In the final twenty-plus minutes of the film, Bernstein seems to have found his way. The cues are powerful, but restrained. They admirably fit the action and, more than that, the emotions associated with that action. It's as if Bernstein had learned by doing, and as he worked his way through the film, got better at it. Unfortunately, some of the earlier, clumsier cues went uncorrected, and the score, though powerful in and of itself, is flawed by its frequent intrusions. *On the Waterfront* won eight Oscars, including Best Picture, Brando for Best Actor, Kazan for Best Director, and Schulberg for writing. Bernstein was nominated, but lost to Dimitri Tiomkin's music for *The High and the Mighty*. Had he wished to do so, there's no doubt that Bernstein could have become one of the screen's finest composers of dramatic scores. But he and the form did not mesh well, and Bernstein never scored another movie. His deepest gifts lay elsewhere.

Now, let's see what the composer did with all this music when he took it to the concert hall. Bernstein worked throughout the first half of 1955 arranging what he called a "symphonic suite" from the film's cues. The result, dedicated to his son, Alexander, premiered on August 11 at Tanglewood. Humphrey Burton has pointed out correctly that this is not so much a suite as a tone poem. I would go one step further and call it a symphony in one movement. At around twenty minutes running time, it is a single statement comprising various interconnected musical gestures and ideas:

We hear a yearning French horn announce the main theme, adagio. The melody arches up, falls back, arcs up again, and finally down. The last gesture changes the minor mode of the theme to major. Flute picks up the theme, echoed by a muted trombone in close imitation. Quiet brass closes out the opening. Suddenly, the pace quickens to an allegro. Softly, timpani and other low drums and eventually cymbals enter in jagged rhythms with a dark and brutal sound, and eventually an alto saxophone announces a two-note stabbing or jabbing motive that metastasizes into a cruel, aggressive theme played by the entire orchestra. The two-note jabbing motive becomes a three-note jabbing motive as the orchestra picks it up and tosses it around. Then, fortissimo, the full orchestra, with an insistent snare drum rhythm in the background, stridently asserts a long passage built on the jabbing motive.

Suddenly stopping the action, pyramiding brass instruments announce a transition to scurrying strings-and-woodwind music that underlies jabs and thrusts of dissonant chords from the brass. The two-note and three-note stabbing motives expand into a lengthy passage that recalls the opening theme, but bent and distorted. After a great deal of working out, this reaches a climax and suddenly everything comes to a halt except for a single held note on the saxophone, which flows into a short, unaccompanied sax solo. Strings reenter with a comforting counterstatement—like a church chorale, but painfully inflected. The stabbing motive now softens into quiet reminiscence from the sax, and then the horn offers up the main theme once more, played alone and as a kind of resigned benediction.

From the quiet of the benediction's end comes a second adagio theme in the flute, with harp and a second flute supporting it. It feels somehow related to the main subject, but sweetened and more optimistic. Even so, though major from the beginning, it contains a tiny "flaw" like a beauty mark, a "blue note" that has the uncanny property of sending the melody to a higher key. Soon the cellos take up the theme, then the trumpet, surrounding by a halo of violins. Both iterations send the melody up, and up again, into new, fresh keys where the theme grows in strength and beauty. Finally, the entire orchestra takes it up and it at last crashes, like a building wave on a shore, and comes to an end. In the distance we hear the solo horn again sound the main theme. The orchestra takes this up and latches on to one aspect of the theme, turning it again into the brutal music of the earlier allegro. But as this subsides, the horn comes back again with the main theme, this time harmonized in a fresh way by the woodwinds and harp.

Now the main theme begins to build, strengthened by the newfound harmonies. Bolstered by strings, then by the full orchestra, it becomes defiant, even triumphant. Briefly and magically, the second adagio theme joins the main theme in perfect counterpoint. The main theme grabs hold of a new key center and, utterly changed by the harmonies that now define it, becomes a majestic hymn to the possibility of overcoming inherent limitations. The score ends on a pair of notes that suggest the brutal jabbing motive has been conquered.

Anyone who has seen the movie and paid a little bit of attention will recognize the various sections of the score and be able to identify the scenes of their origins. But not only is that unnecessary to enjoying and understanding this extraordinary one-movement symphony, it may actually be harder than one assumes. Yes, the "second adagio" theme is the love theme, but in the context of the concert work it takes on a different character. It is still lyrical and suggestive of romance, but what might be called its spiritual element is heightened. Yes, the two- or three-note jagged motive still conjures the docks, if one wishes it to do so, but it also stands on its own as a dark statement that casts deep shadows on the composition's slowly emerging optimism. Some things are entirely new in the concert work, such as the brief saxophone solo. If you listen to a fine recording of the piece, such as that by Marin Alsop leading the Bournemouth Symphony, you will also experience what a professional symphony orchestra and conductor can add to a score previously played rather thinly by studio musicians in Hollywood.

Even as the film of *On the Waterfront* premiered on July 29, 1954, Bernstein was putting the finishing touches on a work that had been commissioned from him back in 1951 by the Koussevitzky Foundation, a nonprofit established upon the death of the elder conductor in July of that year. The commission allowed the composer to choose the format for an extended symphonic work, so Bernstein decided to combine fulfilling the commission with honoring a promise made to his friend, the great violinist Isaac Stern, for a concerto. The result would be his most universally admired concert composition.

The work that cemented Bernstein's reputation as a symphonic composer, the one that is today the most widely performed of his non-theater scores, carries the clumsy full title of *Serenade after Plato's Symposium for Solo Violin, String Orchestra, Harp and Percussion*. Apparently, Bernstein found the absence of winds in his orchestration an element sufficiently significant to warrant being part of the name. The work may be referred to, for brevity's sake, as *Serenade for Violin and Orchestra, after Plato's Symposium*, or simply *Serenade for Violin and Orchestra* or even *Serenade after Plato's Symposium*. Plato's *Symposium*, Bernstein's literary inspiration for this work, praises love of all kinds, but centers on erotic love, either in the literal or as a symbol of more spiritual forms of love. Specifically, the text focuses on the form of Eros most common in Athens at the time, sexual intercourse between an older man and a younger boy. The reason, some would say excuse, for this coming-of-age ritual among Athenian males was the imparting of "virtue" from man to boy. By "virtue," the Greeks meant strength or ability. The boy involved learned from his lover the ways of being a

man. In our time, this would be considered the lowest kind of pedophil-
ia. In ancient Greece, it was the norm.

It's tempting to see in a work based on such an explicitly homoerotic
text the composer's veiled confession of his own proclivities, and perhaps it's not unreasonable to assume that Bernstein chose the *Symposium* over, say, the *Republic* or the *Crito*, for the reason that it "spoke to
his condition," as the Quakers say. But there is a bigger issue in the
Symposium. The text progresses from a discussion of the inherent dual-
ity of man/boy (what we would call the masculine and the feminine) in
the dialogue of Phaedrus and Pausanias, to the mythological and scientific aspects of love (Aristophanes and Eryximachus), arriving at last at
the crux of the matter in Agathon's recitation about the matchless beauty of love. In a final section that is half lecture and half epilogue, Socrates puts a pall over the proceedings and then Alcibiades makes his
famous entrance with a band of merry makers and suddenly, everything
takes a back seat to his party.

Bernstein scored *Serenade* for violin solo with harp; timpani; five
percussionists playing at various times snare drum, tenor drum, bass
drum, triangle, suspended cymbal, xylophone, glockenspiel, chimes,
Chinese blocks, and tambourine; and the usual strings. The solo part
was edited and carefully fingered by Stern, and the completed piece
premiered on September 12, 1954, in Venice, Italy, with Stern as soloist
and Bernstein conducting the Israel Philharmonic Orchestra. Although
Bernstein went through the motion of saying, in his program note, that
the *Serenade* was not intended as a programmatic work, he went on, in
the same program note, to describe how his music paralleled each of
the sections of Plato's original. He always seemed to be of two minds on
the subject.

A note about form: Classical forms are not just a set of molds into
which composers pour notes. They are structural guides that give the
composer a frame, but which also allow great freedom within that
frame. The classical form Bernstein uses for the first movement of the
Serenade is sonata-allegro. Once we get past the dusty-sounding name,
sonata-allegro form is simple to understand. In a sonata-allegro movement, we hear a group of musical gestures or themes—anywhere from
two to four or more—and then we hear them played with, varied, and
tossed about. The laying out of the themes is called the exposition. The
second section is called the development. After the development, we

return to the ideas as originally stated, and yet they are changed in some way peculiar to the composer and his or her treatment of the themes. The last section is called the recapitulation. There is sometimes also a coda, or tailpiece, that serves as a kind of second development; Beethoven employs codas to great effect. But the opening movement of *Serenade* doesn't have one.

PHAEDRUS; PAUSANIAS

Serenade begins in a key signature of six flats at a very slow tempo, *Lento*. Before the sonata-allegro proper, we hear an introduction in which the soloist intones a set of musical ideas that will be expanded on and varied throughout the piece. Five simple notes—a B-flat followed by two higher D-flats, back down to B-flat, and further up to B-flat—form a mini-portrait of desire. This is, of course, the same rising, falling, and rising again that we found frequently in *Age of Anxiety* and *On the Waterfront*. After this comes the same melodic contour but much more broadly drawn. We end up on a B-flat exactly one octave higher than the one we started on. If a melody is a journey, we have journeyed far in a short time, albeit by circuitous paths. Then the orchestral violins enter, with the violas fast on their tail and finally all the strings in fugato, or imitation. An accelerando and a crescendo, aided by a roll of suspended cymbal, take us into the *Allegro marcato*.

Cellos and violas announce a subject made from the elements of the introduction. The meter is more or less seven, or at least 3/8 plus 2/4 (4/8) (though sometimes this is offset by repeated measures of one or the other time signature). The soloist takes up the subject almost violently, and at the finish of her first completing phrase we hear the astonishing entrance of harp and glockenspiel, a glittering coloristic addition. This is a transitional motive, a simple downward sweep of a scale, not unlike the one that forms such an important part of *Age of Anxiety*. The scale is suggestive of one of the seven Church modes; namely, the Mixolydian. This mode is very much like the major scale, but with a flatted seventh (like playing G to G on the piano, all white notes). The orchestra then plays a short, riotous take on the main subject until suddenly, the soloist reenters with whimsical, quieter second subject. If there is such a thing as love-drunk music, it is certainly this second subject, in 3/8 meter but with displaced accents in numbers sufficient to blur the beat like love blurs the senses. About every other note is given a grace note before it, which adds to the already bright sound of the bell-and-harp-obsessed orchestration. A short, heavily accented closing subject brings the exposition to an end.

The development begins with that plunging scale, now turned to a different mode: the Lydian, the equivalent of playing F to F on the piano, all white notes. This will dominate the development, though we also hear new takes on the first and second subjects. The return to the recapitulation is swift, and surprising, as it begins with the transitional subject of the scale—now turned to yet a third mode, the Aeolian, or the equivalent of what we call our minor scale, the white notes on the piano from A to A. We see now that Bernstein the joker has been having a little fun trotting out Church modes with Greek names, singularly appropriate for his literary subject. The rule about recapitulations is that all or most of the themes must come back, but there's no rule about their order. Bernstein grabs us back in with the transitional theme, moves on to the main subject, and ends with a fortissimo reiteration of the second subject, leaving us punch drunk on Eros and wanting more.

ARISTOPHANES

Aristophanes, usually associated with ribald humor like that in his play, *Lysistrata* (in which women withhold sex from men until they stop engaging in their stupid wars), is a gentler soul in Plato's dialogue. Bernstein's program note interprets him as a storyteller armed with "the mythology of love." The atmosphere, Bernstein says, "is one of quiet charm." His music lives up to that description. In a serene *Allegretto* with very few counterparts in the composer's output, all love is true love and all love elevates the soul. The solo violin, softly and *con sordino*—with a mute hushing the strings—utters a cradling little subject in double stops (playing more than one note at a time). Orchestra and soloist exchange musical thoughts, sometimes involving multiple soloists within the violin section. The soloist slowly wends her way to her high register, where she slowly spins out a sweet tune that leads the orchestra to a peaceful conclusion in unambiguous C-sharp major. The score contains the words "tenderly" and "warmly" at various spots.

So many of Bernstein's most distinctive melodic gestures are angular—with large intervals between notes, such as sixths and sevenths—that when he writes more or less stepwise music like the piece at hand, it takes the listener by surprise. Turmoil is Bernstein's natural ground (think of Jeremiah's lamentation and the nail biting in *Age of Anxiety*), and the intent of any given piece is to grasp the turmoil and to transcend it, as the Brando character in *On the Waterfront* transcends it in his bloody march to the ship's hold at movie's end. Serenade is different, and *Aristophanes* is the most different of the work's five movements. The familiar angular melodies show up in the other movements, and there is sufficient conflict in the others to make this a truly Bernsteinian work—we are shortly to get a ferocious scherzo, after all, and a heart-wrenching adagio. But overall, *Serenade* is a more sanguine score than other Bernstein compositions, and Aristophanes in particular affords the listener, to borrow from the title of Bernstein's final work for the lyric stage, a quiet place.

ERIXYMATHUS; PRESTO

Everything in this manic movement is extreme: extreme speed, extreme virtuosity, extremes of dynamics—everything is *pianissimo* and then we turn the corner and wham! All is *fortissimo*. Even the length is extreme: extremely short that is, clocking in at under ninety seconds in most performances. Colors are amazing, such as the doubling of solo violin with xylophone. Our angular melodic gestures have returned and with a bravura vengeance. Some of them are so hard to negotiate that, at one point near the middle, Bernstein writes an asterisked note to the violins: "Play all notes if possible." *If possible!* "Bodily harmony" is the message of this passage in the Plato dialogue.

AGATHON; ADAGIO

"Perhaps the most moving speech of the dialogue," wrote Bernstein of Agathon's speech. To which should be added, apropos the composer's musical paraphrase: "Perhaps the most moving seven minutes in Bernstein's orchestral output." Or even: "One of the most touching slow movements in all twentieth-century symphonic music" ("Serenade [after Plato's "Symposium"]"). This is music as intimate as a kiss, as comforting and as sure as an embrace from a trusted lover. In this movement, Bernstein reveals something pure and simple about human love. It has no name, of course. That's why it's music.

The four-note yearning motive from the very beginning of the concerto returns as an orchestral bed for a love song from the soloist. We have mentioned before the upward-climbing shape of one distinctive brand of Bernstein melody: the melody climbs, falls back, and climbs again, usually higher. The importance of this to the Bernstein sound can almost not be overstressed. The shape, or contour, of a composer's melodies is an important element in the composer's sound, and in Bernstein, the tension, and therefore the beauty, of his melodies often comes from this striving upward. Given that these melodies, when associated with words either sung or unsung, are usually linked to the search for love, it would not be too far to go to suggest that they are sonic symbols of the heart seeking its place in the world. All the love songs in *West Side Story* will show this. (Of course, Bernstein employs a wider range of melodic gesture than merely this one, as we saw, for example, with the songs for *Peter Pan*. But it is characteristic of him in a certain distinctive mood.)

The soloist's love song stretches out freely over a great expanse. Its lyricism is that of passion mixed with wonder. The orchestral accompaniment sometimes amounts to a dialogue with the soloist, and the main voice of the orchestra in these dialogues is often that of the viola. The viola, that unjustly maligned member of the string family, is rarely used with such transparency, as the complaint against its sound is that it can be thin or even scratchy on its own. One of the great advantages enjoyed by Bernstein the composer was his co-identity with Bernstein the conductor. From years of experience conducting orchestras, Bernstein knew each instrument in its strengths and weaknesses, including the viola. He knew the sweet spot in its range and exactly how to get from it the warmth and weight that makes its role in *Agathon* such a perfect fit.

At length, the orchestra takes over in a passage that blooms into purest melancholy. Love's power is a double-edged sword. When it is granted us, we sing and recite poetry and create beauty. But if it is denied, then nothing else can take its place. "[H]e whom Love touches not walks in darkness," says Agathon. The darkness crowds our strings, with the timpani rumbling beneath, until at last the darkness breaks and our soloist returns with a lengthy cadenza. Soloist and orchestra reunited for some last, plangent measures, ending in simple, pure F major.

SOCRATES; ALCIBIADES. MOLTO TENUTO; ALLEGRO MOLTO VIVACE

The last and longest of the *Serenade*'s five movements begins with the somber observations of Socrates, sounded as chime and massed strings, almost as a death knell. The greatest love, Socrates here says in tones, as he says in words in Plato, is not Eros, but the love of wisdom. After all, Socrates reasons in the text, love is the desire for something one doesn't have. Therefore, love has not what it longs for. He goes on in this vein, proving the inadequacies of Eros in perfectly reasoned dialectic. Bernstein's musical parallel is genius: a dialogue between the violin soloist and a solo cello in the orchestra, playing against each other in different keys. The keys (two flats for the violin and two sharps for the cello) are as distant as any pair, yet they work together for an effective duet. This is dialectic musically embodied. In both the dialogue and the musical score we are beginning to think that Socrates is quite the spoilsport when, in the proverbial nick of time, Alcibiades, reputedly the most physically beautiful of Athenians, shows up with a merry band of drunken, happy, lustful friends and Socrates's death knell for love is turned into the ancient Greek equivalent of an Irish wake.

Alcibiades's revelry concludes the *Serenade* with celebratory sounds of music that seem just right for dancing and drinking, either in Athens in the centuries BC, or in New York in the 1950s. For Bernstein, in one of his boldest moves, has interpolated jazz-like riffs into the texture of the string orchestra. In his program note, he admits: "If there is a hint of jazz in the celebration, I hope it will not be taken as anachronistic Greek party music, but rather the natural expression of a contemporary American composer imbued with the spirit of that timeless dinner party" ("Serenade [after Plato's "Symposium"]"). This is the most metrically regular of the movements, a sign of uncomplicated musical ease. It's in gently swinging 6/8 for the most part, until the party reaches its orgiastic climax and the tempo pumps to *Presto vivace*, in common time right to the stunning and unambiguously joyous end.

Serenade, one of but a handful of Bernstein symphonic works without voices, is a miracle of composition from the 1950s. By that time, the leading composers in the tradition of Western art music—so-called classical music—had largely abandoned the harmonies and melodic gestures of traditional tonality. A new style of composing music—called variously "twelve-tone," "serial," and "atonal"—had come to dominate new works for the concert hall in the West. The Soviet Union and the Eastern bloc countries maintained a commitment to tonality, while young composers in Western countries ironically espoused the "historical inevitability" of twelve tone. Tonality, with its major chords and minor chords and do-re-mi scales, was, they said, a thing of the past. The most esteemed composer among the young lions of the 1950s was Austrian Anton Webern (1883–1945), a student of twelve-tone's founder Arnold Schoenberg, and the writer of extremely short, intensely dissonant pieces.

The central tenet of serial composition was that all twelve tones of the chromatic scale should be treated equally. This is far more radical than it may seem, as the tonal tradition, stretching back into antiquity, is based on exactly the opposite assumption: that notes exist in hierarchical relation to one another. In the tonal system, one pitch is the "home tone." This pitch establishes the key center. For instance, if you play all the white notes on the piano from one C to the next C, you will get a do-re-mi scale in which the first and last notes are the obvious headwaters of the scale; the ones in between exist, as it were, in subservience to them. The tones in a scale are ordered in a certain fashion determined by the harmonic series, or overtones. As any guitar player knows, the most common chords are the I, IV, and V. That's because the fourth and fifth steps of the scale are the next in importance after the first. These three together, called the "primary chords," form the "spine" of the key, with the four other steps of the scale making up the rest of the formation. A more elegant metaphor was put forth by Bernstein himself in one of his *Omnibus* television shows. Drawing on his love for sports, Bernstein compared the tonal system to a game of baseball in which "do" ("c" in the key of c) is home base, and all the other pitches are the numbered "bases" to be run in a scale. Instead of three bases, however, the tonal system provides six in addition to home.

Serial music abandoned this idea. Instead of hierarchical relationships between notes, the so-called atonal movement asserted that all notes should relate "equally" to one another. No "do" or "re" or "mi," no I or IV or V, but only Cs and Fs and B-flats and the other nine "pitch classes" in a kind of suspended-animation proximity to one another. Listen to any music by Webern and you will hear its perfect distillation: one note here, a silence perhaps, another note and then the crash of another and, in some distant space yet another, all unrelated except in the sense that the composer has placed them in mutual proximity, as if pitched sounds were neutral sonic objects to be assembled in a manner pleasing somehow to the composer, who has now become a kind of aural designer.

None of this appealed to Leonard Bernstein. Bernstein eschewed the aesthetic of serialism throughout his life, using twelve-tone rows only in a tonal context—that is, to contrast the "disconnect" of dodecaphony with the necessary connections of the tonal language. We encountered this in Symphony No. 2, *The Age of Anxiety*, where Bernstein employed a twelve-tone row to illustrate the alienation of the characters in Auden's poem. We will see Bernstein use rows throughout his career, but always for similar dramatic effect. Once, in the mid-1960s, Bernstein spent an agonizing few months sketching twelve-tone pieces, only to throw them out. Bernstein maintained a loyalty to tonality that made him an outcast among composers that included such champions of serialism as Pierre Boulez and Elliott Carter. (Even Igor Stravinsky, one of the pillars of an expanded tonality through most of his life, capitulated to serialism near the end.) The importance Bernstein placed on tonality would lead him to make an intellectual case for tonality as grounded in nature, in his controversial Harvard lectures of 1973. In the long run, he would prove to be on the right side of music history, as serialism faded and a new generation of eclectic tonal composers emerged. His struggle was even celebrated on the cover of the *New York Times Magazine* in 1986, which pictured the composer and proclaimed: "Bernstein Triumphant."

But in the 1950s, it was serialism that was triumphant, at least in the concert hall. Fortunately, in the commercial theater that was a major locus of Bernstein's work, tonality remained a given. After all, audiences didn't buy tickets to twelve-tone musicals. Dissonance was all well and good, but only if it resolved to a good, solid, tonic chord. In the theater, then, Bernstein worked the mainstream of composing. But the concert world was a strikingly different matter. Among the vanguard composers of concert music in the 1950s, Bernstein was an outsider. That Bernstein's *Serenade* is today one of very few symphonic works of the 1950s to enjoy wide-ranging repertoire status, to be performed and recorded by virtually every living violinist with a solo career, is a magnificent irony.

The Suite from *On the Waterfront* and the *Serenade after Plato's Symposium* are compelling scores in which Bernstein employs his idea of "continuous variation." Musical ideas announced at the head of a piece play out in ways that are unexpected and yet inevitable. A gesture of some sort in one movement is latched onto in the next. This was Bernstein's modus operandi, but what made his music powerful and memorable was an extraordinary ability to shape melodies that opened themselves up to this process. An uninteresting melody may be varied in all sorts of clever ways, but it and its variations will remain uninteresting. It is the melody itself that contains the seed necessary to grow a magnificent tree. At a tribute to Bernstein on the occasion of his sixtieth birthday, Ned Rorem pronounced his old friend "our most beguiling melodist," and that indeed is the core of what made Bernstein Bernstein. In the next two chapters, we will see the role his gift played in the creation, back to back, of two of the most important English-language works for the lyric stage.

6

CANDIDE

We look to a German mathematician/philosopher and a French satirist for the genesis of Bernstein's next project, the brilliant, irresistible, and not infrequently heartbreaking operetta-cum-musical, *Candide*.

Gottfried Leibniz (1646–1716) invented calculus independently of Newton, designed modern mathematical notation, and refined the system of binary numbers. Influenced, perhaps, by the perfections of mathematical processes, he also promulgated the philosophy of optimism: the idea that, out of all the possible worlds God might have created, the one we live in must be the best. Leibniz was a rationalist, basing his thought on first principles rather than on observed events, which explains how he managed to reach a conclusion that ignored the pain and suffering outside his study window.

To François-Marie Arouet, a.k.a. Voltaire (1694–1778), this idea, widely espoused in his time, was hilarious. If a world in which babies died, nations starved, and entire populations were laid waste in natural disasters constituted the "best of all possible worlds," what could possibly be the worst? Voltaire created a character he called Candide, whose master Pangloss (a stand-in for Leibniz) has instilled in him the idea that ours is indeed "the best of all possible worlds," and whose lady love, Cunegonde, waits to give to him her hand in marriage. Voltaire then subjected his characters to a series of utter disasters, among them war, pestilence, murder, rape, tyranny, torture, and an earthquake. (The latter was included in recognition of the 1775 Lisbon earthquake, said to have resulted in up to 100,000 deaths.) Voltaire's ensuing satirical novella, *Candide* (1758), is generally named one of the most important books in European history.

Bernstein talked with playwright Lillian Hellman about a range of collaborative possibilities in the early 1950s. Among these was an idea, put forth by Hellman, for a musical piece about Eva Peron, uncannily presaging the Andrew Lloyd-Webber/Tim Rice rock opera of the 1970s, *Evita*. Bernstein declined the idea, and when Hellman suggested musicalizing *Candide*, he typed a letter to her rejecting that, as well. Then he tore the letter up and wrote another one, accepting it.

Why the change of heart? Bernstein had recently triumphed as a conductor at La Scala, the great opera house in Milan, Italy. The new world of opera was heady stuff for a conductor whose métier until now had been limited to the symphony orchestra. Then, too, he had tried his hand at operatic writing in *Trouble in Tahiti* to real, if limited, success. Now Bernstein must have fantasized his entry into the august repertoire of grand opera. He told his wife Felicia that *Candide* would be "a big, three-act opera with chorus and ballet." It turned out to be a two-act musical-cum-operetta whose eventual history would include at least three distinctly different versions. It would also boast some of Bernstein's brightest and sweetest music, including an overture that is today a mainstay of symphony orchestras around the world.

Many of Bernstein's works from the middle-to-late period of his career exist in numerous revisions or as adaptations of other scores. For example, music for some of the Anniversaries shows up recycled in larger pieces. And as we'll see later, the score for an abandoned musical of the 1960s would become part of *Chichester Psalms*. After the composer's death, adaptations of numerous Bernstein scores were made by his heirs and associates. His last completed musical, *1600 Pennsylvania Avenue*, became *White House Cantata*. Bernstein's daughter Jamie wrote an alternative narration for her father's Symphony No. 3. Even *West Side Story* was eventually offered in an English-and-Spanish revision on Broadway.

But *Candide* tops the list for most versions of one musical theater work, ever. In addition to the original Broadway production of 1956, which we'll shortly examine, the 1958 London staging heavily revised Hellman's book. A 1971 *Candide* by the Los Angeles Civic Light Opera reordered the songs. Most significant, director Harold Prince staged a one-act version Off-Broadway in 1974 that substituted a completely new book by Hugh Wheeler, greatly reduced the size of the forces (a tiny pit band took the place of the original, lavish orchestra), and added some new lyrics by Stephen Sondheim. This became known as the "Chelsea *Candide*," named after the tiny theater where it was staged. This pocket-sized *Candide*, its double-entendres and broad satire infinitely closer to Voltaire than Hellman's libretto, is the earliest version currently available for production.

In 1982, *Candide* finally found its way to an opera house when New York City Opera restored the piece to two acts, reinstated much of the music previously cut in the Chelsea version, and added new scenes. Harold Prince once more directed. In 1988 came the version now standard in opera houses, produced by the Scottish Opera in Glasgow. Directors Jonathan Miller and John Wells amended Wheeler's book, and John Mauceri, who had music-directed the Chelsea version, music-directed this production, which saw the reinstatement of still more music from the original and the addition of a brand new chorus, "Universal Good." Finally, in December 1989, came the premiere at London's Barbican Centre of a concert version that restored yet more music and linked the musical numbers with narration written by Bernstein and director John Wells. This version is available on DVD.

One additional version should be cited: the semistaged concert *Candide* directed by Lonny Price in 2005 as part of the New York Philharmonic's magnificent series of Musicals in Concert. A kind of advance on the Chelsea version, it retains the more ribald and satiric tone of the 1974 production, but returns many of the numbers cut for Chelsea to their rightful place and with many musical numbers and the magnificent original orchestrations restored. It, too, can be found on DVD.

Patience is required to get one's arms around all these rewrites, but the rewards are worth it. Within the myriad *Candides* lie some of the most commanding melodies and brightest lyrical settings of the late twentieth century. Connoisseurs of the work generally treasure the Chelsea version in the theater, the Scottish Opera version in the opera house, both concert versions on video, and the original Broadway cast on CD. The Chelsea staging and New York Philharmonic concert are unmistakably musicals, not operas, while the London concert version, by virtue of its opera-star cast, exhibits the score's affinity with classical singing. The original cast CD falls somewhere in between. It must be said that the 1956 recording, though it contains many numbers later withdrawn or heavily revised, emits an energy of freshness and invention that makes it a keeper.

We'll follow the 1989 concert DVD, the last one authorized before the composer's death. It contains the most music of any readily available version, and is sung at the highest levels of operatic mastery. We'll also take a look at the other *Candide* on video, the New York Philharmonic's semistaged production, performed by a combination of classically trained voices and some of Broadway's leading lights. But before we dive into the world of Pangloss, Cunegonde, Candide, and the Old Lady, a word about *Candide*'s lyricists—all seven of them. That's right: the versions of this show are matched in number by an array of contributing lyricists.

The first lyric written for the show was penned by two Bernsteins—Leonard and Felicia. "I Am Easily Assimilated" is sung by the comic character of the Old Lady, a Pole who finds herself in South America and adapts to new surroundings in order to survive. Felicia, Chilean by birth, contributed Spanish lines to the number. (She is not officially credited, but her contribution is acknowledged.) Hellman wrote one lyric, an ode to Utopian ideals called "El Dorado." Dorothy Parker contributed to the words of another number, "The Venice Gavotte." After that, Hellman and Bernstein engaged lyricist John LaTouche, whose previous credits included the lyrics for Jerome Moross's *succes d'estime*, "the Golden Apple," and collaboration with composer Vernon Duke on numerous songs such as "Taking a Chance on Love." LaTouche's contributions to *Candide* included the opening number, "The Best of All Possible Worlds" (later heavily revised by Stephen Sondheim in his lyrics for the Chelsea version), and "You Were Dead You Know" and "My Love." These last two were amended and completed by the show's next lyricist, who came aboard when LaTouche and the project went separate ways. (LaTouche's departure is clouded in mystery. Around this time, he also collaborated with Bernstein on a popular-song version of the love theme from *On the Waterfront*, which was released as a pop single and then withdrawn by Bernstein. At any rate, LaTouche went on to write the libretto for Douglas Moore's opera, *The Ballad of Baby Doe*.)

Somewhere in the middle of all the work on *Candide*, Bernstein composed an incidental score for Hellman's *The Lark*, produced on Broadway in 1955. Her play, a translation from the French of Jean

Anouilh, portrayed Joan of Arc in her final days, and this required a heavy ambience of the medieval church. Bernstein provided this through modal-laced choruses based on the texts of the Latin mass. Following a performance of the play, choral director Robert Shaw came to Bernstein with the idea of extracting the choruses as a concert piece. It took only thirty-three years for Bernstein to respond. In 1988, the composer arranged the choruses as a setting of the mass (minus the word-busy Credo) for mixed choir, countertenor solo, and incidental percussion. This *Missa Brevis* was Bernstein's last choral work, a fresh work willed with the composer's love of shifting meters and changing modes, but still evocative of medieval in the purity of its sound.

Back to *Candide*. . . . The new lyricist replacing LaTouche was no less than poet Richard Wilbur, who would eventually be credited as the piece's principal lyricist, all other contributors being listed as "additional." Wilbur, thirty-five and a future Poet Laureate of the United States, had recently penned a spectacular translation of Moliere's *Le Misanthrope*, which attained to the daunting task of keeping the playwright's plan of rhymed couplets throughout—a format much more difficult in English than in French. A friend of Hellman's saw the Broadway production of this translation and told the playwright: "If he can do this well with one witty Frenchman, maybe he would do the same with Voltaire" (qtd. in "Happy birthday, Richard Wilbur!").

Bernstein and Hellman met with Wilbur and a certain rapport was established. Wilbur was asked to submit a sample lyric. He complied, Bernstein and Hellman expressed their approval, and at last the project had a stable team of creative talent. The three collaborators spent the summer of 1956 on Martha's Vineyard, completing the long-labored-over effort to bring Voltaire's sardonic saga to the musical stage. By now, Tyrone Guthrie had been hired as director. Guthrie hovered over the creative team, exercising what Wilbur called a "Charles de Gaulle" presence and bringing together the disparate efforts and schedules of composer, lyricist, and book writer. In a videotaped interview, Wilbur later related that he submitted a lyric called "Dear Boy" to Bernstein on a certain date, but that two days later it was not yet set to music. "I can't get inspired," was Bernstein's plaint to Wilbur. Guthrie, who overheard the exchange, interrupted, saying to Bernstein: "Lenny, we all know you've been water-skiing" (qtd. in "Happy birthday, Richard Wilbur!") Chagrined, Bernstein got to work.

That story may suggest some laziness on Bernstein's part, or at least a tendency to procrastinate. But another perspective sheds light on one of Bernstein's modes of stoking the creative fires. Everyone needs fuel. All work and no play doesn't just make Jack a dull boy, it makes him an unproductive boy and possibly even a dead one. The enormous amount of productivity over the course of Bernstein's life is an indication of his work ethic. Athletic activity of all sorts—water skiing, snow skiing, tennis—was a frequent Bernstein outlet for tension as well as a contributor to his well-being. It doubtlessly factored into his survival to age seventy-two despite emphysema and a lifelong smoking habit.

The first *Candide* opened on Broadway on December 1, 1956, and was a decided failure. Hellman's book was dark and brooding, while Bernstein's music was tuneful and cheery. The two didn't mesh, and the public felt it. Hellman's intent had been to draw a parallel between the persecutions portrayed in Voltaire's book, particularly the persecution of Jews by the Church, and the McCarthy-led nightmare of red witch hunts in her own time. While her book went about doing that, Bernstein's score parodied opera in loving terms, sending Cunegonde into hilarious ecstasy in a major virtuoso aria and creating a dazzling array of duets, trios, and larger ensembles, all of them bright as baubles. But while the show failed, the original cast recording became a cult classic and the overture, extracted and set before symphony orchestras, became a concert favorite.

No new lyricists came on board until the Chelsea version, when Stephen Sondheim took scissors and paste to the score, mercilessly chopping some songs completely, rewriting and/or replacing others, all for the purpose of making a legendary flop into a tiny but powerful hit. Sondheim was the last of *Candide*'s incredible cache of lyricists. His biggest changes included grabbing an ensemble number from Act II and making it into a new opener, "Life is Happiness Indeed," and correcting or replacing many of LaTouche's awkward-to-sing phrases and imperfect rhymes, such as one in the song, "The Best of All Possible Worlds" that tries to rhyme "fonder" with "Cunegonde." Along with the new lyrics came a completely different, one-act book by Hugh Wheeler that matched the lightness and breeziness of the music and returned the piece to Voltaire's satiric tone. Hellman withdrew her book, which is today no longer available for staging.

   The remaining history of *Candide* consists of the gradual restoration of most of the original score and the addition by Bernstein of new numbers to his own lyrics. By the time of the 1988 Scottish Opera production and the 1989 London concert version, the new numbers included "We Are Women," a paean to the fairer sex, sung by Cunegonde and the Old Lady; and the penultimate number in the officially approved score, "Nothing More Than This." "Nothing More Than This" was not strictly new. This solo for the title character, which adds a perfect note of sobriety to balance the madness preceding, was written by Bernstein for the 1956 original, but not then used. It provides a serious transition to the solemn beauty of "Make Our Garden Grow." Versions lacking this song suffer too sudden a shift from the piece's general mien of sexual/satirical hilarity to its closing mood of hope and transcendence.

   The DVDs of the London concert and the New York Philharmonic concert are treasures for Bernstein fans. Made less than a year before the composer's death, the London concert features crystalline performances from June Anderson as Cunegonde, Jerry Hadley as Candide, Adolph Green as Pangloss, and Christa Ludwig as the Old Lady. The orchestra is the London Symphony Orchestra, and Bernstein's presence on the podium sparks both cast and orchestra to their finest efforts. The 2005 Philharmonic concert features Paul Groves in the title role, Kristin Chenoweth as Cunegonde, Patti LuPone as the Old Lady, and Thomas Allen as Pangloss. The orchestra is the composer's old band, the New York Philharmonic, led by one of his most famous and successful conducting students, Marin Alsop. Though Groves and Allen are classical singers, the overall production has the unmistakable character of musical comedy, due in no small part to the presence of Broadway superstar Chenoweth and Broadway legend Lupone, but also to the fact that Price's concept draws primarily on the Chelsea *Candide*.

   We are now ready to experience the DVD of the London concert version of *Candide*. Following ecstatic applause for the superstar cast and for Bernstein himself, we begin with words from Bernstein, "a talk from the old professor come to lecture us again," as it puts it in opening remarks. People, he says, have asked him "Why *Candide*?" His answer takes the form of a brief overview of Leibniz and Voltaire, much as the first paragraphs of this chapter. He goes on for a while and at last pokes fun at his own wordiness, saying in summation, "Oh to hell with it, let's play the overture" (*Bernstein Conducts Candide*). The overture, a work by now so familiar to symphony concertgoers that most will be able to hum it, is given a bright and even rollicking performance by the composer leading the London Symphony Orchestra. A blow-by-blow of the overture is given at the conclusion of this chapter as a "Vignette." Suffice it here to say that the piece perfectly prepares the listener for the ensuing operetta's bright-hued contrasts of jollity, serenity, mockery, and solemnity.

The first vocal number is a chorus by the people of Westphalia, the remote region of modern-day Germany that is Candide's homeland. This is a square, note-against-note song rife with strong, traditional harmonies. Surely we are in a settled and even stoically unadventurous part of the world. We won't stay there for every long. Narrator Adolph Green introduces us to the main characters: Candide, "the personification of innocence," but alas, the illegitimate nephew of a baron and baroness, both of whom abuse him horribly. He intones a short paean to his happiness: "I love all my fellow creatures / And the creatures love each other," he sings. We also meet Maximilian, son to the baron and baroness and, in contrast to Candide, the very embodiment of narcissism. More than making up for the fact that Maximilian snobbishly ignores his bastard cousin is the fact that Maximilian's sister, Cunegonde, shows every fondness for Candide—and then some. We also meet Paquette, serving girl to the baroness and oft time more than that to the baron. After all are introduced, Maximilian and Cunegonde boast in song of their respective beauty. "Ev'ry time I look and see me / I'm reminded life is dreamy," sings Maximilian. "The rose," proclaims his equally vain sister, is "my only rival." When they reprise their little patter-tune ode to self-love, they are joined by Candide and Paquette, who sing of their pleasant, if unremarkable, lives to the tune announced by Candide at the start. Voilà, the two melodies dovetail in arresting counterpoint.

Lovers of the 1956 original cast album will wonder what happened to the original opening number, "The Best of All Possible Worlds." Answer: it's coming up, though with Sondheim's revised lyric. This ensemble, titled "Life Is Happiness Indeed," is the opener for the Chelsea version, with a lyric by Sondheim to a tune lifted from Act II. In the Chelsea staging, we never hear that tune again. But in this, the operetta concert, it will return in the second half with a very different, negative attitude attached. This is the "Venice Gavotte," the only song to which Dorothy Parker contributed words. It must be said that "Life Is Happiness Indeed" makes a snappy and mood-setting first number for the musical comedy take of *Candide*, but that one wonders why "The Best of All Possible Worlds" (with Sondheim's superior lyric), which might more vigorously kickstart a work featuring classical singers, wasn't returned to pole position in the operetta.

Pangloss makes his entrance with "The Best of All Possible Worlds," one of Bernstein's most ingratiating Allegros. The notes skip and leap from register to register, landing here and there on strong primary chords that pin them down, only to let fly again. "Mercurial," a word frequently applied to Bernstein melodies, certainly applies here. Pangloss's students—our assembled cast—ask the professor questions and he in turn professes the answers. After all, there is not an answer he lacks when the world is the best it can be, including even its seemingly most vile creatures and conditions. "What about snakes?" he is asked. Without snake, he answers, Eve would not have been tempted and the Christian adventure would not have occurred. "What about war?" he is asked. War unites the noble born and the commoner, thus relieving class tensions. Thus the Theory of Optimism is secured.

Into this placid and settled atmosphere comes trouble in the form of amour. Cousins Candide and Cunegonde are in love (not unusual in the eighteenth century), and they sing of the nuptials they long for it in the duet "Oh, Happy We." The melody of this blossoming little duet, which we first heard as the second subject of the overture, is a simple, folk-like melody at first, but bursts into ecstasy in the release, or middle, section of the piece. The cradling warmth of this musical sentiment keeps its singers from hearing one another; however, as the words put in their mouths by Richard Wilbur betray a couple in complete disagreement. "We'll have a sweet, Westphalian home," Candide sings. Cunegonde's answer: "We'll live in Paris, when we're not in Rome." Cunegonde: "Glowing rubies." Candide: "Glowing logs." And so it goes, but the lovers never hear each other, swept up as they—and we—are in the serene beauty of the melody. It is a picture one recognizes too readily: two people blinded to their radical differences by the rapture of love.

Alas, Candide is a bastard (literally), born to the baron's sister via an unknown gentleman, and the baron, upon hearing of the bastard's plans to wed his daughter, banishes him from the realm. Candide now sees for the first time the possibility that this is not, after all, the best of all possible worlds. Forced to leave his beloved Cunegonde, to flee his native land, Candide nonetheless clings to the teachings of Pangloss and insists, in "It Must Be So," that even this sad state of affairs must have some role in creating a greater good. "There is a sweetness in ev'ry woe" he recalls his master saying. "It must be so."

No sooner is Candide out of Westphalia than he is kidnapped by soldiers of an enemy nation and forced by them into military service. He attempts to escape but is captured and flogged. Meanwhile, the enemy attacks and savages Westphalia, despite its citizens singing a grand hymn to their nation, "Sieg Heil, Westphalia." Cunegonde is repeatedly raped, then run through with a bayonet. In "Candide's Lament," our hero finds Cunegonde's corpse and sings over it an exquisitely sorrowful aria. It seems that this is too much even for someone indoctrinated with Pangloss' "it's all good" philosophy, for he asks in the aria if he shall ever be consoled, and answers, "No, I swear it / By the light of this lover's moon." The central gesture of the song is a rising octave that falls back and rises yet again, the shape by now so familiar in the composer's output. The tune will return, morphed from lament to bright bauble, in the "Paris Waltz."

Candide wanders about the ruin of his country and finds a kindly old beggar with a tin nose. This turns out to be none other than Pangloss. (Voltaire's story contains many such unlikely, and even impossible, coincidences, as we shall soon see.) The professor explains that his tin nose is the result of a flesh-devouring disease, the necessary side effect of "sweet love." Syphilis by name, the disease has come from the New World, infecting all "from bed to bed" as round the globe it goes. And what could possibly be the reason for such a calamity? Why, without the New World, Europe would never have had chocolate or tobacco. The song is "Dear Boy," the one that had found Bernstein water-skiing while Wilbur awaited the setting of his lyric. The bitterly clever words sit on a sturdy, masculine melody in the opening, shifting to a coy little Andantino in the second half. Remarkably, the song never changes meter, staying the course in a direct and powerful cut time, as if to signal Pangloss's dogged belief in the best of all possible worlds, even when his nose is falling off. A note on a note in "Dear Boy": the song contains a single high note, the last one in each verse. Other singers in the cast sing that pitch in place of Adolph Green, who is not a classically trained singer and cannot reach it. It's not covered up; in fact, it's treated as quite the joke during the applause for the piece.

Pangloss and Candide are welcomed aboard a ship bound for Lisbon. Inevitably, a storm arises and the ship sinks. Our pair floats ashore on a wooden plank, just in time to encounter the famous eruption of the Lisbon volcano. While they escape the wrath of the volcano, Candide and Pangloss are arrested on suspicion of heresy and taken to the Spanish Inquisition. As they arrive before the Grand Inquisitor, an auto-da-fé is taking place. An auto-da-fé was a festival surrounding the execution of heathens, heretics, and general enemies of the Church. The chorus exults in the glory of the day. "What a day, what a day, for an Auto-da-fé!" they sing to a jaunty melody. The lyric mixes their delight in seeing people die with their accompanying joy in consumer culture.

As the heretics burn or are hanged, there are combs to buy and alchemists to hire, magicians who can turn the basest metal to gold. Pangloss complains that he can't be executed because he's "too sick to die." He then recounts the lineage of his syphilis, which he got from Paquette. Suddenly the orchestra breaks into Hispanic dance rhythms, and with equal suddenness we hear the roll of drums as the judgments are pronounced. The jaunty tune returns, but then the mood turns darker as the crowd and churchmen offer up Latin exhortations and the hypocritical words, "Pray for us!" Despite his protests, Pangloss is hanged. Candide, inexplicably, gets away with a mere flogging, and is left to sing a reprise of "It Must Be So." Weakened in his resolve to be optimistic by the sinking, the volcano, and the auto-da-fé, Candide decides the fault must be his in not being able to see the good from all this.

He moves on to Paris, a marvelous excuse for Bernstein to write the charming "Paris Waltz," joyfully built from the sad intervals of "Candide's Lament." And whom do we find in Paris but . . . Cunegonde? (Recall the warning about unlikely occurrences in Voltaire's story.) It is at this point that we pause to consider the score's single most popular vocal number, a comic aria to match any in Rossini and all the more amazing for being in English, a notoriously difficult match for the vowel-oriented rigors of classical singing. "Glitter and Be Gay" is a bravura turn for soprano, a showpiece that takes her up to high Cs, Ds, and E-flats, and along the way throws down the challenges of rapid-fire runs and impossible rhythmic negotiations.

The aria's structure betrays the fact that Bernstein-the-conductor was at this point busy leading productions of Italian operas. It could even be said he was consumed with passion for the genre, and this bled inevitably into his work on the operetta. At one point during his collaboration with Bernstein, Wilbur recalled that he absent-mindedly whistled a tune by Verdi, at which point Bernstein ran to the piano and played it, protesting his envy of Verdi's ability to make something powerful out of gestures so simple and even obvious. Nineteenth-century Italian arias frequently exhibited a two-part form, in which the first section was a relatively quiet statement, and the second an animated answer to the first. This latter section was called a "cabaletta" and sometimes an aria with this structure is called a "cabaletta aria." "Glitter and Be Gay" is such an aria, which makes terrific good sense as in the text, Cunegonde finds herself of two minds. She has become the mistress, not to one, but to two men: a rich Jew and the archbishop of Paris. Of course, this is a shameful state that contradicts her earlier devotion to the pure life. In somber minor mode, she bemoans a fate in which she is "forced to glitter, forced to be gay."

"And yet, of course, I rather like to revel," she sings, as the sprightly cabaletta section takes us to bright C major. She goes on to list some of the advantages she enjoys and concludes, "Perhaps it isn't noble to complain." A subtheme of the operetta now reveals itself. Not only is the idea that ours is "the best of all possible worlds" suspect, the very core of our existence is riven by a dichotomy: commitment to love on the one hand, and a lust for material excess on the other. Here again is Bernstein's theme of faith, transposed onto a choice between love and greed. Greed is faithless, requiring belief only in the possession of objects—precious jewels and a wardrobe "expensive as the devil," in Cunegonde's case. Love, on the other hand, demands faith; without it, love falls to pieces. Bernstein's statement, in connection with *Age of Anxiety*, that all his works were somehow bound up in the search for faith, is here vindicated.

The aria repeats, our heroine once more expressing first sadness at her "fallen state," and then giddiness in the wealth and comfort that fall has earned. This time, however, the first, slow section is spoken to orchestral accompaniment rather than sung, conveying unmistakably that she is losing the negative emotion that surrounds her "fall." The second cabaletta section leads into one of the most amazing moments in

American musical theater—a coda so brilliant, so lustrous in musical invention that it rivals the star sapphire of which Cunegonde boasts. For forty-eight measures, the soprano leaps and runs hither and yon in irrepressible excitement. The coda is based on the cabaletta, but takes the material in a completely different direction, one of unadulterated adulteration. At last, those high notes burst out in all their glory, proclaiming Cunegonde's decision to give into a degraded life of wealth, comfort, and glamorous partying.

"Glitter and Be Gay" is a miracle of musical imagination, and is without doubt an operatic moment in a score that, elsewhere for the most part, could go in the direction of either opera or musical theater. When *Candide* is done as a musical, "Glitter and Be Gay" usually suffers, unless a classically trained singer has been cast in the role. (There have been exceptions, of course, the most stunning of which was the original Cunegonde in 1956, the extraordinary Barbara Cook. Asked once how she, a Broadway singer, had managed all those nasty chromatic runs and repeated notes in eight performances a week, Cook responded that nobody had bothered to tell her it was hard.) June Anderson's astonishing performance in the London concert DVD is greeted by a spirited forty-second ovation that would have gone on much longer, had the audience not been made aware of time constraints due to the videotaping.

To return to our story. In yet another impossible happenstance, Candide discovers Cunegonde in Paris, and they sing the hilarious "You Were Dead, You Know," a LaTouche lyric that skillfully skates over the absurdities of the plot. Candide expresses his amazement that Cunegonde, shot and bayoneted in the Westphalian war, stands here before him. "Ah, but love will find a way," she melodically retorts. Again, Bernstein luxuriates in operatic expression, but this time it's strictly for laughs. The duet sends up the tradition of soprano and tenor singing for the sake of ecstatic vocal display when the dramatic situation calls for something more sober. A double cadenza at the end places the pair in a kind of vocal duel that will not resolve (though eventually, of course, it must). At one point, immediately after an interpolated reprise of the "Paris Waltz," they hit high notes and continue on (and on), precisely when you think they are about to conclude.

We now meet the Old Lady, serving woman to Cunegonde, who rushes in to warn her mistress that both her lovers are approaching. The

lovers enter, and the ensuing action is as quickly skimmed as it is ridiculous: "In a flurry of dramatic activity," assures Adolph Green, in his
narrator mode, "Candide inadvertently stabs them both . . . to death."
The archbishop is interred in his cathedral, while the Jew's body is
dumped in a sewer. In a line that breaks the tension of an uncomfortable moment, Bernstein turns to the audience and says, straight-faced,
"I always hated the Jew in this show, anyway."

Candide, Cunegonde, and the Old Lady hit the road for Cadiz—
we're not sure why Cadiz—taking with them Cunegonde's jewels. Of
course, these are stolen en route, but while Cunegonde may have a lot
of fortune in baubles, she and Candide gain a wealth of worldly knowledge when the Old Lady recounts the many tragedies of her life. Used
and abused by a small army of men over the years, she even lost a
buttock when it was cut off and used by soldiers as emergency rations.
To make some money, she offers to sing about her sudden conversion
to all things Spanish, thus charming the locals into making contributions. The song is that half-English, half-Spanish first number written
for the show and mentioned above: "I Am Easily Assimilated."

Before we hear the song, Bernstein regales us with the story of how,
in the lyric, he came to assign the Old Lady a birthplace called "Rovno
Gubernya." (No such village is mentioned in Voltaire.) Bernstein borrowed the name of the place in Ukraine where his father was born, and
moved it to Poland as the Old Lady's hometown. What he doesn't tell us
is why he insisted on using the name of his father's birthplace. Why,
indeed? Perhaps because it sounded funny. Maybe because it was a way
for him to pay secret tribute to the father whose opposition he resented,
but whose support he enjoyed. In any case, once the decision was made,
Bernstein faced the challenge of rhyming the last two syllables of the
strange moniker—BERN-ya—with . . . something. He could think of
nothing in English, so he turned to his wife Felicia, a native Spanish
speaker, for help. She suggested the phrase "Me muero, me sale una
hernia," a Chilean idiom that translates literally as "I'm dying, I'm growing a hernia." It was nonsense, but that didn't matter. Bernstein
grabbed it, and then asked Felicia to write all the Spanish lines in the
lyric, which she did. So, at one point in the number, when the Spaniards
sing back to the Old Lady in a sultry and exotic manner, remember that
what they are actually singing is "I'm dying, I'm growing a hernia."

"I Am Easily Assimilated" doesn't belong in Cadiz, Spain. It's a tango, and the tango is native to Argentina, where Hellman, in the 1956 original, had placed her characters at whim—or perhaps to make it possible for Bernstein to compose a tango. In any case, the characters in Voltaire's novella enjoy their New World adventure in Montevideo, in present-day Uruguay, and in the musical version, that original location will be honored and the song will be performed there, not in Spain. As it turns out, the tango is no more native to Uruguay than to Spain, though it comes a little closer. Its closeness is only geographic; however, as the final joke is that, while the tango does come from Buenos Aires (a location no longer found in any of the various *Candides*), it wasn't devised until more than a century after *Candide*'s eighteenth-century timeframe. It barely matters, anyway. Anachronism is a salient feature of many satires, including this one. What does matter are the exultant Latin rhythms and silky harmonies that make this song a tribute from its composer to the folk-music traditions of the Hispanic world. We'll encounter another, better-known one in *West Side Story*.

We come now to the Act I finale, musically similar to the original finale but with different words. Our trio is forced to flee once again when the double murder in Paris is discovered and Candide is fingered as the culprit. Offered the chance to go to Montevideo as a soldier for the Jesuits, Candide seizes the opportunity to take Cunegonde and the Old Lady to the New World and a new life. The three of them sing of this bold new possibility while the officer in charge urges Candide on. The finale begins with the music of "Candide's Lament" now filled with hope instead of sorrow. A new melody announces itself, first issuing from the Old Lady and then from the Jesuit officer. This will be heard more fully developed and in a completely different context in Act II. The two melodies intertwine and build to a supremely hopeful last few measures. Despite all that had happened, it would seem that Pangloss's Theory of Optimism may yet survive. (Ah, but for how long?)

Act II begins with the hymn, "Universal Good," one of several short, a cappella chorales strung through the score so as to make the arrival of the final massed chorus a more natural, or at least more structurally expected, occurrence. Following this, Bernstein turns to the audience as "the Professor" once more and lectures the audience about the presence of evil that puts the lie to the notion that "everything is for the best." Specifically, he cites the evil that prompted Hellman to pick *Candide*: the communist witch hunts of the 1950s.

Green as narrator returns us to the story. Despite the announcement in Act I that Candide et al. were bound for Montevideo, they arrive in Buenos Aires (too late to do the tango—it's already spent!). There, the governor discovers the beauty of Cunegonde and demands her favors. In "My Love," the theme announced in the Act I finale now becomes the governor's proclamation of pure lust: "Poets have said, love is undying, my love / Don't be misled, they were all lying, my love." The Wilbur/LaTouche lyric is one of the more cynical in the show, yet Bernstein's music is effusive, even embracing. This is true throughout most of the score, especially the core numbers composed for the 1956 original. While Bernstein pokes fun at operatic traditions and forms— the extended ending of "You Were Dead You Know," the over-the-top virtuosity of "Glitter and Be Gay," and so on—he also salutes them, and that means emulating their musical beauty. Imitation is here indeed the sincerest form of flattery.

"My Love" becomes a duet when Cunegonde demands that, if the governor is to have her, he must marry her. Completely enthralled by the prospect, the governor assents. The Old Lady, too, despite her single buttock, catches the eye of some locals, and in self-congratulatory celebration of their wiles, she and Cunegonde sing the duet, "We Are Women," a late addition to the score with a lyric by the composer. Its character is decidedly more musical comedy than opera, and the words feel a little forced into place. It's doubtful, for instance, that a woman's thigh can in any way be described as "sparkling." As a lyricist, Bernstein was hit or miss. But as a composer his intuitions were nearly flawless. The skipping little tune of the duet is just what is needed at this point of the show to freshen our perspective.

No mention is made of Candide's reaction to Cunegonde's betrothal, though by now we're used to the non-sequiturs of what passes for a plot. For no apparent reason, Candide adventures into the jungle—what has happened to his military service, no one seems to know or care. There he meets a Father Superior and Mother Superior who just happen to be Maximilian and Paquette. Joyful to be reunited with Maximilian, Candide exultantly tells him he still wishes to marry Cunegonde. (Someone's forgotten to tell him about the governor.) Maximilian will not hear of it: Candide is still a bastard. Candide, as if to make Maximilian's point, "inadvertently stabs Maximilian to death."

Back in Buenos Aires, Cunegonde and the Old Lady have grown exceedingly bored with their lives in the gubernatorial palace and complain about it in "Quiet." Candide is hardly bored. He has gone further into the jungle, and one day there he finds, to his amazement, a land that might actually be the best of all possible worlds: "El Dorado," the only song with a lyric by Hellman, describes a gentle utopia where people "sing and dance and think and read" without thought of greed or power. Candide remains for some time, but there is a flaw, even in this seemingly perfect place, and that is the absence of Cunegonde. So at length he leaves with the blessings of his new friends, who give him jewels and magical, golden lambs as they send him on his way. "El Dorado," a gentle ballad that finds Bernstein in one of his folksong moods, was a real loss when it was cut from the Chelsea staging and not reinstated in the 1982 New York City Opera version. Only with the Scottish Opera *Candide* and this one did it come back, and what a good thing that was. A direct and emotionally telling setting of the words, this is Bernstein's music at its most unashamedly beautiful. Simple A-B-A structure houses a pair of diatonic melodies that ever so gently push at the edges of their key centers (which are separated by a minor third). The meter is 5/8, producing a sense of almost breathless wonder at the perfection of this hidden sanctuary. It is one of the stranger aspects of the many strange aspects regarding *Candide* that this single, serious-but-joyous song is the only trace left of the person whose idea it was to do the piece to begin with: Lillian Hellman.

Candide, not wishing to return to Buenos Aires for fear of arrest for murder, sends a servant back to ransom Cunegonde from the governor and to give her the message that he will reunite with her in Venice, again for no more apparent reason than their having arrived in Cadiz or Buenos Aires. The word "picaresque" has been used throughout the narration to describe this curious mode of random globe hopping. We hear it now for the last time, as the narrator tells us that Candide stops off in the Dutch colony of Surinam on his way out of the New World. He there meets Martin, a dedicated pessimist who is the reversed-out image of Pangloss, and who is played by the same actor. Martin sings "Words, Words, Words," another song featuring a Bernstein lyric. This one works because it references "The Best of All Possible Worlds" as in a dark mirror.

Candide purchases a ship from a local merchant, and in "Bon Voyage" the merchant admits in jolly song that the ship is a lemon, or more precisely a sinker, and sure enough, the ship goes down. Candide floats to a galley ship, where he meets five kings and his old master Pangloss, all serving as galley slaves. The kings, Candide, and Pangloss sing an ensemble in which they swear to pursue "the simple life" if only they can escape their present condition. The galley eventually arrives in Venice. Candide searches for Cunegonde but finds Maximilian—risen from the dead—and Paquette. Paquette is the most popular prostitute in all Venice, while Maximilian is the prefect of police and the manager of a large, corrupt political organization. Cunegonde and the Old Lady are there, too, working the casino. In a brilliant number from the 1956 original, "What's the Use?," the Old Lady protests that she must pass along what little she makes to the casino owner; the casino owner in turn sings that his profits are destroyed by having to pay off the prefect (Maximilian). The prefect then claims that he loses by having to pay an extortionist, who then bemoans the fact that he loses it all on the roulette wheel, anyway, thus bringing the absurd flow of money full circle. The extortionist may lose at roulette, but as Pangloss sits at the wheel his luck runs super hot. He sings, in the opening of the "Venice Gavotte" (Dorothy Parker's contribution to the cache of lyrics), that he is making money from "the best of all possible banks." The Old Lady complains, Candide offers assistance, the ensemble builds, and at the moment of the song's climax, Candide sees Cunegonde.

As if a veil has been lifted, Candide instantly sees Cunegonde for what she is: a woman who has sold herself for gold. Bernstein's finest lyric of the show and one of his most effective musical settings, "Nothing More Than This" shifts the tone from satire to solemnity. We've been waiting for this moment, the moment when Candide would, as it were, learn his lesson. "Angel face with flaxen hair / Soul as dead as face was fair" he sings, suddenly aware that looking upon Cunegonde through the lens of optimism has blinded him to real life, real values, real love. A final a cappella chorale voices Candide's thoughts: Good and evil, right and wrong, are sewn together into the fabric of life. There is just enough money to buy a little farm outside Venice. He asks Cunegonde to marry him.

Candide begins the closing number, a Bernstein hymn and perhaps the finest of them, "Make Our Garden Grow." This paean to commonplace virtues, to love and work, glows musically with purity and simplicity. Wilbur puts these words in the mouths of Candide and Cunegonde: "We're neither pure nor wise nor good," and yet Bernstein's music is the purest, wisest, and best in the score. In humility, our protagonists have found true nobility. Here is the faith that Bernstein sought his entire life, summed up in the music he set to Wilbur's words: "The sweetest flow'rs, the fairest trees / Are grown in solid ground." Faith is not the belief that "everything is for the good," but that, to flourish, we must connect with the earth and the demands it makes upon us. This idea will be further explored in *Kaddish* and *Mass*, and will become the central theme of Bernstein's Harvard lectures in 1973. In case you have not yet noticed, Bernstein is one of our more intellectually focused composers.

Now we will take a very brief look at the 2005 New York Philharmonic concert, to see how a Broadway-style interpretation of the piece looks. First of all, while still called "a comic operetta" in the opening credits, it is here most definitely a musical comedy. What's the difference, you ask, between opera/operetta on the one hand, and musical comedy on the other? Just prior to the opening of the original *Candide* in 1956, Bernstein explored the differences between the two on one of his Omnibus television appearances. Broadway in the 1940s and 1950s boasted two kinds of musical stage works. One was musical comedy, the other operetta. Examples of operetta were such Rodgers and Hammerstein works as *Oklahoma!* and *The King and I*, while such shows as *Guys and Dolls* and Bernstein's own *Wonderful Town* were clearly musical comedies. If you know the pieces, Bernstein's definitions will make good sense to you. *Oklahoma!* and *The King and I* are operettas because they take place in exotic locales, while the others are New York-specific, with smart, "American" references in their book and lyrics. Locale was not the essence of the matter, however. It was attitude. *Annie Get Your Gun* took place in the Old West, not far from the neighborhood of *Oklahoma!* Its tone, however, was New York City and then some; it cracked wise, and Irving Berlin's songs were Tin Pan Alley, even birthing the great entertainment anthem, "There's No Business Like Show Business." The jokes in *Oklahoma!*, on the other hand, were native to the show's time and place, and Richard Rodgers's score evoked the music of that land and era, such as "Oh, What a Beautiful Morning."

In a follow-up to this matter in one of the many "think pieces" he wrote over the years for the *New York Times*, Bernstein engaged in imaginary dialogue with his "Irrepressible Demon." Wringing his hands over which category fit the specifics of his latest project, Bernstein at last admitted that *Candide* was "perhaps a new kind of show." And that is what, in fact, it is. There are moments that take us into the real, present realm of Candide and his adventures, thus fulfilling the idea of opera, and some that take us out of it and into a contemporary kind of satire. Villagers prancing around and singing joyfully about an imminent execution is pure musical comedy.

The truth is that, with its many versions over several decades, *Candide* is anything a director wants to make it. Our London concert version, its cast populated mostly by opera singers, more resembles operetta than musical comedy, most of the time. The New York Philharmonic concert, its cast primarily Broadway veterans, is more a musical comedy, and not only for the reason that, for example, Patti LuPone is the Old Lady whereas Christa Ludwig sings that role in the London concert. The London concert is unstaged, while the New York Philharmonic version is semistaged by Lonny Price, who takes every opportunity to poke fun in high musical comedy style. As Candide prepares to leave Westphalia, Price has him pack a modern suitcase. One of the items he puts in it is a soundtrack recording of *West Side Story*. The Inquisitor turns out to be Donald Trump. When he is asked whether or not to burn someone, he looks at the victim and says: "You're fired." When Kristin Chenoweth sings "Glitter and Be Gay," she makes fun of the character in broad fashion, underlining each high note with a facial expression, pronouncing "France" like a Texas hick, and so on. Then, too, the Price staging cuts most of the solemn choruses and some of Act II's more operatic numbers. He keeps "We Are Women," but lets go of "Nothing More Than This."

Stephen Sondheim has famously sidestepped defining opera versus musical theater by saying that a piece is an opera when it's staged in an opera house, and a musical when it's in a theater. Of course, this brilliantly begs the question. Bernstein's clarification helps us understand the difference better, but the bottom line in the difference between opera/operetta and musical comedy pertains to priorities assigned to the twin roles of singing and acting. An opera performer is essentially a singer who also acts, while a musical theater performer is an actor who also sings. *Candide* requires hybrids. "Glitter and Be Gay" really needs an operatic voice to do full justice to its many bravura turns and musical subtleties. But "I Am Easily Assimilated" loses many of its words when performed by an opera singer. Classical singing emphasizes vowels and often eclipses consonants, and that song (expect for the Spanish-language lines) is heavy on the snappy consonants. (Because English language is consonant-dominated to begin with, this raises the question of whether opera lies more or less outside the possibility of full realization in English at all. But an answer to that question would require another, different book.)

As one might guess from the prominence of concert versions, *Candide* has never found its perfect form on stage. The Scottish Opera version and the Chelsea staging represent opposite poles of interpretation, each one excluding valuable aspects of the other. Perhaps a perfectly united *Candide*, if any such thing were possible, awaits the hand of some genius director in the future. Film would be an ideal medium for such depth of enterprise.

We move on now to a piece that worked marvelously onstage from the start, as well as on film, the sole Bernstein work without which even mainstream culture would feel an enormous rip in its fabric: *West Side Story*.

OVERTURE TO *CANDIDE*

The music Stephen Sondheim would later call "all bubbles and champagne" begins with a timpani stroke like the popping of a cork, followed by sprays of trumpet fanfares. A comical oompah in the brass underpins a racing melody from the strings and woodwinds that rollercoasters high and low in a mad scurry. The beat is everywhere and nowhere, its displacement assured by the introduction of measures in odd meters such as seven and five.

As if to assure us that the explosion of color we've heard really was intentional, the first fifteen seconds repeat, leading this time to a brassy transitional idea that lands us in a steady, two-beat frame—but only for now. Throughout the piece, we will be cajoled into the comfort of a steady beat, only to have it ruptured and sent lurching, like someone who's had a just little too much of that champagne. A xylophone picks up and expands the brassy tune, and at length it softens and thins into echoes of the opening subject, played by the woodwinds. Then comes the greatest surprise of a surprising overture, a luxurious second subject that is as voluptuous as the opening section was frantic.

The joke is on us, as this seemingly serene tune will appear in the operetta as the duet, "Oh Happy We," in which the lead characters dream of married life together, unaware that their dreams contradict each other. "All will be pink champagne and gold," sings one, while the other looks forward to "feeding the pigs and sweetly growing old." In the wordless overture, however, the tune cradles the listener in a moment of sheer lyrical beauty before suddenly crashing back into the opening group of rambunctious themes.

Suddenly, the lyrical tune returns, this time in a different key and in the woodwinds. Everything is uncannily speeding up, like in a Rossini overture, and you begin to feel things rushing toward an end. When the lyrical tune concludes, there is half a moment of silence before the onset of a closing subject that pushes even more forcefully toward the end—except that we have no idea of where or what the end will be. Surprise is the rule of thumb for the *Candide* overture, even when you've heard it dozens of times. In the middle of this rush, the opening brass salvo returns, and then the rollercoaster subject and then the lyrical tune in comic garb and finally, at precisely the moment you are ready for more of everything—the simplest and most abrupt of endings, a two-chord button like a splash of cold water. Even this tidy ending contains a surprise turn: the first chord is played *pianissimo*, or very softly, and the final chord comes down in loud *fortissimo*.

As with all good overtures to Broadway musicals, this one has introduced the listener to tunes that will appear in the show. What most listeners will not realize, however, is that they have heard an abbreviated sonata-allegro form, complete with contrasts of key centers. In one of his most daring musical coups, Bernstein has combined popular-style tunesmithing with strict classical form to produce the most frequently performed concert overture ever written by an American.

7

WEST SIDE STORY

In 1957, the genre known as American musical comedy (or musical theater) was at flood tide. Once a string of songs and gags put together for a night's entertainment after a hard day's work, a "musical" was now an artistic blend of drama, song, and dance to the end of relating a story and developing a theme. Its home was New York City, but its popularity was ubiquitous, exported across the country by road companies, and across the Atlantic in London productions.

The musical had matured at a glacial pace. The first thing called a "musical" was the 1866 entertainment "The Black Crook," an amalgam of jokes and musical numbers borrowed from popular songs of the day and hung, very loosely, on a story. It ran for years, making a great deal of money and spawning imitations. Theaters bloomed along the numbered streets that intersected Broadway, so inevitably, the shows were soon called "Broadway musicals." Nothing of the earliest musicals remains, the oldest keepers being the shows of George M. Cohan, an Irish-American singer-songwriter-dancer who penned such hits as "Give My Regards to Broadway" and "Over There." By the turn of the twentieth century, when Cohan flourished, the musical had taken on the shape of a true storytelling form, though the stories were flimsy, and the excuses to burst into song often no more than "Hey, I know this great tune!"

Then, in 1927, came *Showboat*, with music by Jerome Kern and book and lyrics by Oscar Hammerstein II, based on Edna Thurber's novel. There had never been anything like it. The show was cohesive in relating a story, and songs were placed to move the action forward or explore a character's feelings. "Ol' Man River," which would later become a signature of the great singer/political activist Paul Robeson, said what no song in American history had ever said before, uttering the truth about labor and the treatment of African Americans. *Showboat* did not, however, spark a series of attempts to move the form further. Perhaps it was the arrival two years later of the Depression (musical theater was a commercial form and the box office ruled, artistic concerns aside), or maybe it was the failure to read *Showboat* as a harbinger of things to come instead of a blip on the radar. In any case, the 1930s saw some isolated political musicals (the Gershwins' *Of Thee I Sing* and *Let 'Em Eat Cake*, and of course, Blitzstein's *The Cradle Will Rock*) and one magnificent leap into the realm where musical theater might meet opera, George Gershwin's *Porgy and Bess*, with words by Dubose Heyward and Ira Gershwin. On the whole, however, the musical remained a breezy, jokey little entertainment without particular artistic quality.

Suddenly there was *Oklahoma!* The first collaboration of Hammerstein with composer Richard Rodgers in 1943 changed everything about the form, and this time, it stuck. The artists were ready to make the changes but just as importantly, audiences were ready. American theatergoers had matured and now were open to something beyond the gags-and-tunes of traditional musical comedy. A famous out-of-town review of *Oklahoma!* (originally titled *Away We Go!*) led with: "No girls, no gags, no chance." What chance could there be for a show that opened on an old woman churning butter and a cowboy singing about the beauty of the morning? Of course, *Oklahoma!* went on to break all box office records and to set the standard for all that was to come. It was the new "integrated" musical, in which song and dance (including a full-fledged ballet-within-the-show) combined with dialogue to tell a story. The story of *Oklahoma!* was a comic romance, but the next Rodgers and Hammerstein musical, *Carousel*, moved into the area of tragedy, including the onstage death of its main character, Billy Bigelow.

Now came the avalanche of new shows following the "integrated" model. Some remained more or less musical comedies with improved books and fresh scores (including *On the Town* and *Wonderful Town*), while others continued to push back the frontiers of the form's expression and even to flirt with opera, including Frank Loesser's *The Most*

Happy Fella (1956) and Harold Rome's now all-but-forgotten *Fanny* (1954). Rodgers and Hammerstein peppered the stage with eclectic song styles from operatic to boogie-woogie to faux-exotic in *South Pacific*, and the new team of writer Alan Jay Lerner and composer Frederick Loewe took audiences to mystical Scotland (*Brigadoon*, 1947), the Old West (*Paint Your Wagon*, 1951), and Edwardian England (*My Fair Lady*, 1956). By the time Bernstein came to focus his composing attention on the form it was ripe for exactly what he had to give it: mastery of song composition, a hunger for innovation, and a breadth of musical knowledge and background. For several years in the mid-1950s he worked almost simultaneously on both *Candide* and the show that confirmed his place in history, *West Side Story*.

Unlike *Candide*, *West Side Story* has no operatic characteristics. The lead female is not required to sing umpteen high Cs and B-flats, the style of the music never references Rossini or Donizetti. It takes place in contemporary times and uses musical materials appropriate to the era. What's more, it is the ultimate triumph of the "integrated musical"—the balance of song, dance, and book. It is dance-heavy, to be sure (appropriate, as the characters are restless teens), and it boasts what has been called the shortest book in musical theater history—all the better to let Bernstein's music and the lyrics by newcomer Stephen Sondheim tell the majority of the story.

Jerome Robbins got the idea in 1949 to do a musical set in contemporary New York with parallels to Shakespeare's *Romeo and Juliet*. It was years in gestation, and early on was tentatively set among Irish Catholics and Jewish immigrants during Passover. In Robbins's initial vision, two young people from these opposite religions/ethnicities fall in love in spite of antipathy from their respective cultures. The working title: *East Side Story*. Robbins collared Bernstein to write the songs (both music and lyrics) and got playwright Arthur Laurents to write the book, but after doing some work on the project, the trio realized they had musically reworked the theme of a recent hit Broadway comedy called *Abie's Irish Rose*. Writer, composer, and choreographer went their separate ways until 1955, when Bernstein and Laurents reconnected in Hollywood, where the one was conducting at the Hollywood Bowl and the other was writing a screenplay. Over dinner, Laurents mentioned the gang warfare that was then plaguing Los Angeles, bitter turf wars between Mexican Americans and Anglos. Bernstein suggested recasting the Catholics and Jews of *East Side Story* as *chicanos* and whites in Los Angeles, but Laurents protested that his greater familiarity with New York City pointed to Puerto Ricans and Anglos on Manhattan's Upper West Side as the more logical switch. Bernstein concurred. Bernstein and Laurents contacted Robbins, who liked the idea, and so *East Side Story* became *West Side Story*—though not before two years of intense work and many setbacks. (And not before it briefly endured the absurd working title of *Gangway!*—a joke of sorts suggested by Laurents.)

After a time, it must have become clear that Bernstein's lyric-writing talent was not nearly up to the level of his compositional talent, because the team started looking for a co-lyricist. Bernstein first asked Comden and Green, but they were busy working with Jule Styne on *Bells are Ringing*. In retrospect, everyone agrees that Comden and Green would have been the wrong match for a tragic musical about gangs. What was needed was an expert craftsman, someone to translate the themes of Bernstein's lyrics into taut verbal expressions of the characters' emotions. Laurents had met a young protégé of Oscar Hammerstein's who filled the bill. And so, with Stephen Sondheim, the fourth and final member of the *West Side Story* creative team was in place. Eventually, Sondheim's lyrics replaced virtually every line of Bernstein's lyrics, and the sole credit was given to him.

Bernstein now faced the challenge of writing two vastly different scores almost at the same time: *Candide* and *West Side Story*, a pair of theater pieces that could hardly have been more unalike. *Candide* leaned toward opera—sometimes falling on it—while *West Side Story* steered the steady course of musical theater. This raises yet again the question, "What's the difference?" Answers come in all forms, but perhaps the best illustration of the distinction comes in a story Bernstein related to his wife in a letter. The writing of *West Side Story* had reached the end of the tragic tale, and Laurents was penning the closing scene, in which Maria holds Tony as he dies. Bernstein took off in an operatic direction: a perfect place for a "mad scene" aria! Think of it: ten minutes of Maria running up and down scales in insane abandon. (Opera is rife with mad scenes, the most famous example being that in *Lucia di Lammermoor*.)

Of course, it was not to be. Robbins, the governor of the project, insisted from the start, aware as he was of his composer's aspirations to opera, that *West Side Story* would be a musical, and only a musical. A mad scene would have gone beyond the bounds of music's role in American musical drama. Musical theater scores comprise songs, and a mad scene is not a song, it is a classical piece of vocal music that demands technical skills above those required to simply sing a song. A song may be easy to sing, or it may be hard to sing, but it is singable by people who do not necessarily have the training to do justice to Lucia's mad scene. In this sense, *Candide*, with its high Cs and B-flats, and its large, complex ensemble numbers, really is a hybrid, with operatically dazzling feats of vocal display and large, complex ensembles, as well as more song-like numbers. (And yet the question is never resolved. What is Sondheim's *Sweeney Todd*, which is often sung by opera singers but hardly requires them, as Tim Burton's film made clear?) The mad scene aria would also have given too much weight to the music over the book, a violation of the tenet central to the "integrated" musical, that the various elements of the show be in balance. The mad scene was not the only Bernstein music cut from the show as it developed. Though the composer complained bitterly about his more operatically inclined numbers being regularly thrown to the floor, his collaborators were vigilant in keeping *West Side Story* from turning into "a damned opera," to use Laurents's blunt phrase.

Yet Bernstein's music, even without the mad scene or other operatic elements, dominates one's memory of the show. Sondheim has given credit for *West Side*'s success to Laurents's book, a script that moves effortlessly from song setup to song setup, never pausing to draw attention to itself. And of course, Robbins's concept and choreography—which are always, by contract, featured prominently on all programs—are the force behind it. But think of *West Side Story* and what likely comes to mind first are not images, but songs: "Maria," "Something's Coming," or "I Feel Pretty." The musical from *Oklahoma!* to *West Side Story* and into the 1960s may have had integration of all its elements as the ideal, but it was still a musical, not a "play with music" or a "dance-ical." Original music and lyrics defined the form. That has changed over the decades, and currently the form is often defined by concept (*Cats, The Book of Mormon*) or by spectacle (*Les Miserables, Phantom of the Opera*) as much as or more than the music. It has even reached a place where original music can be entirely dismissed, as in the many "juke-box" musicals that simply pick up already existing songs (*Jersey Boys,*

Bullets Over Broadway). But in 1957, original music was an important element in a musical, maybe even the primary one.

A composer's work for the stage is always tied to the subject matter and honor-bound to reflect or embody it somehow. His or her musical language must change somewhat as it moves from one subject to another: a musical about, say, the Duke of Wellington should not sound similar to one about Charles Manson—not that musicals about either figure exist (at least at present!). This has been understood by the best stage composers of Western history, going back at least to Mozart, whose fantastical *Magic Flute* sounds musically distant from the sexual realism of *Don Giovanni*. The more that divides any two subjects, the more they will inevitably inhabit different musical universes: a lyric stage score about twentieth-century New York street gangs should not resemble one about Enlightenment-era characters created by a French satirist. So, while Bernstein composed *Candide* and *West Side Story* in tandem, he worked to nurture distinctive voices for each. In seeming contradiction of this, it's often pointed out that two songs in *West Side Story* were originally composed (with different lyrics) for *Candide*: "Gee, Officer Krupke" and "One Hand, One Heart." But that is precisely the point. When Bernstein saw that his melodies were better suited to the feeling and atmosphere of *West Side Story*, he removed them from *Candide*.

In order to compose music that sounded "like the streets," Bernstein researched two relevant genres: Latin-American music, particularly Puerto Rican dance forms; and the popular music of the day, which was in the midst of undergoing a sea change into rock 'n' roll. Roll 'n' roll had not yet arrived in its fullness. Elvis had just burst onto the scene, and rhythm and blues was morphing into classic early rock, but other forms of popular music continued to flourish side by side with the new genre. The ten top-selling singles of 1956, for example, included three Elvis songs, but also the breezy little Latin instrumental "Lisbon Antigua," and Doris Day singing the waltzy "Whatever Will Be, Will Be (Que Sera, Sera)." Bernstein composed *West Side Story* at precisely the moment when it was still possible to ignore rock 'n' roll, to write a love ballad like "Maria" and make it seem like a pop song, to insist that the bop jazz of "Cool" and the bluesy Anglo dance music were truly hip. *West Side Story* is, among other things, a miracle of timing. A few years later, after rock had vanquished other genres, it could not have looked or sounded the way it does and still take place in "the present" of 1964 or 1965. As things transpired, the musical ambience of Bernstein's score captured a fleeting moment in American popular culture.

Beginning with his arrangements of Copland's *El Salon Mexico*, and on into the *Danzon* from *Fancy Free* and "I Am Easily Assimilated" from *Candide*, Bernstein had always had Latin-American moves as part of his stylistic repertoire. But to get the sound of Puerto Rican music in particular he traveled, naturally enough, to Puerto Rico, where little brother Burton Bernstein just happened to be stationed with the U.S. armed forces. In a televised interview, Burton Bernstein recalled taking his brother to a Puerto Rican hotspot and listening to the band, which played mambos and other Latin-American dances, and which always opened its act with the same signature, a sharply syncopated salvo of sixteen intensely rhythmic notes. Bernstein liked this bit so much that he lifted it, note for note, and placed it at the beginning of the famous "Mambo" in *West Side Story*.

The score is, in fact, riddled with allusions and borrowings. The best known of them is the opening of "Somewhere," a song whose distinctive first five notes are identical to those of the slow movement to Beethoven's Piano Concerto No. 5, the "Emperor." Because Sondheim was a trained composer as well as a lyricist (*Saturday Night*, for which he wrote both music and lyrics, was on track to open on Broadway in 1955 when the producer suddenly died), some have suspected the score to be partially his. This is true only at one, isolated spot: the spiky rhythms of "Something's Coming." The backstory changes from one telling to another, but the outcome is that Sondheim took one of the inner parts of Bernstein's setting of the song's opening verse ("Could be! Who knows?") and gave it to his writing partner as the start of the melody for the chorus ("Could it be? Yes, it could!"). The song was the last one written for the show, a mere eleven days before it opened in previews in Washington, DC.

Bernstein's score is unified and given its peculiar character of driven beauty by frequent reference to a particular musical interval, that of the tritone. The tritone is a distinctive distance exactly halfway between a note and the octave above or below that note. Play a C on the piano, then play an F-sharp. Or play an F-natural and a B-natural. Those are the tritones. But their effect is a matter of context. Tritones exist in all standard major and minor scales, and inside those scales they function naturally and without causing the ear to pay undue attention. For instance, on the piano, play all the white notes from C to C (a C major scale) and a tritone will be created by the notes F and B. When, in a C major song, the F and the B show up together, they create the tension necessary to give the scale a sense of "going someplace." Play, for example, the F and the B at the same time. Then, move each finger one note in opposite directions to get E and C: you have resolved the tritone and made a stable statement in the key of C major. The important factor is that, here, the tritone has functioned as a way of "getting to" the relaxed safety of the C major key. Moving from the tritone of F and B to the consonant harmony of E and C is a little like clenching your fist (the tritone) and then unclenching it (the consonant harmony.)

But when tritones go out of the key, their effect is completely different; it's more like clenching your fist and keeping it clenched. With the sound of C major in your ear from playing the scale, now play from C to C again, but this time play F-sharp instead of F-natural. You have created a tritone dissonance between the home note of C and this sudden intrusion of F-sharp. These are the sorts of tritones that show up in *West Side Story*. They are not there to function as a path to consonant harmony; they are there to throw things off just a tiny, delicious bit. We hear one immediately in the second and third notes of the gang whistle of the Prologue. Because this kind of tritone is inherently unstable, those notes set a mood of tension and foreboding. (The whistle starts on a G below C, jumps up to and hangs on to the C, then suddenly arches up to the F-sharp tritone.)

A tritone can be left on its own, or it can be resolved if the composer manipulates that way. For example, it's possible to move from the C to the F-sharp to a G, creating the suggestion that you are in (or at least flirting with) G major. And this, in fact, is exactly what happens in "Maria," one of the best-known songs from the show. The three notes of the song's title word are (in the original key) E-flat, A natural, and B-flat; the tritone of E-flat/A, moving to the resolution on B-flat.

"Maria" and the gang whistle are only the two most obvious of many tritone manipulations in Bernstein's score. Also notable:

- "Something's Coming" is crawling with tritones. The tune of the verse ("Could be! Who knows?") bounces up and down off the tritone on the downbeat of every bar (the first syllable of "something" and "any," etc.), and when the chorus arrives ("Could it be? Yes it could") this continues, in a new key. Tony sings this in anticipation of going to the dance at the gym, so when he meets Maria there and falls in love, the resolving tritone in the song "Maria" announces, in clear musical language, the fulfillment of the expectations expressed in "Something's Coming."

- The harmonies underpinning "I Have a Love" touch on the tritone the first two times the word "love" is sung. Here, the interval is associated with pain, and as Maria's song, which briefly becomes a duet with Anita, nears the end, the troublesome interval fades from the harmony, only to be revived twice, both times underneath the word "life." Thus, the two most urgent words in the lyric are highlighted with a sound that says, in essence, "pain comes with these."

- The melody of "Cool," dramatically a key piece in its depiction of gang energies, is constructed from two sets of tritones: the first in the home key ("Boy, boy, crazy boy"), the second sequenced up a fourth ("Got a rocket in your pocket"). The two sets of tritones— in the original key, C and F-sharp, followed by F-natural and B— make up one-third of a tone row, so of course it was irresistible to Bernstein to expand that into a full twelve-tone row for the instrumental fugue that follows the song.

Bernstein said he never planned to use all those tritones, that it "just came out" that way. But neither was it an accident: it was a product of Bernstein's Jewish upbringing, and of the music he heard in synagogue. Remember that Bernstein's earliest musical experiences were of two things: popular songs and Jewish worship music. Such early experiences never leave a composer; to the contrary, they enter into his/her psyche and become an unconscious part of the everyday business of making music. At this point in his composing career, Bernstein had not created a "Jewish" work since *Hashkeveinu* in 1945, and there hadn't been a major one since the 1942 "Jeremiah" Symphony. His theater subjects had been French Enlightenment satire and all-American suburban ennui; his concert works have touched on modern poetry and ancient philosophy. But here, in the unlikely territory of Jets versus Sharks, an aspect of Jewish music shows up unexpectedly. One of the prominent modes used in the Hebrew worship service is one called the "Ukrainian Dorian," defined by a raised fourth step—a tritone away from the root.

We'll now take a look at the plot of *West Side Story* and the songs that accompany the story, stopping now and then to comment on when the show parallels Romeo and Juliet, and when it does not. The first decision we have to make is whether to follow the stage show or the 1961 film. There are major differences between the two, especially in the order of the songs. In the stage show, "Cool" is in the first act and "Gee, Officer Krupke" is in the second act. This is reversed in the film. In the stage show, "I Feel Pretty" opens the second act, and because this is after the rumble, there is a horrible irony in that fact that Maria is rejoicing in the newness of her love for Tony, completely unaware that Tony has just killed her brother. In the movie, it occupies a pre-rumble spot in the lineup. The stage show includes the song "Somewhere" sung offstage during a ballet sequence that was cut from the film. "Somewhere" in the movie shows up only at the end, as the farewell duet of Tony and Maria.

While the stage show represents the artists' original intent, the movie is far more accessible via DVD, and in several ways it can actually be seen as an improvement. No less an authority than Sondheim has commented that the Jets' hilarity in "Gee, Officer Krupke" hardly makes sense when the gang has just lost their leader, Riff, and everything is coming apart. The movie's earlier placement of the song corrects this. The movie also restores the original lyric to "America," which is sharper and tougher than the one in the stage show. Robbins's first idea had been to make "America" a dance number for the Sharks' men and women. Sondheim accordingly wrote a lyric in which the women sing the praises of America, while the men give a more realistic perspective. But in rehearsal the number changed to the Sharks' women only, causing Sondheim to write a revised set of noticeably softer words. The original lyric, restored in the movie, is a radical statement about American hypocrisy, a culture that says you are "free to be anything you choose," when the reality is that you will "clean up the dishes and shine shoes."

For these reasons and others, but primarily because the movie, codirected by Robbins and Robert Wise, is a quality piece of cinema and readily accessible—we will follow it, rather than the stage play.

The Overture. The stage play has no overture, which in 1957 was an innovation—no warming up the audience, just plunge into the action. The movie gives it one that starts with the gang whistle, three times, then moves on to the usual mélange of songs from the show: "Tonight," "Maria," etc. The accompanying graphics prepare us for the opening shot of Manhattan.

"Prologue." It's more than twice as long as the stage version. The reason once given was that film lacks the immediate energy of the stage, that more time was needed to get the audience into the ambience. The gang whistle is heard several times over sputtering bongo drums and the camera zooms down closer and closer until we at last see the profile of a young man snapping his fingers. This is Riff, leader of the Jets. We see other members of the gang, all snapping their fingers in time, and at length they start to walk the length of a community basketball court. At first it's just a walk, but the movements become slowly more and more "choreographed" until the Jets are dancing classical steps. The transition tells us that what we're going to see will combine the real and the stylized. The Jets meet up with members of the Sharks, the Puerto Rican gang, and throughout the rest of the piece, the two gangs will fight and tussle, sometimes humorously, but ultimately violently enough that the Jets' "Baby John" gets bloodied and the cops show up. Bernstein's music follows the action exactly, and we hear foreshadowings of the "Jet Song" and the Mambo from the "Dance at the Gym." The opening is a close parallel to that of *Romeo and Juliet*, in which the Capulets and Montagues draw swords and have at it.

"Jet Song." Bernstein and Sondheim wrote this song, then substituted a tougher one called "A Bit of Turf," then reinstated the original. Marked "boogie-woogie" in the score, the music saunters to an off-beat dissonance that gives it a bravado matching the boastful words. ("We're gonna beat / Ev'ry last buggin' gang on the whole buggin' street.") Words like "buggin'," obvious substitutes for more street-wise words, were necessary in 1961, when the film was made.

"Something's Coming." The last song written for the show was necessary to "give Tony some balls" as Bernstein put it in a letter to his wife. Even so, it is still a rather ethereal song for a gang member, even a reformed one. We meet Tony, Riff's best friend, who is working at Pop's drugstore. Riff wants him to rejoin the gang, but Tony has moved on and is looking for something more—he just doesn't know what. The song, both music and lyric, is full of the sense of expectation, maybe because of all those tritones. Tony agrees to go to the dance that night at the gym when Riff says, "Maybe what you're looking for will be twitchin' at the dance." Again the parallel with Romeo and Juliet is fairly exact: Mercutio (Riff) has convinced the dreamy Romeo (Tony) to come out with him that night. Only in the Shakespeare, the pair will be crashing a party given by the rival family.

"Dance at the Gym." We meet Shark family members Maria, her brother Bernardo (the Sharks' leader), Bernardo's girlfriend Anita, and Chino, a shy young man whom the family has "set up" with Maria. In *Romeo and Juliet* terms, Maria is Juliet, of course, Bernando is the doomed Tybalt, and Chino is the hapless Paris. But who is Anita? Tybalt has no lady love in the Shakespeare. Anita, it will turn out, is the *West Side Story* equivalent of the Nurse, who is absent from the musical. When Maria swirls in her new dress, cinema magic takes over and we are transported to the gym, even as we hear the first notes of what will become the song, "Maria." Suddenly we see Sharks and Jets couple dancing to some hot, big band jazz. The dancing ends, Riff and Bernardo approach each other menacingly, but are interrupted by a comically silly school official who announces a get together dance. Girls in an inside circle, boys on the outside, they circle in opposite directions and are then supposed to dance with whomever is opposite when the music stops. The music stops, Sharks girls are opposite Jets boys and vice versa, so of course everyone ignores the rule and grabs their original partners. Then comes the blast of rhythm Bernstein lifted from the Puerto Rican bar band, and the justly famous "Mambo" section begins. Soon it becomes a contest between the rival factions. Into the middle of this enter Maria and Tony, who notice each other across the dance floor. The astonishing choreography and its music fade as the two approach and, in some fantasy quite apart from the reality of the gym, dance a piquant little duet to the music of "Maria." They speak Laurents's perfect speech that replace with contemporary love words the words of meeting spoken by Romeo and Juliet. "You're not making a joke?" Tony asks. "I have not yet learned to joke that way," Maria answers. "Now I think I never will." The music here is shaped expertly to meet the spoken words but not overpower them. Sondheim praised Bernstein's ability to write underscoring, and it seems that here, as elsewhere in *West Side Story*, he had learned a great deal from the successes and mistakes of *On the Waterfront*. The music ends as Bernardo breaks up the love-at-first-sight couple.

"Maria." Tony doesn't know who she is but he hears Chino call her "Maria" as they leave. That's enough for him: the name is an emblem of his sudden rush of feeling, and he celebrates it in this eponymous song. Sondheim has told a story, which has become famous, of Robbins confronting Sondheim with the unanswerable question, "What happens in this song?" And quite obviously, nothing "happens" in the song. The implication of the story is that Robbins had a point. He didn't. Or, if he had one, it flew in the face of the entire history of lyric theater. What "happens" when Liza Doolittle in *My Fair Lady* sings of wanting "a room somewhere / Far away from the cold night air"? What "happens" when Sarah sings, "If I were a bell, I'd be ringing" in *Guys and Dolls*? What, for that matter, "happens" when Curly sings, "Oh, What a Beautiful Morning," at the start of *Oklahoma!*? All of these characters are telling us their feelings: Liza of her longing for warmth and security; Sarah of her glee at the discovery of sexual ecstasy; Curly of his astonishment at the glory of the land at sunrise. Tony, in "Maria," quite naturally and perfectly expresses his love for this slip of a Puerto Rican girl, the fulfillment of the "something" that was on its way that morning. It is as indispensable to the wholeness of the show as "Celeste Aida"—an aria in which nothing "happens"—is to Verdi's opera. Bernstein's ability to express the exultation of a feeling like young love owes to his ability to spin convincing melodies that soar high, higher, and still higher—the "Bernstein rollercoaster," I like to call it. Think of the melody to this song, following the verse that begins things ("The most beautiful sound I've ever heard"). It starts with an upward gesture on the three syllables of the blessed name, the ascending tritone that resolves to the G above. It repeats this obsessively, then pulls back slightly. It starts again, but this time it spins higher and "breaks"—just as a wave breaks on shore—on the words "Maria, say it loud and there's music playing." After a short resolution on the home tone, it enters a place where Tony simply sings the name again and again, and each time it goes breathtakingly higher than the last time! At last, the tune comes down, but only briefly. It then climbs again on a return to the verse ("The most beautiful sound I ever heard") and ends with the singer having to "float" (that is, sing softly, not belt loudly) a high note on the final syllable of her name.

"America." After the dance, the Sharks convene on the roof of their building. Bernardo taunts Anita that she is "queer for Uncle Sam." With a sultry verse section ("I like the island Manhattan"), Anita begins the song that proved to be the biggest hit of the show with early audiences. The rhythm is not Puerto Rican, but Mexican, a dance piece in the style of the *huapango*. It may sound as if the count changes from one measure to the next, but in fact it's all in 6/8. What alternates are the accents: ONE-two-three-FOUR-five-six/ONE-two-THREE-four-FIVE-six.

This gives the impression of two beats followed by a faster set of three beats. In his excellent book, *Something's Coming, Something Good: West Side Story and the American Imagination*, Misha Berson identifies the melody as one of Bernstein's "trunk songs," meaning a tune written for no particular purpose, put away, then used later. Bernstein spent a fair amount of time in Mexico, so it's possible he wrote this after hearing a mariachi group play a tune with a similar, typical rhythm. Sondheim's words for this version are the most incisive of any in the show. The girls sing idealistically of material things like Cadillacs and washing machines, but the boys burst their bubbles. "I'll get a terrace apartment," sings Anita. "Better get rid of your accent," Bernardo admonishes. And in the most astonishing (for 1961) pair of lines of all, the girls sing that "Life is all right in America," bringing on the boys' rejoinder: "If you're all white in America."

"Tonight" (Balcony Scene). The second-to-last song written for the show was a substitute for the original balcony scene (or "fire escape" scene) song: "One Hand, One Heart." (This is according to Berman. Humphrey Burton claims that "Somewhere," with a different lyric, was the original balcony scene number.) That gentle duet was deemed too serene to represent the passion of Tony and Maria's first time alone together. Bernstein and Sondheim raided their own product, taking Tony's and Maria's parts from the Act I closer, the extraordinary Quintet, and expanding them into a stand-alone duet. The result is so completely effective that one assumes the duet must have been written first, and then blended into the Quintet. (This, despite Sondheim's famous qualms about a street kid like Tony says things like, "Today the world was just an address.") Again we ride the marvelous Bernstein melodic rollercoaster that goes up, up, and further up, seemingly never to come down. The highest note is reached on the second syllable of the word "today" in "Today, all day I had the feeling." But the ending phrase doesn't settle back into its place, and the last note is an octave above where the song began. Given all this excitement, it may come as a surprise that the song undergoes two key changes, each one of them down a half step. The first change comes with the words, "Tonight, tonight / The world is full of light," and the second one arrives with the tender last words, "Good night, good night." The lower keys relax the feeling of the song, so these changes are the perfect sonic picture of the energy of a first encounter: Initially bursting at the seams, then calming somewhat, and finally falling into a peaceful place of "good night." This flow nicely imitates the emotional arc in Shakespeare's original, which progresses from Romeo's exuberance in comparing Juliet to the sun; to Juliet's command to Romeo that, if he loves, he "pronounce it faithfully"; to the reluctant goodbyes ("parting is such sweet sorrow"). At the end of the duet, we hear the orchestra play a few notes of "Somewhere," foreshadowing the tragedy that will ensue.

"Gee, Officer Krupke." While the Jets wait outside Doc's Soda Shop for word from the Sharks, they sing the show's sole comic relief number. In the movie, the lead singer is Riff (in the stage play, where the song happens in the second act, Riff was dead before the song was sung). He is dragged around a cycle of pretend authority figures, starting with one gang member as "Officer Krupke," a stand-in for the actual Officer Krupke, a pear-shaped buffoon who's just told them to get off the streets. "Krupke" takes him to a "judge" and Riff tells His Honor that life with his parents is rough, since "With all their marijuana / They won't give me a puff." The "judge" sends him to a "head-shrinker" and Riff's complaint is, essentially, that everyone around him is screwed up ("My sister wears a moustache / My brother wears a dress"). The cycle continues, as Riff is dragged to a social worker, and then back to Krupke. The song ends with "Gee, Officer Krupke, Krup you!" For "Krup," of course, substitute a different set of four letters.

"I Feel Pretty." The most widely satirized number from the show (it was mercilessly skewered on *Saturday Night Live*) still makes Sondheim blush, or so the lyricist says. Yet, it provides a moment for Maria, in the company of girlfriends at the bridal shop where she works, to revel in the promise of a love she does not know will come to a tragic end. The feeling is Latin American, though nothing of it is especially Puerto Rican.

"One Hand, One Heart." Another song sometimes poked fun at, and actively disliked by all members of the creative team except Bernstein, this duet actually balances the emotions of Tony and Maria, grounding them as a serious couple, not just two people in the throes of infatuation. The melody is emphatically not one of Bernstein's roller-coasters. It moves stepwise or modestly by thirds and fourths, leading with dignity to a high note not far from the song's starting place. Berman points out that the closing words, "Even death won't part us now," both foreshadow the couple's fate, and echo the words of Romeo to Friar Laurence when he weds Juliet: "Do thou but close our hands with holy words / Then love-devouring death do what he will." Unlike Romeo and Juliet, Tony and Maria do not actually marry. The bridal shop scene takes the place of the wedding.

Quintet. Twice in the score, Bernstein will get his wish to bend in the direction of opera (albeit remaining in the arena of musical theater). This is the first time. Nearly six decades after the first production of *West Side Story*, nothing has come along to challenge this perfectly realized ensemble for tautness and concision of expression balanced with richness of textures. Most musical theater songs are solos, duets, or massed choruses. Here is a true quintet, the sort one might very well encounter in an opera where it is relatively common to hear five different groups or individuals singing about different-yet-related things to different strands of melody at the same time. In musical theater, this is a rarity. Only one other number comes immediately to mind, and that is "Someone in a Tree" from Sondheim's *Pacific Overtures* (1976), but there the counterpoint is not as consistent and the final minute or so is sung in unison. In this number, Tony, Maria, Anita, the Jets, and the Sharks all sing their anticipation of the coming night in separate musical statements that magically coalesce. The Jets and Sharks look forward to the fight, Anita looks forward to lovemaking from Bernardo, and Tony and Maria anticipate seeing each other again. We hear the music of "Tonight" reprised, though as it's been pointed out, this was where the song actually originated.

The Rumble. Moved by the fact that he is in love with a Shark girl, Tony has already convinced both gangs to ditch the rumble and substitute a "fair fight" between Bernardo and Ice (a Jets character invented for the movie). But that's not enough for Maria, who demands that Tony stop all violence between the rival groups. Obediently, Tony shows up at the desolate spot beneath the highway and physically puts himself between Ice and Bernardo. This only enrages the Sharks, who taunt him and back him away until, disgusted with the treatment of his friend, Riff steps into the fight and lands a punch on Bernardo. The music starts up and tensions shift into high gear. Switchblades come out. Confusion reigns. The music, which owes something to Bernstein's score to *On the Waterfront*, grows more and more percussive and dissonant. Tony tries to come between Riff and Bernardo but is restrained. He breaks free and pulls Riff away from the fight, but Riff in turn breaks away and runs directly into Bernardo's knife. Blinded by raged at the death of his closest friend, Tony stabs Bernardo with Riff's knife. An all-out fight erupts until police sirens stop the scene, and the music. The music picks up again in subtle little percussion moves. Tony, realizing what he has done, screams "Maria!"

"Somewhere." Chino tells Maria that Tony has killed her brother. When Tony arrives, she screams "Murderer!" at him, but she cannot sustain her hatred. The two sing the song as a duet, one of the more famous numbers from the show and now a standard. Afterward, they consummate their love, just as Romeo and Juliet do in their parallel circumstance. In this number, the stage version succeeds where the film fails. To have Tony and Maria sing at such a moment makes no sense. Onstage, the song is sung by a distant voice, as the pair dance a fantasy ballet that takes them "far, far away." The ballet works to suggest the unreality of Tony's and Maria's situation, whereas the song as a duet is too "real." Sondheim, who frequently denigrates his own lyrics for this show, says that other songwriters call this his "a" song, after the second note, a high note which carries the word "a," as in "There's A place for us." It's considered poor craftsmanship in professional songwriting to place an unimportant word on a high note. That opening pair of notes constitute a large leap up (a minor seventh), but this is no rollercoaster. The melody will progress steadily along the defining lines of its subtle harmony, ending on a pair of yearning notes that barely hang on to their place at the top of the range. The four love songs in the score have described an arc of emotions from ecstasy (the ever-higher spinning melody in "Maria") to anticipation (the constantly lowering key centers of "Tonight") to solemnity (the stateliness of "One Hand, One Heart") to the heartbreaking hope of "Somewhere."

"Cool." The Jets are in hiding and bursting to get further vengeance against the "dirty Sharks." Ice takes over as their leader and tells them to stay cool, advice he repeats in song. The song is followed by a highly expressive dance to Bernstein's twelve-tone fugue. In theater or in concert, Bernstein used twelve-tone rows only in isolation. In actual serial writing, rows are subjects to be developed along certain prescribed lines. Bernstein instead uses them by themselves to suggest dislocation, ennui, or emotional distance. In other words, he uses tone rows in the context of tonality. In his later lectures at Harvard, he will essentially argue that tone rows can only be used in a tonal context, some composers' intent notwithstanding, since all perception of music is necessarily tonal. This observation ranks among the most important in Bernstein's life, a theme central to his musical ethos and, as we shall see, to his idea of "faith."

"A Boy Like That"/"I Have a Love." Bernstein's second act of smuggling opera into the show is this linked pair of songs that do what no dialogue could possibly have done: reconcile Anita, who has lost Bernardo to Tony's knife, with Maria, who loves Tony in spite of all that has happened. This is a true operatic *scena*, or sung scene, not an expression of attitude ("Jet Song," "Cool") or emotion (the love songs), but the action of a scene made fuller and given more power by being sung rather than spoken. Anita musically spits her words at Maria through notes that land on the downbeat with fierceness. Maria implores her, gently at first ("Oh no, Anita, no") then more aggressively ("You should know better"). This segues directly into "I Have a Love," in which Maria floats notes in protest of her love for Tony, a love that transcends such petty business as murder. It's completely unrealistic to expect Anita, whose boyfriend's body is barely cold, to forgive and even reach out to Maria; in dramatic terms, it is unbelievable. And yet, the music makes us believe it—and that's pure opera. The creative team had painted themselves into a plot corner here. In *Romeo and Juliet*, there is no character corresponding to Anita, no "girlfriend" for Juliet's cousin (not brother) Tybalt. In her place is the nurse, a character who, though she grieves for Tybalt, was neither related to him nor his bed partner. But Maria's "Romeo" has just killed Anita's lover! Why would she acquiesce to Maria's requests? Why, indeed, would she not slap Maria silly and curse her? Because Bernstein's soaring music tells her not to—that's the only reason why. So, when a police officer shows up to interview Maria about the murder, Anita agrees to take a message to Doc's and tell Tony that Maria has been "detained." (*West Side Story* skips over the whole bit of the drug that puts Juliet into a death-like sleep.) But once at Doc's, Anita is harassed and mock-raped by the Jets, who don't buy for a minute that she is there to help Tony. In spiteful revenge, Anita, instead of telling them to have Tony wait for Maria, announces that Maria is dead. Doc passes the bad news along to Tony, who's been hiding in the cellar, and he then wanders the night, shouting for Chino to come kill him. Just as he spots Maria still alive, Tony is gunned down. Maria reprises "Somewhere" as Tony dies in her arms. The Jets approach the Sharks, keen on revenge, but Maria grabs Chino's gun and declares, "You all killed him, and Bernardo, and Riff, not with guns and bullets but with hate." Together, Jets and Sharks carry Tony's body away to the sounds of "Somewhere." The last music we hear is the final two notes of "Somewhere" underpinned by a dissonant tritone.

West Side Story opened out of town in August 1957 in Washington, DC, and for once, the talk of the nation's capital was a work of art. The premiere was attended, in Bernstein's phrase, "by Nixon and 35 admirals"; in other words, dignitaries and officials en masse. It opened at New York's Winter Garden Theater the following month to almost unanimous raves and tumultuous audience response, ran for over 700 performances, toured the country, and returned to Broadway for another 200-plus performances, and was then made into the hugely popular film we have just described. It's difficult to convey to a culture that currently marginalizes Broadway music just how ubiquitous the Bernstein-Sondheim songs became, but here's an illustration: The soundtrack of *West Side Story* was the number one selling album in America for more than a year (fifty-four weeks). That's a record that's never been broken, the closest runner-up being Michael Jackson's *Thriller*, which maintained the number one spot for thirty-seven weeks.

Almost exactly concurrent with the opening of *West Side Story* came the announcement that Leonard Bernstein would become the first American-born music director of the nation's oldest orchestra, the New York Philharmonic, effective the fall of 1958. So, precisely at the moment when he had arrived as a major force in theater composition, Bernstein turned from composing full time and conducting on the side, to conducting full time (and then some, the position was an enormous responsibility) and composing in the cracks. Scores would come less frequently now, spaced out over years instead of months. If it was a time of few and far between, it was also a time to get "serious": the next three major compositions would directly tackle Bernstein's stated life theme of the search for faith; two of them in Hebrew, and one of them, the most controversial of all his controversial pieces, a theater work in which the subject is holy sacrament.

SYMPHONIC DANCES FROM *WEST SIDE STORY*

Of all Bernstein's concert works, none shows up more often on symphony orchestra concerts than the arrangement Bernstein made in 1960 of melodies from *West Side Story*. Bernstein had previously excerpted Three Dance Episodes from *On the Town,* and had turned the Overture to *Candide* into a concert staple. Arranging a suite of pieces from *West Side Story* for symphony orchestra was a natural. Assisted by Sid Ramin and Irwin Kostal, his orchestrators for the Broadway show, Bernstein put together a cohesive and compelling sampling of *West Side Story* moments. The pieces selected for the suite do not follow the order in which they appear in the show, nor is the suite a complete representation of the musical's most popular moments. Rather, as the title suggests, the score hits the dance highlights of the show, re-ordered for maximum contrast.

Symphonic Dances opens as the show opens, with the Jets and Sharks pitted against each other to the rough-edged music of the Prologue. The first interval heard is the feared tritone, signaling unrest and the coming drama. This may be the only piece of music in the mainstream repertoire that requires members of the orchestra to snap their fingers. The Prologue dives straight into "Somewhere" from the show's second act. The song is first heard (in the stage version, not the film) as the offstage accompaniment to a fantasy ballet in which Tony and Maria search for a place and time where they might be free from the violence that rages around them. The music dies away into a dirge that will recur as Tony's funeral march at the show's end.

The suite proceeds with sprightly music (Scherzo), also from the ballet sequence, before plunging directly into the sweat and swelter of the intense Mambo, danced by the Sharks at the fateful dance at the gym. It's there that Tony and Maria meet, accompanied by the piquant Cha-Cha and Meeting Scene that immediately follow. (The melody is that of the song, "Maria," sung by Tony after he leaves the dance.) The Cool Fugue that comes next is the centerpiece of the suite's second half, an elaborate fugal working-out to a simple subject derived from the language of bop, the form of jazz then most current, but also comprising a twelve-tone row.

Out of the fugue erupts the violent music of the rumble, followed immediately by the only excerpt not taken from a dance section of the show: "I Have a Love" is the duet between Maria and her brother's girlfriend, Anita. It is a Bernstein hymn, like the one he wrote for Marlon Brando striding toward the corrupt union bosses in the score to the film *On the Waterfront*. Its lesson is the supreme message of love. At the very close, the muted sound of Tony's funeral music returns to conclude the Symphonic Dances on a somber note.

8

KADDISH **AND** *CHICHESTER PSALMS*

The position of music director of a symphony orchestra demands much more than waving a baton in front of a hundred musicians. A music director conducts the lion's share of concerts, auditions musicians, plans seasons, schedules tours, selects repertoire, consults on soloists, and last but far from least in the minds of board members, serves as liaison to the community of concertgoers and patrons, providing a "face" for an organization that is otherwise a sea of musicians without distinct profile.

In other words, Lenny was a busy man during the New York Philharmonic years of 1958 to 1969. During that time, he made New York's orchestra the nation's orchestra, through groundbreaking tours such as that to the USSR in 1959, with high-quality recordings of the major repertoire, and via the Young People's Concerts that brought classical music and the ideas surrounding it to the ubiquitous little screen in American homes. Bernstein's personality and style of delivery were made for television. Because of him, millions of people who otherwise might have had no exposure to "classical" music learned about Beethoven, Mahler, and Strauss; about what made jazz "jazz"; and why the new popular music of the mid-1960s was so important and so different.

Only, where did this leave him as a composer? Stranded, for the most part. Except for a short bit of incidental music for a play in 1958, and some tiny brass pieces in the spring of 1959, the early Philharmonic years saw a dearth of new Bernstein compositions. And yet, he worked steadily on a big project, a new work in Hebrew. It would be his final numbered symphony, Symphony No. 3, *Kaddish*.

The *Kaddish* Symphony is the problem child of Bernstein's oeuvre, the black sheep in the herd. For those of us who love it, nothing else quite matches the intensity of its angry address to God, the sorrowful power of its Mahler-tinged soprano solo, or the exultance of the closing fugue, with its heaven-lifting "Amen." To others, it is marred by the composer's self-indulgent fantasies of dialogue with the Deity in the form of a spoken narrative. While Bernstein was first and always a musician, he was also a writer of strength, clarity, and grace. There is a gulf, however, between being able to write well and being a poet. Bernstein may not have been aware of that gulf, or perhaps he thought he spanned it, so it was without qualm that he conceived of a choral symphony sung in Hebrew, but overlaid with his own, English-language commentary.

This would be his third and last numbered symphony, meaning it had to deal with father in some manner. Bernstein had dedicated his first symphony to his biological father, a work dealing with the woeful prophecies of a biblical father figure, and had dedicated his second to Serge Koussevitzky, his musical father. Though Sam would not again be the dedicatee of the newest symphony, his presence hangs over it. Humphrey Burton relates that in 1962, Bernstein gave a speech in honor of his father's birthday, an address that compared a father to God, "because he caused me to exist." Now a father himself, Bernstein said he had a greater understanding of that role's challenges. Every child at some point, Bernstein's speech continued, "fights his father, leaves him, and then returns to him." As it was with the earthly father, so it was with the heavenly one. The theme of the new symphony was born.

The *kaddish* is a Jewish prayer sequence that thanks God, praises Him, and concludes in a plea for universal peace. A central, repeated part of the prayer asks that God's name be "magnified and sanctified." The *kaddish* is usually associated with mourning rituals, where the prayer is used to proclaim that, despite the loss of a loved one, the person praying still loves God. This *Job*-like challenge to love a God who in the long run destroys all of us must have held deep significance for Bernstein. In his score, he will set the prayer three times in succession, and each time will change context and meaning as the English-language text—by turns a plea to God, an accusation hurled at God, and a reconciliation—shades it. The work was commissioned by the Boston Symphony Orchestra with help from the Koussevitzky Foundation, bringing in yet another "father."

And there is one more. In the early 1960s, the Bernsteins became friends with President John F. Kennedy and his wife Jacqueline. They had supported Kennedy's candidacy in 1960 and Lenny, at the request of Frank Sinatra, had fashioned two fanfares for the president at his inauguration. Frequent visitors to the White House, the Bernsteins were not only on the official guest list, but were often invited to stay after official gatherings had ended. Bernstein had met presidents before, but this one was different, and for the first time he could say he was on a first-name basis with one. In terms of age, Kennedy was no "father figure" (the two men were close contemporaries), but the office of president represented paternal authority. Bernstein would be at work the afternoon of November 22, 1963, putting the finishing touches on the orchestration of *Kaddish*, when word came of Kennedy's assassination. Suddenly, the mournful aspects of the symphony took on a horrible new dimension. Bernstein dedicated the symphony "to the beloved memory of John F. Kennedy."

Again with this symphony, as with so many Bernstein scores, we face the question of extremely different versions of the same work. For the original, Bernstein stipulated a female speaker, on the premise that only the feminine side of man that dared to address God. Felicia Bernstein, an actor before she largely sacrificed her career to be the composer's wife, was the first speaker of the *Kaddish* text and is heard on the 1964 recording, with her husband leading the New York Philharmonic. The recording won that year's Grammy for Best Classical Album. Years later, Bernstein decided the narrator could be of either gender and he revised the text accordingly, along with small changes to the music. The narrator for many performances after that was the composer's friend, Michael Wager. But even the revised text struck many people as overreaching. "Pretentious" and "embarrassing" were two words commonly used by denigrators of the text. Critic Michael Steinberg pulled no punches, calling Bernstein's prose, and by extension the symphony itself, "plain junk." Jamie Bernstein, the composer's daughter, agreed about the text, though not the music. In 2002, she fashioned a new text that dealt with, not the Creator, but the creator—with the composer of the symphony, her own father. The result is a daughter's address to a father, via a work composed by that very father, and in turn intended to call to account the Heavenly Father. Jamie Bernstein's text deals with her father's eccentricities, with his God obsession, and even with what she hears as his overly complicated music with its "barbed dissonances." At one point, she exhorts him to be "Simple! Simple!" The controversial narration, in performance and on CD, has helped acquaint a new generation of listeners with the extraordinary music—barbed dissonance and all—that otherwise might go unheard.

Reviewing all of these versions, I find the original by far the most powerful. "Pretentious" though the address to God may be, it speaks to something inside every human being. Who has not thought, "If God is so great, why is there death? Why does violence rage everywhere? Who allows this? Why should I praise such an entity? You—whoever You may be—are not in charge, I am. You want me to believe in You? Try believing in me." Reduced to its essence, that is the argument of Bernstein's text. Such sentiments may indeed be "embarrassing" when aired in the form of a public address, but that doesn't keep them from being true. When uttered by a woman, rather than a man, they take on additional power somehow. Bernstein, I believe, was intuitively in track when he required a female narrator, for, in the words of G. K. Chesterton, "Men are men, but Man is a Woman." (I also believe those who object to Bernstein's text to be thrall to a contemporary sensibility that forbids them to take God or metaphysics or eternity or truth seriously, but only ironically. When the age of irony is gone, the original *Kaddish* will seem less "embarrassing" than awe-inspiring.)

The texts being controversial, we'll focus on the music, using the original version of the text only as a guidepost. The most immediately arresting thing about any version of *Kaddish*, and what must have startled the audiences who first heard the piece in 1964, is the unique power of the Jewish music. It's like nothing else ever heard to issue from a symphony orchestra; the middle movement of *Jeremiah* comes close, but this outstrips it with the *Les Noces*-like sonic fundamentalism of its modes and rhythms. Bernstein had not written vocal music on a Hebrew text since *Jeremiah* and *Hashkivenu* in the 1940s, with one tiny exception. In the spring of 1958, he contributed a short work for chorus and percussion called "Israelite Chorus" to a Broadway play. The work was withdrawn and for decades went unheard until recently, when it was included with *Hashkivenu* and other Jewish-themed Bernstein works on a CD from Naxos. It is a thunderous, tribal, "primitive" choral shout that makes no apologies for being Middle Eastern. It's my belief that Bernstein startled even himself with this music, and that this in turn influenced him to compose a symphonic work with these very traits.

Symphony No. 3, scored for orchestra, mixed chorus, boys choir, soprano solo, and speaker, begins with an indeterminate humming in the chorus, setting up a sense of entering a different space. The speaker offers her address to "Lonely, disappointed Father," an "Angry, wrinkled old Majesty." Harp and flutes announce a three-note ascending motive: up a minor second, up a minor sixth. This will color the ensuing forty-five minutes. The speaker wants to say *Kaddish*, her own *Kaddish*, a prayer connected to her own death. The three-note motive repeats, now in biting brass and woodwinds. Strings play a version of the motive that droops at the last instead of ascending. Alto saxophone announces a mysterious theme picked up by the strings. The speaker announces that the time has arrived to say the *kaddish*, uttering its opening words, "Magnified and Sanctified be the Great Name. Amen." Chorus and orchestra begin a respectful treatment that shortly turns into an angry, rhythmic shout that is half praise and half accusation. The melody is that of the saxophone, but set to jagged rhythms. The main rhythm is in eight, but the measures are subdivided 3+2+3. The "Amen" is shouted/ sung fortissimo with wildly glissando-ing harps and chimes struck with metal hammers.

"Amen! Amen! Do You hear that, Father?" the speaker shouts in turn. The speaker wants to know why God, who can "spin moons," can't seem to produce "a touch of order" here below. And she wonders if God recognizes her as that part of humanity that resists death, the part "that insists on You," as Bernstein's text so eloquently puts it. Here begins the bitter "Din-Torah." The chorus hums the mysterious melody as the speaker grows more and more impatient with God's silence. Where is the rainbow He promised? "Tin God!" she screams, as the orchestra reaches a peak of dissonance and the percussion section blows out all its limitations in thundering fortissimos. The release of anger takes all forms. There is a sudden little bluesy figure in the lower strings marked "grotesque," piles of wrong orchestral notes that throw themselves on each other, and a final eight-part chorus that goes off in eight different directions at once.

The Din-Torah over, the speaker now wishes to rock God in her arms as if He were a child in need of comfort after such an attack from His own child. A soprano solo starts a long-lined melody shaped like the opening three-note motive, but greatly expanded. This is the second setting of the prayer, once again starting with the speaker's intoning of "Magnified and Sanctified be the Great Name." It's important to note that the "Great Name" isn't, well, named. That will figure into things coming up. The central musical idea here is of stepwise movement followed by suddenly larger intervals. The chorus joins her and the crushing beauty of this impossible desire to comfort the ruler of the universe. When Bernstein composed *Kaddish*, he had recently started recording his first series of Mahler symphonies with the New York Philharmonic, and the influence of that composer shows in the strangely unsettling serenity of this solo, which embraces while also questioning. The solo over, the speaker decides to hold God's hand and, with Him, visit "the workings of perfectedness" that He has posited as our ideal.

This starts the scherzo. As speaker and God view the "star most worthy" of God's creation, some ideal realm where everything is as it should be. But "something is wrong." Everything is *too* perfect. All is static. There's "nowhere to go, nothing to know." In a flurry of amazingly complex and dramatically perfect writing, the musical action builds to a climax in which the speaker finally concludes the phrase, "Magnified and Sanctified be the Great Name . . . of Man!" This phrase, which in the Jamie Bernstein rewrite literally prompts her to say, "Ugh," is the very heart of Bernstein's text. What is the Great Name but our own? Who is God but ourselves? What sparks faith but the burning desire to go beyond the restraints of human limitations?

The scherzo becomes frenzied with rhythmic eruptions of muscular musical strength, then softens to a trio of unparalleled sweetness. A melody that expands the opening three-note motive, pushing the intervals further until they take the shape of a Bernstein rollercoaster, grows from the violas, doubled by English horn (one of Bernstein's favorite and most effective doublings), into the full orchestra in dreamy triumph. This chorus sings *kaddish* for a third and final time, in perfect harmony and without a hint of anger. And yet it has, after all, been only a dream. Speaker and God awake, and the "dawn is chilly."

A downward plunge recalls the Din-Torah, signaling that chilly dawn, and as the tragic music concludes, the speaker makes intimate and Quaker-quiet reconciliation with the deity, knowing know that her own questing, questioning spirit is the Father Himself, as He is her questing spirit. Forever, the speaker concludes, the two will "recreate each other." A magnificent fugue, a form symbolic of compromise for the sake of beauty, ends the symphony.

No description can do justice to the drama of the piece, whether you think it is drama in the best or worst sense. Listeners who concur that the text is embarrassing should try the Jamie Bernstein version, bearing in mind that her words constitute a kind of memoir of her father, and are only peripherally related to the original text.

Here we have had another in a series of Bernstein meditations on faith. At the height of *Kaddish*'s man-affirming scherzo the speaker says "Believe! Believe!" Only, believe *what*? A pact between God and Man to "forever recreate each other" is all well and good, faith reconstituted from the dashed trust of an infantile humanity into a mature, psychic relationship between Self and God feels right, but what is it that we are to believe in? Faith, its loss and recovery, are the enduring themes of Bernstein's work, never more so than in this most personal of all his scores. Yet we are left with the question what, exactly, is it we are to have faith *in*? For the answer, we will have to wait another few years. But the answer will come. Have faith.

Return for a moment to "Glitter and Be Gay" from *Candide* and listen to the closing section or *cabaletta* in which Cunegonde sings "ah" all over the place. You will hear her sing a measure, and then you'll hear the same measure played in the orchestra immediately after. Go back to the Quintet from *West Side Story* and listen to Maria sing "Tonight, tonight." The same thing happens: she sings a measure, and the orchestra comes in on the same measure right after her. Check out the beginning of the Symphonic Suite from *On the Waterfront*, and there it is again: after the horn announces the theme, we hear it again, this time by the woodwinds, which are echoed instantly by muted brass. Everyone's playing or singing the same music, but some are starting a measure later than the others, like the rounds we used to sing as children (*Frére Jacques*, etc.), but much tighter. This is "close imitation," a favorite device of Bernstein's. We'll hear it exploited to magnificent effect in our next Bernstein experience, the *Chichester Psalms*.

By now, we are aware of many Bernstein earmarks. We frequently ride the Bernstein rollercoaster, with angular intervals pushing us ever higher. An alternative to the rollercoaster is the magisterial Bernstein hymn. In faster tempo pieces, time signatures are often in flux, and yet, the melody falls naturally on displaced accents. The use of the tritone, the raised fourth step of the major scale, dominated *West Side Story* but shows up in many other pieces as one of the composer's most natural melodic and harmonic gestures. To this we've added "close imitation," a technique that in fugue is called *stretto*, and is generally used near the end of a fugue to accelerate the excitement of the imitative device. In *Chichester Psalms*, we will see all of these traits in full array. After the Symphonic Dances from *West Side Story* and the Overture to *Candide*, *Chichester Psalms* is the third most performed Bernstein work in the concert hall. (It is also the only one of the three that started in the concert hall, rather than the theater.)

One reason for *Chichester Psalms'* popularity may be that it exhibits every one of the above traits in profusion. Another is certainly the serene beauty of its mood. It contains struggle, yes, but without the ambiguity of *Kaddish*. The music Bernstein gives to the words of young King David will praise God and peace, inveigh against the "goyim"—the nations of the earth—for their violence, then turn gently again to the renewal of trust in the Lord and His people. *Chichester Psalms* is the *Kaddish* Symphony's happy little brother. Where the symphony is riddled with problems and controversies, and where its ambience is somewhat saddened by the reduction of God to the level of man, this score sings of unclouded innocence. It is also slight. At just under twenty minutes, it is the shortest of Bernstein's concert pieces other than the overtures. It leaves the listener wanting more.

Bernstein took a sabbatical from his position at the New York Philharmonic for the season 1964–1965. The plan was to reunite with his old chums and collaborators Betty Comden and Adolph Green to adapt Thornton Wilder's play, *The Skin of Our Teeth*, as a musical. Perhaps because there was too much time ("a plan and not quite enough time," remember?), or more likely because the play resisted musicalization, the project was abandoned. Somewhere in the midst of this final attempt at collaboration by the team of Bernstein, Comden, and Green, a commission arrived for Bernstein from Chichester Cathedral in England. Would Bernstein write a choral piece for them? Bernstein plotted out three movements, each containing one complete psalm of David and a portion of another. The first movement (Psalm 108, verse 2, and Psalm 100, entire) finds David dancing in ecstasy around the Ark of the Covenant, praising God with "psaltery and harp." The second movement pits the entirety of the famous twenty-third Psalm ("The Lord is my shepherd") against the first four verses of Psalm 2, "Why do the nations rage?" The closing movement sings of humility in the presence of God (Psalm 131, "My heart is not haughty") and ends with the first verse of Psalm 133: "Behold how good / And how pleasant it is / For brethren to dwell / Together in unity." The orchestration is for strings, harps, brass, and percussion with no woodwinds.

Chichester Psalms begins with a great orchestral crash on B-flats with added noes, marked *Maestoso*. The chorus, fortissimo, proclaims "Awake, psaltery and harp: I will rouse the dawn!" The words are actually in Hebrew, as they are throughout the work, but there is no mistaking the vibrancy of the emotion, whether you know Hebrew or not. After this short introduction, there ensues the most exultant four minutes of music in all Bernstein, a dance in 7/4 that shouts to the heavens the prefect glory of belief. When Bernstein plugs into a seven-beat groove, the result is generally joyous, but this time goes beyond the others in its whirling-dervish-like forgetfulness of anything but the pure ecstasy of *now*.

The second movement startles with a sweet dissonance from the harps, a dissonance made sweet, we are unsurprised to find, by a tritone. A boy solo begins to sing. This is the voice of David watching the flocks and finding himself watched over by *Adonai*. Harp notes ring out as they might have on David's own harp, and the melody that rises above them is what we have called the Bernstein rollercoaster, but which here might more appropriately be renamed the Bernstein magical ladder. It rises at first abruptly, falls back, rises again even higher, then levels off. A "bridge" takes the line downward, so the return to the upward gesture is all that more comforting and right. The sopranos in the chorus pick up the melody, singing it divided, in close imitation, to almost mystical effect. As one group of sopranos is arching high, the other is poised to follow in the next measure, like flowers opening in speeded-up action so you can see one petal follow another in blossom-ing.

With a shock, our peace is interrupted. "Lamah ra-g'-shu goyim?" shout the tenors and basses. Why do the nations rage? This aggressive motive is also given the close imitation treatment. For a while the men rage, but then the women enter with David's gentle song and for a while the forces of peace and compete in tight counterpoint. The boy solo reenters, the women echo him, and David's psalm is apparently triumphant. The movement ends with the uneasy feeling that the forces of war may return at any time.

The strings at the start of the final movement are in anguish over the struggle they have witnessed. A brief but intense prelude intones their almost post-Romantic protest, a dissonantly chromatic exhortation worthy of *Elektra*-era Richard Strauss. At one point, a distant-sounding trumpet sounds eleven notes of David's melody from the beginning of the second movement, a reminder of the song praising God's steward-ship. Yet the sorrowful mood will not be altered or stopped. Instead it plays itself out, and only when the feelings of disappointment and de-spair have been fully experienced does the chorus begin to sing a cra-dling little Bernstein hymn, a gently flowing confession of humility writ-ten in 10/4, but felt in five counts times two. Sung mostly in unison but with close imitation to enrich the texture, this is a hymn of uncalculated warmth and forgiveness. An a cappella, note-against-note benediction closes the movement and this most popular of the composer's concert compositions.

Chichester Psalms makes no apologies for relative tonal stability, nor for its simple theme of innocence versus violence. In a poem Bernstein published in the *New York Times* on the occasion of the work's pre-miere, he said the work was "Certain to sicken a stout John Cager / With its tonics and triads in E-flat major." This the "simple" statement that daughter Jamie Bernstein wanted *Kaddish* to be in her revised narration of Symphony No. 3. Perhaps it is simple because some of the material, notably the boy solo song in the second movement, came from the abandoned *Skin of Our Teeth* musical. As hard as it is for lovers of *Chichester Psalms* to comprehend, that solo, which begins in transliter-ated Hebrew with, "Adonai, ro-i, lo ehsar," was first a melody that framed the words: "Winds may blow, and snows may snow." We'll cover that in the next vignette.

CHICHESTER PSALMS: SECOND MOVEMENT—"SPRING WILL COME AGAIN"

Bernstein's penchant for reusing material reaches an uncanny peak in the transformation of the song, "Spring Will Come Again," into the main subject of the second movement to his *Chichester Psalms*. The two texts to which this music is set could not be more different. The lyric to "Spring Will Come Again" was written by Betty Comden and Adolph Green for a proposed musical based on Thornton Wilder's play, *The Skin of Our Teeth*. In the play, the characters face a coming Ice Age. The song was to be sung by two characters expressing a cautious but genuine optimism that even such a horror as the destruction of the world will someday be past, that spring will truly return to humankind. The *Chichester Psalms* movement is in Hebrew rather than English and comes from the most famous of David's biblical psalms: No. 23, "The Lord is my shepherd." David faces, not the end of the world, but the "raging nations," and his gentle song represents an outpost of peace amidst the noise of war. With the exception of a handful of notes that repeat in one version but not in the other, the two pieces are note-for-note identical, though they represent contrasting expressions in different languages.

1. "Spring Will Come Again" begins with a "wintry" chord—a blend of gently dissonant notes in a high register that instantly paints a picture of isolation. The traditional function of harmony is to provide grounding in a certain key center. From classical minuets to the blues, we "feel" harmonies as signposts: when a twelve-bar blues returns to the home chord from its brief journey to other chords, we know where we are. But the first chord of "Spring Will Come Again" is deliberately enigmatic. Tonally, we don't know where we are any more than the protagonists of Wilder's play know what will happen to them in the coming Ice Age. Out of the chord, a solo singer latches on to one note as if to a life raft, and sings a three-note, upward cresting motif, which then repeats, starting higher. The remainder of the song is a tonal working-out of this opening. The singer searches for a secure tonal base, as the text longs for spring.

2. The second movement of *Chichester Psalms* begins with the same chord as the song, but now, instead of evoking a winter of despair, it is played on the harp to conjure David gently plucking the strings of his instrument. The upward-thrusting three-note motif is now set to the Hebrew word that transliterates as "Adonai"—in Judaism, one of many names for the single god YHWH. Adonai is that aspect of YHWH that represents the protective master, the "shepherd" of Psalm 23. The second, still higher iteration of the motif comes with the words "I shall not want." The overall effect is of a growing confidence in the Lord's ability to provide—so perfect a piece of tone painting that it's easy to assume the music was written expressly for those words.

MASS AND THE NORTON LECTURES

Bernstein's introductory essay to his 1966 book, *The Infinite Variety of Music*, is a remarkable document. In five scant pages in the form of an open letter to "My Dear and Gentle Reader," the author addresses the crisis in music that was at that precise moment approaching climax. About a century previous, the tonal system of Western music had begun its breakdown, culminating in the assertion, by Arnold Schoenberg and his so-called Second Viennese School (the first was Haydn-Mozart-Beethoven), that the future of music lay solely in what is called serial music or dodecaphony. Serial music had been the origin of the twelve-tone rows so fondly used by Bernstein-the-composer in various nonserial contexts. Twelve-tone rows (the ordering of all twelve tones available in a given octave so as never to repeat one before all the others have sounded) appear in Bernstein at, among other junctures, the portrayal of angst in *The Age of Anxiety*; the appearance of ennui among the characters of *Candide* in the ensemble, "Quiet"; and in the notes of the fugal subject in "Cool" from *West Side Story*, when the Jets are trying to cool their jets in order to remain distant and aloof from the action. In other words, the twelve-tone row for Bernstein is the very embodiment of crisis, specifically the crisis of *alienation from reality*. And this, in turn, can be restated as Bernstein's old recurring theme, the loss of faith.

Bernstein's conclusion in the essay is that the crisis in tonality is a throbbing symbol of the broader crisis in faith. Nietzsche proclaimed God to be dead in 1883, Bernstein points out, the very same year in which Richard Wagner, the last champion of tonality's progress and, once upon a time, Nietzsche's idol, died. Coincidence? Bernstein thinks not. After Wagner, and especially after *Tristan und Isolde*, the work Bernstein identified (in agreement with many others) as the turning point in modern music history, nothing is the same. Although many post-Wagnerians asserted a conservative musical ideology (Brahms, for example), the main historical thrust was toward ever-increasing ambiguity of tonality until at last, in the 1920s, Arnold Schoenberg asserted the "inevitability" of music written within the confines of the twelve-tone system, a system the stated aim of which is to wipe away completely the key centers Wagner had so effectively obscured.

The ascendance of serialism in the mid-twentieth century contributed to the decay that had already progressed upon the body of Western art music, and by 1966 the leading edge of classical music was a kind of antimusic, typified by John Cage's aleatory experiments, "chance" music that further distanced the artist from his or her creation by making him or her the neutral vessel of random sounds. But—and this is enormous—Bernstein asserts in his essay that there can be no such thing as anti-music. He does not say that music is better than antimusic, or that people shouldn't write antimusic, he claims that anti-music *cannot exist*. Why? Because the ear hears pitched sound as belonging to a harmonic series. The ear automatically infers tonal relations even when the composer intends otherwise. To put it as succinctly as possible, no note is an island. Every pitch stands in relation to other pitches, and not because the composer says so, but because it cannot be otherwise. All music is necessarily tonal, not in the sense of conforming to the specific rules of the Western system of tonality, but in the larger sense that every note will be heard as suggestive of some kind of pitch hierarchy, even if the composer doesn't want to suggest one. There are not and cannot be random notes. John Cage is either making a fool of himself or of us when he insists there can be. This idea, which flies in the face of all modern thinking by asserting a kind of natural law is at work, will be greatly elaborated and linked to no less than the linguistic theories of Noam Chomsky in Bernstein's 1973 lectures as occupant of the Charles Eliot Norton Chair of Poetry at Harvard University. In those lectures, Bernstein will fulfill the promise of his studies with aesthetics professor David Prall at Harvard. Their impact will be considered at the end of this chapter.

But before the lectures, the music. In *Mass* (1971), the work we are about to examine, Bernstein brings to a climax his musical search for faith. Subtitled *A Theatre Piece for Singers, Players and Dancers*, *Mass* is the capstone of Bernstein's composing career. *Age of Anxiety* announced his mastery, *Candide* and *West Side Story* confirmed it, and *Mass* crowns it. Its origins were of the highest official order. In 1969, Jacqueline Kennedy (by now Mrs. Aristotle Onassis) commissioned Bernstein to compose a major work to celebrate the opening of an arts center in Washington, DC, to be named for her late husband, the president: the Kennedy Center for the Performing Arts. Having just left his celebrated position as the New York Philharmonic's music director ("I'm really a composer" was the reason he gave the orchestra's board), Bernstein's decks were now relatively cleared—except for dozens of guest-conducting engagements. He accepted the commission. Only, what could possibly be a sufficiently worthy subject for a ninety-minute composition intended for the grand opening of the country's most important new venue, named after its beloved, recently fallen leader?

In June 1968, Bernstein had stood in sorrowful awe as the Catholic requiem mass was said for Senator Robert Kennedy, the president's brother, also struck down by an assassin. As part of the funeral rites, Bernstein led members of the New York Philharmonic in the Adagietto from Mahler's Symphony No. 5. Humphrey Burton credits this soul-shaking experience as one inspiration for Bernstein's choice of the Catholic mass. Another was the composer's recent project, abandoned before fruition, involving the score to a film about St. Francis of Assisi. That the Kennedy family was Irish Catholic may also have contributed to the choice. Whatever the reason, Bernstein's decision to deal with the Roman Catholic mass, in its original Latin form, taking on its history and spiritual significance, celebrating the ritual, and confronting the doubts surrounding its proclamations of faith, was pure Lenny. So was his decision to amp up the eclecticism. Despite some critics' insistent voices to the contrary, Bernstein for the most part strove to tame the many streams of influence in his music. *Candide*, *West Side Story*, and *Kaddish* had all had unifying stylistic elements, whether found in mock-opera, tritone-laden bop, or Hebrew cantillation. They hang together because of common threads throughout. Ditto *On the Waterfront* and *Trouble in Tahiti*. But *Mass* is a glittering jewel box of genres: blues, hymns, 1960s rock, Mediterranean folk dance rhythms, musical comedy, brass band. This was not a composer to make facile decisions. The eclecticism must have been intentional, and there must have been a reason, because the whole score shouted it.

The prominence of popular forms of music in a "serious" piece have caused some to dismiss *Mass* as too light for the gravitas of the subject. To Bernstein, however, the then-current sort of serious music was no match for the youthful power of popular music. In the above-mentioned essay, Bernstein startled the contemporary classical world by stating flat-out that he was no longer listening to avant-garde Western art music, but to popular music, preferring "the musical adventures of Simon and Garfunkel" to Cage, Boulez, Berio, and so on. The sudden explosion of rock-based popular music in the mid-1960s had made everything else "old-fashioned" overnight, Bernstein wrote, from serialism to chance music and "even jazz." In this, he was acutely perceptive, sensing the sea change that many colleagues missed. After the 1960s, music would no longer continue the tradition of structured tonality in popular music or the structured "atonality" that had replaced it in the concert world. In development was a musical language intensely beat-driven, almost as if in defiance of the disappearing bar-lines of contemporary classical music and avant-garde jazz, and more modal than tonal. ("Modal" here does not imply atonal, but is simply contrasted with systematic tonality. Modal cadences defined rock harmonically from the start. Cream's "Sunshine of Your Love" is an early archetype.) Nor would the classical music world drive the engine any longer, with popular music chugging along behind. The hierarchy was in the midst of a reversal, and very soon, "new music" would mean new *popular* music. Not long after that, commercial popular music would be calling the stylistic shots for classical, not the other way round. The arrival of Minimalism in the mid-to-late 1970s signaled the completion of this metamorphosis. The phased repetitions of Terry Riley and Phillip Glass have more in common with Iron Butterfly's "In-A-Gadda-Da-Vida" than with Elliott Carter or Krzysztof Penderecki.

In such circumstances, what is a Leonard Bernstein to do but embrace the change and emulate it? After all, it gave him a great excuse to let loose a torrent of music making, freed of any preconceptions. For whatever else it is or is not, *Mass* is an energetic overflow of melodic invention sparked by the composer's encounters with the new forms and freedoms of popular music. "Simple Song" evokes the folk music revival of the era. Hard blues dominates the "Confiteor." To a cynical, rock-inflected tune, a young man sings, "I believe in God, but does God believe in me?" The muscular "Gloria" is a gospel shout crossbred with chant. "In nomine patris" returns to more familiar ground, a Sephardic swirl, a deeply Hebraic sound etched in Bernstein's usual mix of meters but basically in "Turkish nine"—3/4 followed by 3/8. Musical theater gestures show up more than any other single element, though these are sometimes limned with electric guitars to give them a rock "feel." Anyone with an awareness of Bernstein's style will find the usual markers. "Simple Song" rides the Bernstein rollercoaster, reaching the top at the words "or the moon by night." Even in songs with a steady beat, the count is thrown "off" here and there to keep things rhythmically interesting. An a cappella chorus, "Almighty Father," could slip into *Candide* unnoticed. The finger-snapping "Mea culpa" might be the work of the Jets. People who complain of "eclecticism" often neglect the distinction between idiomatic style and personal style. An idiom is the cup, while personal style is the wine. Beethoven composed within the classical idioms of symphony, sonata, etc. But his music was not generic. Personal style, what is often called "gesture" by composers, was the differentiating element. Listening to *Mass*, one can focus on the myriad influences that prompt the "e" word from so many critics, or one can choose to hear the Bernstein style, which is present and at flood tide in this amazing score.

Smack on the heels of the high honor of the Kennedy Center commission came Bernstein's worst public relations moment: the Black Panther affair. In January 1970, Felicia Bernstein, who frequently organized for political causes, hosted a fund-raising event to assist twenty-seven members of the radical Black Panther party arrested on dubious charges. Rich celebrities crowded the Bernstein apartment on Park Avenue and the pitch was made for contributions. The man of the house pledged the check from his next engagement conducting Mascagni's *Cavalleria Rusticana*—an amount that came to around $2,000. Another $10,000 or so was raised during the evening, which featured brief speeches from the Panthers' attorneys and from a member of the group. Felicia erred, most everyone agrees, in welcoming the press to the event, and that's where things went horribly wrong. Lenny could not resist talking with the Panther member, who proceeded to lecture Lenny in his organization's politics. At one point, the Panther member said something general about his group's aims, punctuated with "You dig?" And Bernstein, just to be polite, answered with "I dig absolutely." The next day in the *New York Times*, the conversation reported was quite different. Panther: "We need to seize the means of production." Bernstein: "I dig absolutely." (The Panther's "You dig?" was left out.)

It was bad enough that Bernstein was quoted out of context and in faux-street lingo to make him appear in favor of the violent overthrow of the status quo. But when the Jewish community got wind of the Panthers' anti-Zionist position, the Jewish Defense League picketed the Bernsteins' apartment. Nor did it stop there. Five months later, journalist Tom Wolfe published his now-famous bit of long-form reportage, *Radical Chic*, which portrayed the evening as a bungled attempt on the part of the Bernsteins to appear fashionably leftist. This only added to a busy conducting schedule to cause still greater distraction from the enormous project at hand. (As an aside, Felicia Bernstein was vindicated when the flimsy case against the Panthers was thrown out of court.)

In Bernstein's usual fashion, one thing or another was allowed to interfere with the work's steady progress, and by September 1970, just twelve months before the center's scheduled opening, little had been accomplished. (At least the project now fit his famous parameters of having a plan, and not quite enough time.) Bernstein was seriously stalemated by the lack of a lyric-writing partner. His concept was to present the Latin of the traditional mass interlaced with English-language tropes by way of comment and criticism. But as had happened with *West Side Story*, his own skills as a lyricist were inadequate to the occasion. This time, however, Sondheim was unavailable. Once "just" a lyricist, Sondheim had re-emerged as the composer-lyricist he always really was, and had begun to write a string of musicals that would redefine the genre in the coming decade. His *Company* was the most talked-about show on Broadway, soon to be outdone by his *Follies*.

Lenny's sister Shirley, now an agent for theater talent, mentioned to her brother a particularly gifted young songwriter named Stephen Schwartz, whose show *Godspell* had just opened. Bernstein saw the show and liked it, and in the proverbial nick of time, Bernstein had the partner he needed. This time around, however, the new lyricist would not take over the sung text entirely, as Sondheim had in *West Side Story*. The words for *Mass* remained a mix of Bernstein and Schwartz, effectively blended so as not to make obvious whose lyrics are whose.

Because of that socialist-affirming "I dig absolutely," abetted no doubt by Bernstein's leftist past, the Nixon administration did not look kindly upon *Mass*. Their disdain only increased when they learned the composer was consulting with Phillip Berrigan on the matter of Catholic liturgy. Berrigan, a high-profile antiwar activist, was in prison on dubious charges, and Bernstein had to limit his visits to an hour. The year 1970 was the height of the Vietnam War, now a six-year-old conflict that showed no signs of abating. It was the year that four peacefully protesting students were gunned down by the National Guard at Kent State University. Tensions were high, and the Nixon White House gang nursed suspicions that *Mass* was going to contain "secret messages" promoting peace. Apparently no one told them that the Catholic mass, quite without Bernstein and Schwartz, ends with the words "Dona nobis pacem" (Grant us peace). Nixon did not attend the premiere. Henry Kissinger did.

Of the many daggers hanging over the success of *Mass*—its politics, the dated feeling of some of its language, the charges of disrespect for Catholicism—the biggest may be the form of the piece. What is *Mass*? Throughout the rest of his life, when asked this question, Bernstein would answer with the work's subtitle: "A Theatre Piece for Singers, Players and Dancers." He must have known that this is an evasion, not an answer. He was certainly right that *Mass* is a "theater piece," for while it has been frequently presented in concert, nonstaged versions lack punch. (Look up the BBC Proms concert of 2012, available on YouTube.) It is not an opera. So, is it a musical? Critic and musicologist Robert Craft once condemned the work as "Mass, the Musical." Negative connotations aside, the statement exhibits some validity.

The musical language of *Mass* is largely that of the American musical, with infusions of the new popular style. Yet, except for the Celebrant, there are no characters, per se. Nameless "characters" do show up throughout—a jailed protestor here, a cynical hippie there. They are not, however, what the story is about. Is there a story at all? Oh yes, it's a story with exactly two characters: Christianity and the People (called "street people" or "street chorus" in the score). This is not a "musical about the mass," though it has been called that. It's a musical that uses the Catholic mass as a structure in order to examine the relationship between humanity and the promise of Christianity. A big subject? Remember, this is the composer who shook his fist at God in the *Kaddish*

Symphony. In many ways, *Mass* is an extension of the themes in that earlier work.

Bernstein's *Mass* is presented in alternations of live and pre-recorded performance. This is a theatrical aspect that, unfortunately, does not come across in a CD or MP3. The idea is simple: the recorded performances represent, for the most part, that aspect of spirituality that has become ossified, while the live performances bring a refreshed, or at least contrary, point of view. This is most effective in the *Credo* section, where the Latin text delivers its orthodox belief system in direct terms via recorded music, while the live performers pull at it mercilessly until, at last, the structure of belief falls. This dichotomy is announced at the very start in clear musico-dramatic terms, when the first thing we hear in a darkened auditorium a fiercely dissonant "Kyrie" blasted at us from four loudspeakers. "Kyrie eleison" is the first section of the traditional mass, and the only part in Greek rather than Latin. Its entire text is: *Kyrie eleison, Christe eleison, Kyrie eleison* ("God have mercy on us, Christ have mercy on us, God have mercy on us"). But its meaning here is obscured by the fact that none of the four bits of music coming from different speakers is in sync with, or can be comprehended as being in harmony with, any of the others. It is complete discord. It reaches a climax of ugliness, and at that exact moment we hear an open chord on an acoustic guitar and a living voice singing, "Sing God a simple song." Here is Bernstein's contrast of established modernism with the emerging popular music aesthetic.

"Simple Song," the best-known excerpt from *Mass*, was originally written for the St. Francis movie Bernstein had begun with director Franco Zeffirelli. (According to Humphrey Burton, Bernstein also raided many "trunk songs"—tunes composed for no particular reason and then put away—for *Mass*.) Far from simple, it requires a voice with range and an ear for distantly separated intervals. The lyric is in English, but mixes in many *laudas* and *laudes*, forms of the Latin word for praise. You know you're in for an unusual musical experience when the second line of the lyric is "Make it up as you go along." *Make it up as you go along*? Are we in for an evening of improvisation? No, the admonition is not to be taken literally; it's there to oppose the strict preconceptions of the recorded *Kyrie*. We are starting again. Something old has died and something new is being born. The chorus (the main part) of "Simple Song" arches up at the beginning, but stays "close to the ground" after that, until the release (or "bridge"), when the line rises and rises, like an aerial shot in a movie, until the magical word, "moon." The phrase "The sun shall not strike me by day, nor the moon by night" comes from Psalm 121. It asserts a kind of pact between God and the people: that the people will praise God, and in return, God will set suns and moons spinning in perfect order, a symbol of His protection through the regularities of nature. It is, of course, a song of faith.

To the sound of a pop-ish little shuffle on the loudspeakers—the "Simple Song" has apparently defeated (for now) the convolutions of orthodoxy—our hippie-like interloper is adorned with vestments and becomes the Celebrant. The Celebrant is a bravura role of almost impossible demands. He will be on stage consistently for the next ninety-plus minutes, and will sing for much of that time, including a punishing, fourteen-minute soliloquy in the second half.

What is a Celebrant but a reason to celebrate? Enter a brass band, marching down the aisles in one of Bernstein's most over-the-top theatricalisms. And yet, it is exactly right. The baritone who interrupted the ossified *Kyrie* has refreshed the faith, swept away the cobwebs of religion, and awakened the people anew to the beauty of belief. This is an American show, and what is more American than a brass band to welcome the morning of belief? In the middle of this, a boys chorus sings in sweet tones of going up "to the altar of God" as if it were a self-evident truth. The boys are there to reflect the Celebrant's continuing innocence. And just when you think Bernstein has pulled out all the stops, the singers double the brass band tune . . . on kazoos.

Then, the strangest shift in the show, the most radically eclectic moment of them all. On the Latin words "In nomine Patris, et Filii, et Spiritus Sancti" (In the name of the Father, the Son, and the Holy Spirit)—the proclamation of the Trinity, exclusive to Christian belief— we hear the most Jewish music of the score. It's sometimes even called the "Hebrew dance," and in the BBC Proms version a Star of David shines side-by-side with a cross during its performance. This is the piece in "Turkish nine" plus a mesmerizing parade of other meters that defy a regular count. It was fortunate for the premiere production of *Mass* that no less than Alvin Ailey was the choreographer. Ailey and his dancers were absolute masters of the count.

Bernstein is throwing beauty at us from every direction. No sooner do the brass band rhythms grab us and the kazoos raise our eyebrows than we are dazzled by the mesmerizing meters of the "Hebrew" dance. We barely latch onto this when a soaring French horn solo underscores the Celebrant's noble call, "Let us rise and pray." This leads to the glow of the a cappella chorus, "Almighty Father," at which point the first scene might be said to come to an end. It's hard to blame the many listeners who, getting no further than this, wonder, "What on earth is this piece up to?" Indeed, *Mass* is, in isolated spots, a lot of fun, which should not surprise if you stop to remember that its composer, even in his fifties, enjoyed jumping fully clothed into swimming pools at cocktail parties. Only, don't let the fun fool you into thinking that's all there is. We are going to get something much more serious than we bargained for when the brass band marched down the aisle.

(In fact, you've already gotten it, or a part of it. Listen again to the *In nomine Patris* a.k.a. "Hebrew Dance" and the "Almighty Father" chorus, back to back. They mirror one another. Each *is* the other, more or less, slowed down or sped up and given a different time signature. Judaism and Christianity are, after all, kin.)

The second scene opens with the angry jabbing of notes on pre-recorded oboe. The notes form no melody; they are as shapeless as the "Kyries" of the opening, a specter of the fractured orthodoxy that the young man vanquished with his guitar chord. (Or did he?) The order of the liturgy next calls for the *Confiteor*—declaration of confession. Darkness falls swiftly where once kazoos buzzed. The chorus and percussion intone gothic sounds, which suddenly shift to a finger-snapping five-beat with electric guitar and electric bass. At last, two young men called only "First Rock Singer" and "Second Rock Singer" begin to protest the requirement to confess one's moral failings. He could confess, says First Rock Singer, "But why, Lord? I don't know." This is the first of many English-language "tropes" or interventions, if you will, that question the liturgy. The singer admits that he doesn't know "what is real." The original text had him say he didn't know why he was so "freaky-minded," a 1960s phrase that falls with a thud on contemporary ears. Recent productions generally substitute "crazy-minded." Rock and blues vocal lines alternate as various singers admit to lust, to not knowing what they want, to creating poetry that's all style and no content. These are all forms of alienation, sins the confession of which can do nothing to assuage. The final singer sums it up: "Living is easy when you're half alive." The first of three meditations follows. Meditation No.

1, for orchestra alone, is a dialectic between anguish and endearment that finds no synthesis. The sweetness of singing the Lord a "simple song" has become much more complicated. Is it even possible?

It remains possible to sing the Latin mass, at least, and the happy words of praise, *Gloria tibi*, come pouring out of the Celebrant and the boys' choir in a dancey five-beat melody of inextinguishable joy. The people pick up the *Gloria* text, but their music is less dancey than striding. It's praise with a stick, a heavy-footed shout where a light footfall would be more suitable. It is exciting, however, in an almost self-propelling way. Into the Latin suddenly comes the most famous English-language quatrain of the piece. Ironically, it was written neither by Bernstein nor by Schwartz. Bernstein's lyric-writing partner on the abandoned St. Francis project had been Paul Simon, one half of the Simon and Garfunkel whose musical adventures Bernstein so coura-geously said he preferred to the classical avant-garde. Rooting around in the notes from their brief collaboration, Bernstein found four lines he thought fit perfectly the sensibility of the street chorus in the *Gloria*: "Half the people are stoned / And the other half are waiting for the next election. / Half the people are drowned / And the other half are swim-ming in the wrong direction." Simon gave the lines to Bernstein as a Christmas present.

The *Gloria* shuts down and a soprano solo sings the most poignant moment of the score, "Thank You." She is nostalgic for the thankfulness she used to feel when she was young in her faith, and singing "Gloria" meant something. Now that feeling is gone, and she wants it back.

Meditation No. 2, again for orchestra alone, ushers in what might be called the third scene. The first scene established the person of the Celebrant, the second introduced the first of the tropes questioning the values of the mass. This third sends the piece in a new direction. Subti-tled "On a sequence by Beethoven," the second meditation uses a pas-sage sung by the male choristers near the end of the "Ode to Joy" movement of Symphony No. 9. Amazingly, it is 11/12ths of a twelve-tone row—Bernstein's old bête noire. A theme suggests itself: the loca-tion of meaning. Is it in the words of the mass? Is it in words at all? Or does meaning reside in the establishment of concord where there is discord? Beethoven's eleven-note row, a discord, searches fitfully for a tonal base, and of course, finds one firmly back in D major. Meaning may reside there, in the alignment of our values with the real rather than the contrived and the artificial.

The reading of the Gospel prompts another dialectical trope. A moving section portrays war protestors as latter-day apostles, standing up for "the word of the Lord." But on the heels of this comes a crazed preacher who uses the same "word of the Lord" to justify all kinds of abuses. Here is one of the more the controversial quotes in the script: "And it was good / And it was Goddamned good!" There is no way to reconcile these opposites who both claim the same authority for their contrary actions.

The *Credo* or Creed leads to the defining dialectic of the piece. A recorded *Credo* proclaims the belief that God was made man. "Et homo factus est," the male street chorus sings, interrupting the tape at that point in the text. The male singers take over in a trope that cynically dismisses God's incarnation. God, after all, knew what he was doing beforehand, right? Easy for him to face life and death, knowing all and seeing all, but "I don't know why I should live / If only to die," as one of the men sings.

The recording of the *Credo* continues and so do the tropes with their increasingly critical interruptions. Two back-to-back mezzo-soprano solos question if "You will ever come again" (the actual name of Jesus Christ is never uttered in *Mass* in English, though it slips past all but unnoticed in Latin) and whether the idea of "world without end that "turns mindlessly round" is such a great idea. (This echoes a similar passage in the *Kaddish* Symphony in which the speaker finds the kingdom of heaven "flat and sterile.") A rock singer asks the key question, "I believe in God / But does God believe in me?" "I believe in F-sharp / I believe in G," he adds. A recorded performance of *De profundis* ("From the depths"), called Meditation No. 3—though this one is choral, not exclusively orchestral—stops the surging anger of the street chorus. The Middle Eastern dance music returns, as if in triumph, and the first act ends.

Act II begins with the Celebrant, distracted, singing a quasi-improvisational "Our Father," and a brief song about going on, no matter what. The boys' choir provides a necessary infusion of innocence in a Sanctus sung in Latin and also in the original Hebrew (the text is sourced in the Old Testament book of Isaiah). The melody is purity itself—the unruffled and unworried praise of all that is good. The sweetness of singing

"Holy, Holy, Holy" will not, however, keep the street chorus from its outrageous demands. Intermission has not quelled them, and with the mass's final movement, *Agnus dei* (Lamb of God), the crowd becomes vicious. *Dona nobis pacem* (Give us peace), the famous final words of the mass, become a demand for fulfillment, a challenge hurled at the feet of the Celebrant to "Give us peace now, and we don't mean later." The music is a roiling, hard, blues-cum-rock riff that swells violently as the crowd threatens to take what the Celebrant refuses to give them. At the climax of this confrontation, the Celebrant throws the sacramental wine and chalice to the floor, the chalice shatters, and the wine splatters like blood.

What follows might be thought of as "the revenge of Maria's mad scene." Bernstein may have been kept from composing a mad scene for Maria in *West Side Story*, but in this project he was the boss, and no one could stop him from giving the Celebrant what amounts to an operatic *scena*. Here is a fourteen-minute solo called "Fraction," in which the Celebrant works through the contradictions of the previous ninety minutes, all the while at the edge of losing it. Chards of the songs return as memories, and the Meditation No. 1 is given words. Beethoven's eleven-tone row from Meditation No. 2 is toyed with and varied. The Celebrant ends his scene in hopelessness and despair.

But innocence will not die, and a boy soprano soloist begins to reprise a portion of the "Simple Song," now renamed "Secret Song." One by one, members of the street chorus pick it up, until at last the Celebrant musters what is left of his strength and sings it in unison with the boy. Then begins a round of *Laudas* and *Laudes* so perfect and rich and deep that the street people are transformed and throw off their ugly demands. Here is true Communion. The musical subject comes from the "Lauda, laude" section of "Simple Song," and it is sung in the close imitation that Bernstein so loved. The sound swells and then fades, a sound in perfect concord, the opposite of the flinty, recorded discords that began the piece. The boys' choir goes out into the audience to deliver the touch of peace that was a part of the old mass service. The two characters of our musical—Christianity and the People—have reached a place of understanding. The people will take from the church what it can—the beauty of praise, the love of brother and sister—and work it out, each for himself or herself.

Here at the end, Bernstein's intent is laid out for all to see, if anyone chooses to see it. For all the great tunes and Hippie allusions and musical comedy techniques and kazoos and Middle Eastern dancing, Bernstein's *Mass* delivers a startling message: "The mass is ended" are the final words of the Catholic service, but in light of the struggle we have just witnessed, it is organized religion's attempt to serve the spiritual needs of humanity that has ended. Not only ended, but ended in failure. All dogma ossifies, all pre-conceptions lead to questioning. All promises lead to outrageous demands. No, the spiritual needs of humanity are to be filled by humanity itself. It won't do to turn away from those needs, to "swim in the wrong direction" of worldly concern alone. That is to ignore a dimension of humanity that makes us more than eating-defecting-dying machines. But to depend on an organization to supply them for us is to court disaster. The better way is to take "the peace" that the church passes to you out into the world, singing your own "lauda, laude" in harmony with everyone else's, and to dwell in unity of one's own accord.

Reports of opening night put the silence following those final words—"The mass is ended, go in peace"—at three minutes, and the ensuing ovation at nearly half an hour. Word spread of this amazing, unique, and powerful work. Because its composer did not have collaborators to curb his most extreme enthusiasms, *Mass* is sloppy, uneven, and sometimes self-indulgent. It doesn't matter. The music is irresistible and the drama potent. The cast album sold so well, first on LP and later on compact disc, that it remains today (2014) the best-selling multiple-disc classical recording in the industry's history.

As usual, the press was out of step with classical audiences. Paul Hume in the *Washington Post* said the music was the best Bernstein had ever composed, but in the *New York Times*, Harold C. Schonberg led the charge against Bernstein in a vicious review that called the work "a combination of superficiality and pretentiousness, and the greatest mélange of styles since the ladies' magazine recipe for steak fried in peanut butter and marshmallow sauce" (qtd. in Davis). Many other critics echoed this objection to that most obvious of Bernstein traits, his "eclecticism."

A word must here be said about the quality of American classical music criticism in the mid-twentieth century. Largely self-serving or even anti-intellectual, American music critics of that era focused almost entirely on performance rather than on new works, and when they did deal with the new, it was either to compare it against their own conception of what the new should be, or to deal with its surface factors (again, the element of performance over creativity) and to turn away from ideas. American classical music criticism was then, and remains today to a large degree, a promoter of opinions and "taste," nothing more. Harold Schonberg cared little for new music, preferring to remain comfortable among myriad interpretations of the Romantic piano repertoire. His review of *Mass* is not merely bad criticism, it is not criticism at all. It's an attack for the sake of an attack, with nothing to back it but that most persistent of art's enemies, "good taste." Such was the cultural milieu in which Bernstein worked.

There were exceptions, and one of them was *New York* magazine's Peter G. Davis. Davis championed *Mass* from its beginnings, and in a piece for the *New York Times* in 2008, on the occasion of a concert version of the work at Carnegie Hall, wrote astutely that "beneath the original dramatic conception, the creative exuberance, the showbiz glitter and the ear-catching set numbers is a sophisticated, carefully controlled piece of musical craftsmanship that repays close scrutiny" (qtd. in Davis). Davis went on to find unifying gestures among the seemingly wild array of "styles." Bernstein's point in underlining the eclecticism was to show that, however different we may be, we share common roots.

Mass has been on a trajectory toward revival since the turn of the present century, with performances that range from high-profile, professional productions to community affairs. The enormous forces required by the score—around 200 participants including sixty choristers and a twenty-member boys' choir; vocal soloists; massive winds onstage, strings and percussion in the pit; guitars and rock drums and a marching band—make it a challenge for many. Not so challenging anymore is the implied theology. In 1971, Catholic bishops condemned it as blasphemy. In the sharpest imaginable contrast, in 2000 Pope John Paul II requested that Bernstein's *Mass* be staged at the Vatican, which it was four years later. The production is available on DVD as *Leonard Bernstein: Mass at The Vatican City*.

The intensity around the composing and staging of *Mass* knocked the wind out of Bernstein, but this only gave him the perfect opportunity to turn elsewhere, away from composing for a while, and even away from conducting. Since his days studying aesthetics with David Prall at Harvard, Bernstein had grappled with the ideas attending music: What makes music such a force? Why make music at all? What distinguishes the wheat from the chaff? He was born into a time when ideas collided with the arts in a way that made it impossible to ignore these questions. Practitioners and critics alike of early twentieth-century literature, visual arts, and music had called into question all the assumptions so long taken for granted. Why must a painting "look like" something? Why must meter and rhyme dominate poetry? Why must narratives "make sense"? In music, the greatest challenge came in the form of serialism or dodecaphony, which we've touched on earlier. The fundamental premise of the Schoenberg school was that music could be and, given recent music history, should be, reconceived as "atonal." Until serialism, notes related to each other in a hierarchy. For example, in a scale of seven notes, the first, fourth, and fifth had greater weight. That's why countless songs maintain a chord progression involving the I, IV, and V chords of a given key. (Music analysis always uses Roman numerals.) This is tonality. Other notes and chords are used, of course, but they are there to support the hierarchical system.

In so-called atonal serial music, the idea is to disassociate those normally associated hierarchies, to make each pitch sovereign. Arnold Schoenberg (1874–1951) thus invented the idea of the "row," a series of pitches (usually all twelve) that must all be sounded before any of them can be repeated. Repetition is key to tonal music, since the hierarchy is strengthened by emphasizing some tones more than others. But if I play two notes—say, G and C—and am then forbidden by the rules of this new game to play them again until I have played all the others (D, A, A-flat, F-sharp, F, D-flat, B, B-flat, E, E-flat), then my attempt to establish a tonal center, a key, is subverted. (Try playing the row I just invented on the piano; it will sound inherently "modern.") And this is precisely what Schoenberg and his adherents had in mind: the subversion and abandonment of tonality in favor of this new way of composing.

The row, or series, was just the beginning. Schoenberg proffered rules for manipulating the series by playing it backward, upside down, and upside down and backward, and by transposing it to other starting pitches, creating twelve possible rows, plus their retrogrades (played backward), inversions (played upside down), and retrograde inversions (played upside down and backward). All this was considered quite "scientific" by an intellectual community that had long ago abandoned the idea that experience contains inherent values. Giving some notes more weight than others—Is and IVs and Vs over all the others, for example—was just one way of conceiving music, a way that had run its course. Wagner had pushed the hierarchies of tonality to their very breaking point and Schoenberg essentially said, fine, let's just break them and move on. Serialism became the gold standard for new composition. Schoenberg's student Anton Webern was lionized as the great hope of the future and hundreds of young hopefuls worldwide emulated his spare, acerbic scores. Composers who ignored serialism or, like Bernstein, used rows only in dramatic contrast to otherwise tonal music (usually connoting darkness or negativity) were considered hopelessly old fashioned, destined for the trash heap of history.

Having just dragged the 1960s onstage in front of Henry Kissinger, invoking the (accurate) judgment of White House aide John Dean of being "antiwar and antiestablishment," having just composed a piece so wide in its embrace of popular idioms and so stunning in its message that it would be decades before the world understood it, Leonard Bernstein now decided to take a ball peen hammer to serialism and its premises, and by extension, to its intellectual underpinnings.

That was one of the spookier aspects of Leonard Bernstein: his external personality did not match his internal ambition. In the public eye and in the imagination of the press, he was flamboyant, excessive, and narcissistic. "Lenny" was what we would now call a party animal, making the rounds of social gatherings, smiling, joking, drinking, smoking (cigarettes were never far from him), and posing jocularly for the popular media. In private, he was deadly serious about music, ideas, the flow of history, the fate of humanity, and he thought—no, he knew—that he could play a role in the latter. Bernstein was a radical in the pure sense: he took ideas to their logical, if sometimes necessarily extreme ends, and refused to allow opinion or prestige to interfere with his conclusions. When Harvard University offered him the Charles Eliot Norton chair of poetry, with its obligation of delivering lectures on the aesthetic subject of his choice, he grabbed the opportunity to do justice to the influence of his old aesthetics professor, David Prall. Here was a chance to add his name to a list of Norton lecturers that included T. S. Eliot, Igor Stravinsky, and Jorge Luis Borges. The resultant lecture series, titled *The Unanswered Question* after a composition by Charles Ives, is dedicated to Prall. (The lectures were transcribed into the book, *The Unanswered Question*, and were made into a DVD set that includes many major musical illustrations featuring Bernstein leading the Boston Symphony Orchestra.)

Bernstein was not an academic and he needed a place to begin. He found that place in the work of linguist Noam Chomsky. Chomsky had pioneered the idea of generative grammar, one premise of which is that grammar is inborn in the human mind. The idea that a musical grammar might also be similarly inborn "haunted" Bernstein, to use his word, and so he set about making parallels between linguistic and musical grammars. After all, an inborn musical grammar would eliminate the possibility of Schoenberg's artificially constructed "atonality." But the Chomsky connection was really a shield against potential critics; if Bernstein could link his idea of tonality-as-inherent to a similar idea in another discipline, it would help make his case. Citing Chomsky turned out to be controversial; exact parallels between language and music were incongruent.

Bernstein found much more solid footing via the approach he'd taken in his introduction to *The Infinite Variety of Music*: the inescapable presence of the harmonic or overtone series. When the human ear hears a pitch, it always hears within it the subtle presence of other pitches, and these other pitches always conform to a hierarchy that we have subsequently translated into our tonal system: the octave, the fifth, the third, and so on. Tonality is inherent in the way we hear pitched sound, and therefore hearing isolated pitches as "sovereign" is not merely wrong, it is impossible. That is what Bernstein is saying in his Norton lectures. Many critics interpreted him to mean that tonality is preferable or "more natural" or something like that. That's not the point at all. Again, that seminal essay from *The Infinite Variety of Music* summarizes what becomes much more expansive in the lectures: "We cannot hear two isolated tones . . . without immediately imputing a tonal meaning to them," not because our culture gives them a meaning, but because meaning is there in how we as humans hear pitched sound. The working-out of Beethoven's eleven-tone row in the "Fraction" section of *Mass* had been the musical precursor of the Norton lectures. Only when the Celebrant can find his way back from the unreality of that "atonal" tangle, only when he makes cuts through the seeming nonmeaning can he regain his innocence and sing again the "Secret Songs."

And this is it, the thing we've been looking for, the thing Bernstein said was at the heart of everything he composed. This is faith. Not belief in God or a creed, not being able to rest assured that a heavenly Father is looking out after our interests, but the knowledge that meaning is inherent in human experience. Music—tonal music, for all music is tonal or at least we necessarily hear it as such—is an emblem of this inherent meaning that persists in all things, not just music. Music is the very symbol of faith, the experiential proof that existence is not, despite claims to the contrary by the Existentialists (with whom Bernstein took issue), void of meaning until we give it some. The meaning is there, waiting. It will differ from person to person, exactly as one composer's music differs from all others, but it is there, in the way we experience reality. This embrace of what was once called "natural law," a concept long out of favor, outraged many in the intellectual community. If Bernstein cared, he didn't show it. After all, he was really a composer.

10

LAST WORKS AND LEGACY

After *Mass* and the Norton lectures, everything changed. By the end of the 1970s, Bernstein would experience personal crisis when he came out as gay and left his wife, followed by personal tragedy when Felicia died shortly thereafter. The story is complex in the way that all such stories are complex, but it is simple enough in outline. During his work on the Norton lectures, Bernstein met a young man named Tom Cothran. They fell in love and began a long-term relationship. Bernstein had had other male lovers during his marriage (recently published letters reveal that Felicia was fully aware and accepting of her husband's orientation), but none had prompted the emotions sparked by this twenty-four-year-old classical radio professional. Details are beyond the scope of this book; suffice it to say that Bernstein left Felicia, then moved back in but too late—she had been diagnosed with the cancer that killed her in 1978. Cothran would die of AIDS in 1981.

Along with this bitter personal sorrow came a huge professional defeat. In the mid-1970s, Bernstein worked with librettist-lyricist Alan Jay Lerner (*My Fair Lady, Camelot*) on a musical about the White House called *1600 Pennsylvania Avenue*. The show opened in the spring of 1976 in observance of America's bicentennial, and closed after seven performances. It was enormously ambitious, a telling of the White House story from 1792 to 1902 from the point of view, not of power or of politics, but of race relations. Subjects included Thomas Jefferson's relationship with his slave Sally Hemmings, the shameful history of slavery in the District of Columbia, and the effects of the Civil

War. One actor played all the presidents and one actress all the first
ladies.

The original concept involved a framing device in which a group of
actors are both depicting the incidents in the show and discussing race
relations from a contemporary viewpoint. Along the way, the frame was
thrown out, along with a lot of Bernstein's music, and the original director and choreographer left the show. What was left was a disaster, and
critics ravaged it. Bernstein was sufficiently angry at how things turned
out that he refused to okay an original cast recording. After Bernstein's
death in 1990, a concert version was published called *White House
Cantata*. One song from it has taken hold in the culture: "Take Care of
This House," a farewell song to the White House sung by one of the
first ladies. Bernstein would relocate some of the score's other numbers
to various upcoming pieces: the Whitman song in *Songfest*, a passage in
A Quiet Place, and both sections of the tiny curtain raiser, *Slava! A
Political Overture. 1600 Pennsylvania Avenue* was Bernstein's last musical to open on Broadway.

In addition to professional failure and personal tragedy, two other
factors contributed to a change in the sound and feeling of Bernstein's
post-*Mass* music. One, *Mass* and the Harvard talks were the climax of
everything Bernstein had sought. *Mass* said something big in a unique
way to an audience that needed to hear it. The Norton lectures codified
Bernstein's restless intellectual explorations and made what might be
called his one big point: the unavoidable necessity of tonality. After
these two achievements, it's a bit of a coast downhill. To be sure, there
was still more to compose. The last decade and a half or so of Bernstein's life gave us many new works. But they are of a different flavor
than the earlier ones. Artists change, and we cannot expect the composer of *Candide, West Side Story, Chichester Psalms*, and *Mass* to give us
those things again. We shall not hear them or their like in the later
scores. Some traits will remain: a certain air clings to a Bernstein melody, no matter its vintage. Overall, the late works will be edgier, somewhat more removed and cerebral, and certainly less extroverted than
the earlier compositions. It will require future considerations to put
them into the context of the recent past, and of classical music history,
which has been sufficiently marginalized by the hegemony of popular
music (the very thing Bernstein welcomed in the 1960s, ironically) that
we may actually be seeing its end. Therefore, for our purposes, we'll

take only brief looks at some of the scores Bernstein composed between 1973 and 1990.

The first work after Bernstein gave the Norton lectures was a last collaboration with choreographer Jerome Robbins. Robbins and Bernstein's final ballet together was *Dybbuk*, a story piece based on a 1919 play by Yiddish playwright S. Ansky about obsessive love and possession by spirits. Until now, Bernstein's Judaic works had dealt with the exoteric, or surface elements of the religion. With *Dybbuk* he delves into the esoteric in the form of Kabbalah, Judaism's mystical arm. In Kabbalah, significance is given to the fact that the twenty-two letters of the Hebrew alphabet have commensurate numerical value. Bernstein seized on this to create a scale paralleling the use of the number nine— sacred in Kabbalah—and its multiple eighteen, which is the number of the word *chai*, meaning "life." This scale was octatonic, meaning that from one name note to another, there were not seven different name notes, as in a standard major or minor scale, but eight. With the repetition of the tonic note at the top of the scale, Bernstein had nine notes, or eighteen when two octatonic scales were deployed, side by side.

Bernstein then manipulated the notes of his octatonic scale in the fashion of a serial composer: presenting the scale forward, backward, upside down, and so on. The result is a thorny score, much "edgier" than most Bernstein works, as Jack Gottlieb has pointed out, and it has been unsuccessful in penetrating the repertoire, either as a ballet or in the two symphonic suites Bernstein pulled from it. *Dybbuk*, which does not consistently exhibit the earmarks of the composer's style, escapes this writer's full understanding. Its day, perhaps, awaits.

In the wake of the failure of *1600 Pennsylvania Avenue* came the greatest success of the late period compositions and one of the most gratifying of all of Bernstein's scores: *Songfest*. Commissioned to write a song cycle on poems by Americans for the country's bicentennial, Bernstein could not complete *Songfest* in time for the actual bicentennial in 1976, so the work was premiered in October of 1977, part of an incredible concert by the National Symphony Orchestra that also featured two other Bernstein premieres: the Three Meditations from *Mass* for Cello and Orchestra, and *Slava!, A Political Overture*, dedicated to cellist/conductor Mstislav Rostropovich. *Songfest* is a cycle of a dozen songs on thirteen poems (two poems together make up one of the songs) for six singers, one of each vocal range: soprano, mezzo-soprano, alto, tenor, baritone, and bass. All the poets are Americans, ranging from the seven-teenth-century Anne Bradstreet to living practitioners. The result is a panorama of American perspective on love, loss, social norms, and self-hood. Here follows brief descriptions of the twelve songs:

OPENING HYMN: *TO THE POEM*

The opening song is a pseudo-fanfare on some lines by Bernstein's fellow Harvard alum, the poet-art curator Frank O'Hara. In "To the poem," O'Hara calls for us to do "something grand," which he then changes to "something small and important and un-American." The lines are half pronouncement/half sendup of such lyric exhortations. Bernstein plays it straight, with flourishes from trumpets and drums and, except for a brief passage near the beginning, note-against-note singing from his six vocal artists.

THE PENNYCANDY STORE BEYOND THE EL

A Fender bass lick introduces the jazzy rhythms of the song, a setting for baritone solo of beat poet's Lawrence Ferlinghetti's famous paean to "falling in love with unreality." The poem is full of color and a kind of magical realism, but Bernstein's music takes it in a completely different direction. The tempo indication includes the words "like a quick, dark dream," and in fact, after the bass riff is exhausted, the energy thickens and the last image, that of the leaves saying as they fall, "too soon," is not whimsical, but nightmarish. What has happened? The seemingly innocent bass lick at the start was a twelve-tone row, and the conse-quent working-out of the piece has adhered (very unusually for Bern-stein) to the rules of dodecaphonic procedure. Thus the darkness of the song's climax. (We should've known by now.)

A JULIA DE BURGOS (TO JULIA DE BURGOS)

Julia de Burgos was a Puerto Rican poet who died young (1914–1953) and whom many consider the greatest poet produced by that forgotten corner of U.S. territories. The poem is a brittle and beautiful condemnation by the poet of her public persona, the persona that is a "frosty doll of social conceit" while the true Julia de Burgos is "a virile flash of human truth." These are words from the translation by the composer's daughter, Jamie Bernstein, but the song itself is in the original Spanish. Bernstein shapes a powerful song for solo soprano from this sentiment, and along the way reminds us how effectively he writes for the trumpet, which here displays both aggressive and reflective expressive modes as an instrumental alter-ego to the singer.

TO WHAT YOU SAID . . .

This is one of Walt Whitman's overtly homoerotic poems, in which he declines an advance from a potential lover too concerned with appearances, preferring instead the company of "these young men that travel with me." Bernstein's setting uses the vibraphone in an eerie fashion, producing a C minor triad throughout, where most of the song is in C major. Adding to the sense of mystical awe is that while the bass solo intones Whitman's words, the other five singers hum in unison a gentle melody, introduced by the orchestra, that aims in its contours toward a high note that is the very E-flat of the vibraphone's C minor triad. This beautiful song is among Bernstein's most perfectly realized short vocal works.

I, TOO, SING AMERICA/OKAY "NEGROES"

This duet for mezzo-soprano and baritone combines two texts by different poets in counterpoint at the same time. Both poets are African American. Langston Hughes's poem proclaims in heroic gestures that he is the "darker brother" sent to the kitchen to eat, where he laughs off the insult and eats and grows strong. June Jordan's puts down African American efforts to appear "white" in action and demeanor. Bernstein interweaves the two effectively as music, though "getting" all those words will take more than one hearing. The song is unique: none other I can think of involves the simultaneous singing of two different poems by two different poets.

TO MY DEAR AND LOVING HUSBAND

America's earliest major poet was Anne Bradstreet (1612–1672). This poem is a loving message to a husband whose love, she says, "is such I can in no way repay." The setting for the three women of the ensemble—soprano, mezzo-soprano, and alto—is stately and embracing. According to Jack Gottlieb, Bernstein chose to set the poem for three women in order to "depersonalize" the emotion and make it less "quaintly naïve." It is an unusually serene score from the composer. The writing for the three women's voices produces a "bell" effect.

STORYETTE H. M.

The antithesis of Bradstreet's portrait of domestic happiness is this poem by Gertrude Stein that tells of "one's" desire to roam and the other "one's" resentment. Bernstein sets it as a soprano vs. bass kind of anti-duet. The straight-faced baby talk so typical of Stein is matched by mechanical, "perpetual motion" music, long on percussion and even note values in the voices.

"IF YOU CAN'T EAT YOU GOT TO"

A poem by e.e. cummings about the rougher aspects of the Bohemian life begins with a comical little tuba solo, and then the three men protest that "if you got nothing to eat, you got to smoke." The women join in. It seems there are no cigarettes, either. So they decide to sing, but they can't sing, so they sleep. But without dreams, they might as well die. Even so, they finally settle on sleep. The whole thing scoots by in little over two minutes, a phantasmagoria of the mental anguish around living for art and being rewarded with poverty.

MUSIC I HEARD WITH YOU

A well-known poem by Conrad Aiken explores the melancholy of recalling, in solitary desolation, the music heard, the food eaten, the hands touched that are now gone. A sad little melodic gesture that will be developed in the upcoming *Halil*, a set of four notes that hang on to a precipice and then plunge, is sounded in the oboe and the mezzo-soprano enters on the title words. A middle section goes twelve-tone and more alienated than sorrowful. A trumpet restates the plunging melody and the singer returns to her earlier mood.

ZIZI'S LAMENT

Lines by beat poet Gregory Corso evoke the Middle East of camels, hashish, and "Fatimas." If only, the poet's voice complains, he could catch "the laughing sickness," he might be more comfortable amid all these exoticisms. Bernstein gives us snaky oboe lines, finger cymbals, and evocative scales for this tenor solo.

SONNET: "WHAT LIPS MY LIPS HAVE KISSED "

Bernstein pronounced this farewell to love his favorite of the dozen, and certainly Edna St. Vincent Millay's complaint that summer, which once sang in her, sings no more, was at the edge of Bernstein's thoughts. Despite his still ongoing love affair with Tom Cothran (and the domestic disaster it had produced) Bernstein was soon to turn sixty. He must have felt it, for in an interview concerning this text he protested, a little too much perhaps, that the summer still sang in him, though "not as often." The music begins grimly. This is not a sentimental setting. The memories are not fond, they are fading, and the alto solo knows what she would rather not know: that love will not return.

CLOSING HYMN: *ISRAFEL*

The finale is a bright and celebratory setting for all six singers of Edgar Allen Poe's ode to the Muslim angel of music. The poem seems to imply that Israfel would have a much harder time maintaining his passionate melodies if he had to dwell here on earth, but Bernstein's music proclaims no difference between heaven and music.

A brief compositional lull followed the tragedy of Felicia's death in 1978 and the trauma that summer of the composer's sixtieth birthday. Then, suddenly, Bernstein entered a period of renewed creativity. In a burst of energy, perhaps brought on by the very specter of aging and death that had recently paid a visit, he composed more between 1979 and 1983 than at any other time since the mid-1950s. In 1980 came two new orchestral scores: the bright little overture, *A Musical Toast*; and the *Divertimento* for orchestra, commissioned and premiered by his "hometown" band, the Boston Symphony Orchestra. The following year saw the premieres of Bernstein's longest mature solo piano composition, *Touches*, and the ambitious and unique flute concerto, *Halil*. The following year was also busy with work on revisions for the opera house version of *Candide*, premiered a year later by New York City Opera. Bernstein's opera, *A Quiet Place*, his final completed stage work, premiered in its first version in 1983, and in revision the year after that.

After this second wind of compositional intensity, the pace did slow somewhat. The composer's daughter Nina has recalled that "the notes came harder for him" late in life, and daughter Jamie remembers that her father's transitions from conducting mode to composing mode took much longer than his schedule allowed. In his final handful of years, Bernstein wrote additional numbers for the Scottish Opera staging of *Candide*, penned some of his loveliest *Anniversaries*, and composed two valedictory pieces: the Concerto for Orchestra, and the whimsical song cycle, *Arias and Barcarolles*. In December 1989, came the famous concerts of Beethoven's Ninth at the fall of the Berlin Wall; the following month he wrote his last completed work, the tiny Dance Suite for brass quintet. His emphysema worsened considerably, and following concerts in the summer of 1990 at Tanglewood, Bernstein announced his retirement from conducting. He would, he said, devote the rest of his life to music education; composition, his statement implied, had come to an end along with conducting. But whether or not he ever intended to write another note was soon of no relevance. On October 14, Leonard Bernstein died from cardiac arrest due to side effects from a medicine he was taking for mesothelioma.

Divertimento is Bernstein's most unusual concert work, a suite of pieces without a program or story but resonant with memories and attachments. The suite is a study in pastiche, and is full of allusions to and even literal quotations from famous repertoire. There are eight movements: Sennets and Tuckets, Waltz, Mazurka, Samba, Turkey Trot, Sphinxes, Blues, and In Memoriam/March. The overall effect is of memories altered by time and refashioned into something new. The opener is lopsided fanfare, a call to audience attention; the beginning evokes Bernstein's own Overture to *Candide*. The Waltz is not in three, as would be usual, but in seven, and recalls Tchaikovsky's similar remetering of a waltz in 5/4 in that composer's final symphony. In the Mazurka, a movement for double reeds alone, Bernstein quotes one of the oboe's most famous solo moments: that from the first movement of Beethoven's Fifth Symphony. The most touching moment is the In Memoriam section of the last movement, featuring three flutes in longbreathed melody over a steady funeral beat. The memories of musicians past are interrupted by the explosion of the concluding march.

By this time (1980), the influence of Judaism on Bernstein's music had made itself felt in two symphonies and the *Chichester Psalms*. His next work would deal, not with Judaism per se, but with the state of Israel. Bernstein's relationship to Israel was an important part of his life. He was present in 1948 when the country was founded amidst war and bloodshed, conducting what was then called the Palestine Philharmonic Orchestra (later the Israel Philharmonic Orchestra). As the battle raged around them, Bernstein and company performed Mahler's Symphony No. 2, "Resurrection." The performance attracted so many people, and so many among them military personnel, that Egyptian reconnaissance aircraft mistook the assemblage for troop movements and reported them as such. Thus, inadvertently, Bernstein actually contributed to the new nation's military success. That relationship continued over the years, culminating musically in *Halil*, subtitled a "Nocturne" for solo flute and orchestra. The designation "nocturne" was employed, the composer said in a program note, because sleep is "Death's twin," and the subject of *Halil* is death, as either an end or a kind of eternal beginning, depending on perspective.

The score is dedicated to "the spirit of Yadin and to his Fallen Brothers." Yadin was Yadin Tanenbaum, a nineteen-year-old flutist killed in his tank in Sinai during the 1973 Yom Kippur War. Composed in 1980–1981, *Halil* (a Hebrew word for "flute") was "formally unlike any other work" he had written before, Bernstein claimed. Yet here again we encounter the clash between two opposing musical forces. Bernstein calls these forces "tonal and non-tonal," yet in the context of his Harvard lectures, where he made a clear-cut case that all pitched sound is experienced tonally, a more accurate distinction might be "the affirmation of tonality and the attempt to deny it." The composer is in no way bashful about which side in the struggle for life these forces respectively fall. On the one side are "wars and the threat of wars," or the denial of life/tonality while, on the other, lie the urge to live as well as "the consolations of art, love and the hope for peace"—faith, in the Bernstein sense, represented by the acceptance of tonality as the necessary medium of our musical experience. Yet the complete victory here is lacking. The announcement of a twelve-tone row at the start is only partially overcome, and the final cadence, though very clearly in D-flat major, feels almost as much of a resignation as a triumph.

Halil is scored for solo flute plus an orchestra of piccolo, alto flute, harp, strings, and a very large percussion battery. The piccolo and alto flute are instructed in the score to be hidden from sight, since they serve as doppelgangers for the solo flute, commentators who, like psychic presences, speak for the soloist "beyond itself." Bernstein's usually brilliant use of percussion for color, support, and emphasis is at its peak in this score, which calls for timpani, four snare drums (used at the same time for relative pitch differences), four tom toms, bass drum, pair of cymbals, two suspended cymbals, two gongs, tam-tam, two triangles, four wood blocks, whip, glockenspiel, xylophone, vibraphone, and chimes. Percussion is so deeply integrated into the process of the work that a reduction for flute and piano is not available; the closest to this standard practice format is a reduction for flute, piano, and percussion.

The work begins with a violent spray of notes from strings, harp, vibraphone, and gongs, followed by the flute, *forte*, and crescendoing on a high F-flat to fortissimo, in a shouted, arrhythmic pronouncement of a twelve-tone row. The soloist continues to expand the idea at hand, and is soon shadowed by the alto flute, which, hidden in the percussion section, echoes the soloist darkly as if uttering a premonition. Suddenly we are in the middle of an unapologetically beautiful melody, a falling line of repose and simplicity. Interaction with the orchestra changes the feeling of the melody and there emerges a struggle between F-flat and F-natural—no small battle, since this note will determine the major or minor status of the work's main key center, D-flat. Solo viola engages with the solo flute, an almost foreboding biblical presence to offset the purity of the flute's expression.

Timpani and the low strings on the harp announce a coming conflict and before long we are a pitched battle of bowed versus pizzicato strings and spiky, accented tom toms. The soloist flies above all this for a while, with the part marked in three- and two-measure phrases that define it against the maelstrom of sound below. But the orchestra thickens, activity increases, the 3/4 meter shrinks to 5/8, and with this compression things become increasingly hostile for the solo flute, who fights back with fortissimo salvos of high notes and flutter-tonguing. With the crash of tam-tam and the roll of timpani and bass drum, the struggle ends with a scream of a cadenza. A rimshot on snare drum sends the soloist into a two-note tizzy that leads to an unexpectedly plaintive memory of the lyrical theme. The soloist continues to dialogue with percussion instruments—with wood block, timpani, suspended cymbal, triangle, bass drum, vibraphone, glockenspiel.

A sudden, cold fortississimo entrance by the strings ends the struggle and brings on the pain of loss. The soloist is gone. In his place come, at length, the sound of alto flute and piccolo (both remain hidden from view) affirming, in highly theatrical fashion, the continuation of the soloist's spirit. The lyric theme returns and with it, a sure sense of the D-flat major tonality toward which the piece has been aiming from the start. At last, the soloist returns, though with but two notes: a leading tone and the tonic or home note of D-flat. Thus, with hard-won hope, this orchestral musical drama concludes.

Formally, as Bernstein said, *Halil* may not have been like anything he'd written before, but its theme of faith embattled, the theatrical nature of the theme's depiction, and the mastery of orchestral expression in every measure are pure Bernstein. *Halil* was premiered in May 1981 by soloist Jean-Pierre Rampal and the Israel Philharmonic Orchestra, the composer conducting, and was given its American premiere in July that year at Tanglewood by flutist Doriot Anthony Dwyer, the Boston Symphony Orchestra, and Bernstein on the podium. Despite an absurd review in the *New York Times* suggesting Bernstein had "laid an egg," *Halil* was accepted globally as a major work. Along with *Songfest*, it is, in this writer's opinion, the most artistically satisfying of Bernstein's later scores.

A Quiet Place, Bernstein's last completed work for the stage, was intended as a continuation of the lives of characters he created for *Trouble in Tahiti*. Opera director Stephen Wadsworth wrote the libretto, based on the composer's story idea. In the first version, composed for the Houston Opera, which premiered it in 1983, the earlier one-act opera was performed as the first act, with the new material making up the second act. It was such a resounding failure (the headline over one review read "Bernstein's Trouble in Houston") that Bernstein and Wadsworth completely reworked it as a three-act opera, with scenes from *Trouble in Tahiti* integrated into the second act as flashbacks. This is the production currently licensed. *Trouble in Tahiti* continues to be licensed as a separate, stand-alone piece as well.

A *Quiet Place* opens with a car crash that has killed Dinah, the wife from *Trouble in Tahiti*. Her death and funeral will reunite Sam with his and Dinah's children: a son, Junior (whom we remember from *Trouble in Tahiti*), and a daughter, Dede. Junior and Dede live in Quebec with a French Canadian named François; Dede is married to him and Junior is his lover. This is not exactly a situation that finds favor with Sam, who explodes in anger at the three. Act I contains a trio for Junior, Dede, and Francois in which they all recall once having been close to their fathers. This is Bernstein's final expression of father love/hate. At length, with many bumps along the way, the family dynamic is worked out and Sam, his children, and his son-in-law decide to try to reach out to one another.

There is no dearth of invention in Bernstein's music, and there is much beauty (the Act I postlude is a concert-worthy intermezzo), but the kitchen-sink nature of the story strikes many people as dated, and the confrontation between old values and new ones is forced. The fresh-minted orchestration includes electric bass (which Bernstein had first used in *Songfest*), a Yamaha keyboard doubled by the pianist, and a percussion battery huge even by Bernstein's percussion-loving standards. Four players perform on twenty-five different instruments, including steel pipe and sandpaper blocks. A broader issue with *A Quiet Place* is much of it is through-composed; that is, the music rolls along with the text not stopping, for the most part, to shape words into lyrics for songs. Even when it does, as in Dede's Act III aria, the feeling is more of accompanied recitative than of blossoming song. This contrasts with *Trouble in Tahiti*, made up of songs for the most part, or of through-composed passages that take on songlike shapes. Bernstein was a song composer, and a great one. I've never seen a production of *A Quiet Place* (few have, productions are rare) but in listening to the recording I grow frustrated waiting for "Bernstein songs" that don't come—except when the interpolation of *Trouble in Tahiti* takes over. But the staging can make all the difference, and *A Quiet Place* has begun to receive restagings and rethinkings, especially in a critically approved 2010 production at New York City Opera. The time for this work, as for *Dybbuk*, may well lie in the future.

The title of Bernstein's final song cycle comes from a curious phrase dropped by President Eisenhower, who said casually to Bernstein upon hearing something he had enjoyed, that he liked it, as opposed to all those "arias and barcarolles." It's a nonsensical remark from a no doubt well-meaning but musically wholly incompetent man. *Arias and Barcarolles*, which contains neither arias nor barcarolles (the latter being a boat-song), is a collection of eight songs, six of them on Bernstein's own texts; one of them, a "kid's song," to a text by his mother, Jennie; and one in Yiddish by Yankev-Yitskhok Segal. The theme is romantic love in all its mystery and frustration. The original (1988) was scored for mezzo-soprano, baritone, and piano, four hands (two people at one piano). Bernstein orchestrated the cycle with assistance from Bright Sheng for strings and percussion, and after the composer's death, Bruce Coughlin arranged it for chamber orchestra. The songs outline a love relationship, from the first tentative outreach, to marriage and children, to the domestic life of family that scrapes the nerves and challenges one's patience. The songs contain some of Bernstein's most honest thoughts on the subject, how love has its own existence almost apart from the lovers. The second song, "Love Duet," includes the words, "Scary, the way it flows, as if it knows the mystery." The setting employs one of the composer's most effective uses of close imitation.

Bernstein's final major score had its genesis in 1986 as a two-movement work called *Jubilee Games*. The title comes from the original idea of "Jubilee"—a Hebrew custom involving the release of all debts and servants in the years following every seven times seven years—in other words, every half-century. Bernstein composed it for the Israel Philharmonic Orchestra, and perhaps had in mind the upcoming fiftieth anniversary of the founding of Israel (1998), which he would not live to see. The first movement, called, after his enthusiasm for sports, "Free-Style Events," is rife with the number seven, whether in the form of seven-beat meters or, more overtly, when the players are required to shout "*Sheva!*" (Hebrew for "seven" seven times). Brass swoops and shofar-like horn calls evoke Joshua and Jericho. Near the end comes the biggest pile-up of pure dissonance in Bernstein's composing career.

The original *Jubilee Games* (1986) concluded with what is now its third movement. In 1989, Bernstein pieced together a larger-scale composition by placing a set of variations on his octatonic scale from *Dybbuk* in the role of an Adagio movement, coming between the Allegro "Free-Style Events" and the scherzo. This movement he dubbed "Mixed Doubles," another sports allusion. It is also perfectly descriptive of what happens in the movement, where pairs of instruments take up variations, one after the other. The scherzo comes next, an easy-going, easy-to-identify-as-Bernstein piece called "Diaspora Dances." In meters of eighteen beats, it evokes the klezmer musicians of the Jewish diaspora. (Lenny's dad had been right, after all: his son ended up a *klezmorim*!) We now have an Allegro, an Adagio, and a scherzo. Where we might expect the usual closing Allegro we get instead a brief, warmly melodic piece for baritone and orchestra that Bernstein had written for the reopening of the refurbished Carnegie Hall in 1986. At Carnegie Hall, it had been billed as an "Opening Prayer." Now, Bernstein placed it in the final slot of his new four-movement work and called it "Benediction." To this last, cobbled-together score Bernstein gave the name "Concerto for Orchestra."

It is somehow perfect that the last words of the last Bernstein composition are these, here translated from the Hebrew, words that traditionally end the Jewish service, and which aptly leave Bernstein's fans with the message he had been trying to impart his entire life: "May the Lord bless you and keep you. May he make His face to shine upon you and be gracious unto you. May He lift up His countenance and give you the blessing of peace."

While writing this book, I fully expected Bernstein the composer to shrink. By that I mean: I expected that getting a grasp on his output would likely reduce, rather than increase, its general significance. But as research into the scores cleared the detritus surrounding Bernstein's life, from its outrageousness to its sorrows, the trajectory of his work emerged, and this had the opposite effect. His catalogue now looms larger than before in depth, power, and meaning. Marin Alsop's opinion that Bernstein was not merely a twentieth-century composer, but one of the best the century had to offer, is buttressed by a clear comprehension of what Bernstein accomplished in his work. What he achieved, embodied in score after score and supported by written (verbal) materials, was nothing less than a twofold cultural project: the reassertion of music as an emblem of experience, and the case for tonality as inherent in the way he hear music. Music for Bernstein was no casual entertainment and no mere "cultural expression" (though he frequently turned, as we all do, to his own cultural roots for inspiration). Bernstein heard and felt music as a communication of reality, of my reality to you, and yours to me. Ideally, music in a Bernsteinian universe is the language of peace, the language with which we say to each other how we see the world, the language through which we understand one another.

This is his compositional legacy—this, and the many works he left us that will, if we are lucky, never leave us. He was also a model for the next generation of composers. John Corigliano, a Pulitzer Prize-winning concert composer and an Oscar winner for his movie score, *The Red Violin*, has said, "Leonard Bernstein was an enormous influence on me. I loved his music, but more than that I learned so much from it. His eclecticism made it possible for me to produce works like my opera, *The Ghosts of Versailles*, and my first symphony. And his bravery, in a time of strict modernism, gave me the courage to write all the music that I have."

Leonard Bernstein was so many things. It is impossible to think of American conducting without thinking of him, and the current treasury of American classical musical talent would be considerably less had he not been there as a teacher. But above all, I believe he was the thing he always wanted to be. He reached for the note, and grabbed it. He was a composer.

SELECTED READING

Bernstein, Burton, and Barbara Haws, eds. *Leonard Bernstein: American Original*. Harper-Collins, New York, 2008. Bernstein's brother and New York Philharmonic archivist Barbara Haws have commissioned a number of essays by, among others, author Joseph Horowitz on Bernstein as music director, critic Tim Page on Bernstein's television persona, and composer John Adams on the distinctly American voice of Bernstein's music.

Bernstein, Leonard. *Findings: Fifty Years of Meditation on Music*. Anchor Press, New York, 1982. Bernstein's final volume of thoughts on his art.

Bernstein, Leonard. *The Infinite Variety of Music*. Amadeus Press, New York, 2004. (Originally published in 1966.) This collection provides a taste of Bernstein's ability to make the most arcane subjects clear and cogent, and to make the music of Dvorak, Brahms, and Tchaikovsky take on the urgency of this morning's news. Also contains his open letter challenging the hegemony of serial music.

Bernstein, Leonard. *The Joy of Music*. Amadeus Press, New York, 2004. (Originally published in 1959.) The first compilation of Bernstein's writings and television presentations, it bursts with the author's excitement and insight.

Bernstein, Leonard. *The Unanswered Question: Six Talks at Harvard*. Harvard University Press, Cambridge, 1976. In lectures representing the pinnacle of his work as a thinker about music, Bernstein uses Noam Chomsky's linguistic theory to spark a discussion of inherent musical values. Not only intellectually compelling (if controversial), but touching in its author's obvious passion for the subject.

Berson, Misha. *Something's Coming, Something Good: West Side Story and the American Imagination*. Applause Theatre and Cinema Books, New York, 2011. A thorough and captivating look at the creation, production, and impact of *West Side Story*.

Broadrubb, Donald. *An Attempt to Delineate the Characteristic Structure of Classical (Biblical) Hebrew Poetry*. Bookleaf Publishing, Australia, 1995.

Burton, Humphrey. *Leonard Bernstein*. Doubleday, New York, 1994. Bernstein's official biographer knew the man, knew the music, and knew how to balance the two in perspective. "Official" his book may be, but Burton does not spare his subject from the truth, even when that truth is less than flattering.

Chisholm, Kate. "Symphony No 2: The Age of Anxiety." http://www.leonardbernstein.com/works_anxiety.htm.

Davis, Peter G. "Celebrating Bernstein's 'Mass' Anew." *New York Times*, October 17, 2008.

Ewen, David. *Leonard Bernstein: A Biography for Young People*. Chilton Co., Philadelphia 1960. Published only halfway through Bernstein's career, this nonetheless remains a great introduction for children, and leaves the composer's life at its peak of just having composed *West Side Story* and taken the helm of the New York Philharmonic.

"Gilbert   Concert."   *Leonard*   *Bernstein*.   http://www.leonardbernstein.com/
news_detail.php?Gilbert-Concert-67. November 3, 2008.

Gottlieb, Jack. *Working with Bernstein*. Amadeus Press, New York, 2010. A chatty but loving
memoir from Bernstein's longtime assistant, with peeks into the composer's methods and
habits.

"Happy birthday, Richard Wilbur! The poet speaks of *Candide*, Russian poets, and meeting
'the right girl.'" http://bookhaven.stanford.edu/2012/03/happy-birthday-richard-wilbur-
the-poet-speaks-of-candide-russian-poets-and-meeting-the-right-girl/.

Ledbetter, Steven. *Sennets and Tuckets: A Bernstein Celebration*. Boston Symphony Orchestra in association with David Godine Publisher, Inc., Boston 1988. A volume of tributes to
Bernstein on the occasion of his seventieth birthday.

Secrest, Meryle. *Leonard Bernstein: A Life*. Alfred A. Knopf, New York, 1994. Published the
same year as Humphrey Burton's biography, Secrest's tome is long on psychological
theories and somewhat short on musical savvy, but it gives good perspective on Bernstein's place in American society.

Secrest, Meryle. *Stephen Sondheim: A Life*. Alfred A. Knopf, New York, 1998. The standard
biography of Bernstein's *West Side Story* collaborator and friend.

"Serenade (after Plato's 'Symposium')." http://leonardbernstein.com/works_serenade.htm.

Simeone, Nigel, ed. *The Leonard Bernstein Letters*. Yale University Press, London and New
Haven, 2013. Not many insights, but a wonderful glimpse into the relationships Bernstein
maintained over the decades.

Wolfe, Tom. *Radical Chic* and *Mau Mauing the Flak Catchers*. Farrar, Straus & Giroux, New
York, 1987. The first of the two title essays in this book is the famous attack on the
Bernsteins' party for the Black Panthers. In retrospect, it seems like an attack for the sake
of an attack.

SELECTED LISTENING

DVD

American Masters. Dir. Kathryn Walker. Perf. Leonard Bernstein, Richard Rodgers, and Dorothy Fields. Wellspring, 2004.

Bernstein Conducts Candide. Dir. Leonard Bernstein. Deutsche Grammaphon, 2006. DVD.

Candide. Deutsche Grammophon, 2006. The BBC concert performance from 1989, with June Anderson and Jerry Hadley, conducted by Bernstein.

Leonard Bernstein: Mass at the Vatican City. Kultur Video, 2000. The remarkable production of Bernstein's *Mass* performed at the request of the Vatican.

Leonard Bernstein: West Side Story, Special Edition. In 1985, Bernstein decided to record *West Side Story* with major opera singers, including Kiri Te Kanawa and Jose Carreras. The result was a curious blend of genres. This set combines the CD, plus a video documenting the making of the recording.

Leonard Bernstein: Young People's Concerts. New York Philharmonic, 2004. A multiple-disc compilation (twenty-five hours) of Bernstein's famous concerts with explication.

Leonard Bernstein's Candide. Image Entertainment, 2005. The New York Philharmonic's concert version, heavily favoring the score's musical comedy side, starring Kristin Chenoweth and Patti Lupone.

Teachers and Teaching: An Autobiographical Essay by Leonard Bernstein. Dir. Humphrey Burton, 1985. Currently out of print.

CD

Bernstein: The Age of Anxiety and Serenade after Plato's Symposium. Sony, 1998. Isaac Stern, violin, with the New York Philharmonic conducted by Leonard Bernstein. The Serenade has become a staple of every violinist's repertoire, from Hilary Hahn to Anne-Sophie Mutter to Joshua Bell. Here the original dedicatee plays it, plus the original version of Bernstein's Symphony No. 2, *Age of Anxiety*.

Bernstein: Chichester Psalms/On the Waterfront/Three Dance Episodes from "On the Town." The Bournemouth Symphony, [with Bernstein protégé] Marin Alsop conducting. Naxos, 2003.

A trio of Bernstein scores from three different decades: 1940s (*On the Town*), 1950s (*On the Waterfront*), and 1960s (*Chichester Psalms*).

Bernstein: Kaddish (Symphony No. 3)/Chichester Psalms. Sony, 1998. A reissue of the first recordings of these works, with the composer conducting.

Bernstein: Kaddish (Symphony No. 3)/Chichester Psalms/Missa Brevis. Chandos 2004. Jamie Bernstein, speaker. Leonard Slatkin leading the BBC Symphony Chorus and Orchestra. This is the composer's daughter's take on Bernstein's most problematic score, plus *Chichester Psalms* and the only complete recording of the *Missa Brevis.*

Bernstein: Mass. Sony, 1997. A reissue of the original 1971 recording, the biggest-selling, multiple-disc classical recording in history. Later recordings, such as Marin Alsop's, have their strengths, but Bernstein's own conducting is, unsurprisingly, immensely compelling.

Bernstein: Overture to Candide/Symphonic Dances from West Side Story/On the Water-front/Fancy Free. Sony, 1998. Reissues of some of Bernstein's most popular music.

Bernstein Conducts Bernstein. Deutsche Grammophon, 2008. A seven-disc compilation containing some of the composer's most popular pieces (Symphonic Dances from *West Side Story*, Overture to *Candide, Serenade, Chichester Psalms*) plus harder-to-find earlier scores (Symphony No. 1, *Facsimile* and *Prelude, Fugue and Riffs*) and a treasury of his later works (*Halil, Songfest, Divertimento, Dybbuk,* and Concerto for Orchestra.)

Candide. Original Broadway Cast, Columbia, 2003. A reissue of the 1956 original in all its sparkle.

West Side Story. Original soundtrack, Columbia, 1998. The album that spent time at the No. 1 sales slot longer than any other in history continues to be a popular seller.

INDEX

ABOUT THE AUTHOR

Kenneth LaFave has worked as a music journalist, a composer, a teacher, and a New York pit musician. In addition to writing thousands of articles about music, dance, and the arts for the *Kansas City Star*, the *Arizona Republic*, *Dance Magazine*, *Opera News*, and many other publications, LaFave has composed works on commission for the Tucson Symphony Orchestra, the Phoenix Symphony, the Kansas City Chorale, the Chicago String Quartet, Ballet Arizona, cellist Yehuda Hanani, clarinetist Robert Spring, and the New York Philharmonic's late timpanist Roland Kohloff. LaFave fell in love with the music of Leonard Bernstein while still in his teens, singing as a chorister in Bernstein's *Chichester Psalms*. He currently lives in Scottsdale with two highly musical sons, Max and Emmett, and a pair of black cats, Luna and Lucky. He is working toward a PhD in philosophy at Switzerland's European Graduate School.

9 781442 235434